Cambridge Texts in the History of Political
Thought

Cicero
On Duties

CAMBRIDGE TEXTS IN THE HISTORY OF POLITICAL THOUGHT

Series editors

RAYMOND GEUSS
Reader in Philosophy, University of Cambridge

QUENTIN SKINNER
Regius Professor of Modern History, University of Cambridge

Cambridge Texts in the History of Political Thought is now firmly established as the major student textbook series in political theory. It aims to make available to students all the most important texts in the history of Western political thought, from ancient Greece to the early twentieth century. All the familiar classic texts will be included but the series seeks at the same time to enlarge the conventional canon by incorporating an extensive range of less well-known works, many of them never before available in a modern English edition. Wherever possible, texts are published in complete and unabridged form, and translations are specially commissioned for the series. Each volume contains a critical introduction together with chronologies, biographical sketches, a guide to further reading and any necessary glossaries and textual apparatus. When completed, the series will aim to offer an outline of the entire evolution of Western political thought.

For a list of titles published in the series, please see end of book.

CICERO

On Duties

EDITED BY

M. T. GRIFFIN

Tutorial Fellow in Ancient History
Somerville College
Oxford

and

E. M. ATKINS

Research Fellow
Christ's College
Cambridge

CAMBRIDGE
UNIVERSITY PRESS

PUBLISHED BY THE PRESS SYNDICATE OF THE UNIVERSITY OF CAMBRIDGE
The Pitt Building, Trumpington Street, Cambridge, United Kingdom

CAMBRIDGE UNIVERSITY PRESS
The Edinburgh Building, Cambridge CB2 2RU, UK
40 West 20th Street, New York, NY 10011–4211, USA
477 Williamstown Road, Port Melbourne, VIC 3207, Australia
Ruiz de Alarcón 13, 28014 Madrid, Spain
Dock House, The Waterfront, Cape Town 8001, South Africa

http://www.cambridge.org

© Cambridge University Press 1991

First published 1991
Ninth printing 2003

Printed in the United Kingdom at the University Press, Cambridge

British Library Cataloguing in Publication data
Cicero, Marcus, Tullius *106BC – 43BC*
On Duties. – (Cambridge texts in the history of
political thought)
1. Politics. Ethical aspects
I. Title   II. Griffin, Miriam T. (Miriam Tamara)
172

Library of Congress Cataloguing in Publication data
Cicero, Marcus Tullius.
Cicero On Duty / edited by M. T. Griffin and E. M. Atkins
p. cm. – Cambridge texts in the history of political thought)
Includes bibliographical references.
ISBN 0 521 34338 0 (hardback)   0 521 34835 8 (paperback)
I. Ethics, Ancient.   T. Griffin, M. T. (Mirain T.)   II. Atkins,
E. M. (E. Margaret)   III. Title.   IV. Series.
PA6296.D5   1990
171'.2–dc20
89–25428
CIP

ISBN 0 521 34338 0 hardback
ISBN 0 521 34835 8 paperback

Contents

Editors' Note

There has been consultation and collaboration between us on every aspect and at every stage. The primary division of responsibility, however, is as follows. The Introduction was written by Miriam Griffin, who also furnished the list of Principal Dates, the Bibliography, the Biographical Notes, and most of the annotations on the text. The translation was the work of Margaret Atkins, who also prepared the Plan of the Hellenistic Schools, the Summary of the Doctrines of the Hellenistic Schools and the Notes on Translation. She also contributed to the Biographical Notes and the annotations. The Synopsis of *De Officiis* was a joint enterprise.

Miriam Griffin is grateful to Quentin Skinner for his comments on the Introduction and to the Institute for Advanced Study at Princeton for providing ideal conditions for the project. Margaret Atkins would like to thank Malcolm Schofield and Merton Atkins, each of whom read earlier drafts of the translation with generous attention and contributed greatly to the final version.

This volume is dedicated to the memory of Elizabeth Rawson.

Introduction

The author

Marcus Tullius Cicero was born in 106 BC and was thus an exact contemporary of Pompey the Great and slightly older than Caesar the Dictator. Members of the last generation of the Roman Republic, all three were to die by violence in the decade of the forties, when the Republic itself was in the death throes of civil war. Pompey had said in public that, without Cicero's service to his country as consul, there would have been no Rome to witness his third triumph (*Off.* 1.78); Caesar had written of Cicero's service to Latin letters: 'You have won greater laurels than the triumphal wreath, for it is a greater achievement to have extended the frontiers of the Roman genius than those of Rome's empire' (Pliny *NH* VII.117). Yet these were two of the greatest generals in a state that admired, above all, military victory and conquest. What feats of statesmanship and eloquence had made such praise, or flattery, appropriate?

Unlike his great coevals, Cicero was a 'new man', the first of his family to hold public office (see p. 54, n. 1). He came from Arpinum, a town that had enjoyed Roman citizenship since 188 BC and had so far produced one great Roman general and statesman, Gaius Marius, who had saved Rome when a barbarian invasion threatened from the north in the decade of Cicero's birth. The Cicerones were local aristocrats, landed, leisured, educated, and involved in local politics. Cicero's grandfather had attracted attention at Rome by his conservative zeal in opposing the introduction of the secret ballot in Arpinum (see p. 30, n. 3). His father, sickly and thus confined

ix

to scholarly pursuits, was nonetheless set on giving his two sons, Marcus and his younger and less talented brother Quintus, the opportunities necessary for entering Roman public life. He took them to Rome where, at the house of the great orator L. Licinius Crassus, they were entrusted to the best teachers of rhetoric.

At the same period Cicero made his first acquaintance with law and philosophy, encountering among others the Stoic Diodotus, who was later to live and die in his house, and Philo of Larissa, the head of Plato's Academy in Athens, who fled to Rome in 88 BC to escape the invasion of King Mithridates of Pontus. Cicero then went to Greece in 79–77 to continue his study of rhetoric and philosophy. When he says in *De Officiis* that philosophy had not only been a great interest of his youth (II.4), but the source of his achievements in public life (I.155), he was thinking of its importance in the training of an orator. Diodotus had taught him dialectic; the Peripatetics, who had developed the theory of rhetoric, taught one to argue both sides of a question; the Academics taught one to refute any argument. They remained the most important for Cicero. While abroad, he had heard two charismatic philosophers, Antiochus of Ascalon (see p. xxxvi), and Posidonius, the Stoic polymath; but Cicero remained essentially true to Philo's early sceptical teaching, rejecting the possibility of certain knowledge and asserting his right to adopt what position seemed most persuasive on any occasion (II.7, III.20, cf. I.2, I.6).

Cicero had made his debut in the lawcourts during Sulla's dictatorship (II.51). After his return to Rome, he was elected to his first public office, that of quaestor, or financial officer, in Sicily. Six years later he prosecuted the rapacious governor Verres on behalf of the island (II.50). He went on to hold the aedileship, in which he gave the expected public entertainment but at moderate expense; despite this frugality, he tells us, he secured election to the two top offices ahead of the other candidates and at the earliest possible age (II.59). He thus became praetor at the age of forty and consul at the age of forty-three. It was a remarkable feat for a man of his origins.

The consulship of 63 BC, in which he completely overshadowed his colleague, was the summit of his career. He had no desire to command armies or govern a province of the empire, though some years later when he was sent to Cilicia, he performed his administrative, judicial, and indeed military duties conscientiously, while working to ensure his prompt return to Rome. The boastful allusions to his consulship that adorn every book of *De Officiis* (1.77, 11.84, 111.3) give only a faint idea of the importance Cicero attached to it. He celebrated it in Greek and Latin, in prose and verse, 'not without cause, but without end', as Seneca later remarked. For the conspiracy of Catiline, which Cicero provoked by frustrating both radical proposals for debt relief and the electoral ambitions of the blue-blooded Catiline, and which he then exposed and thwarted, would certainly have meant bloodshed and social upheaval. Cicero was shortsighted in ignoring genuine grievances in Rome and Italy, but he showed no lack of courage in confronting the consequences.

His prompt action, which included the execution of Roman citizens without trial, was resented in some quarters, and Pompey, though prepared to praise him, did nothing to prevent the tribune P. Clodius sending him into exile in 58. In retrospect, Cicero saw his suffering as that of a patriotic martyr (11.58), though Pompey secured his recall in the next year.

There was indeed a sense in which Cicero's change of fortune was linked with that of Rome. For the political alliance of Pompey, Caesar and Crassus, formed in 60, not only restricted the influence and activity of men like Cicero, but also subjected to military coercion the institutions of the Roman Republic – the popular assemblies which elected and legislated, the annual magistrates who convened them, and the Senate, composed of ex-magistrates, which provided the one element of continuity in policy.

Cicero had once suggested to his brother that his consulship was the realization of Plato's dream of the philosopher ruler (*Qfr*. 1.1.29). Now, impeded in his service to Rome as a statesman, he turned to instructing her in rhetoric and political philosophy, writing dialogues inspired by the literary masterpieces of Plato. After his governorship and his subsequent involvement on Pompey's side in the civil war, Cicero was pardoned by Caesar, now Dictator, and resumed his literary activity: with the defeat of the Republican cause, independent and hence honourable political activity, he felt, was closed to him (*Off.* 11.2).

Cicero turned to philosophy partly because it provided distraction and comfort, which became particularly necessary after the death of his beloved daughter Tullia in February of 45. It was also an honourable use of his leisure for the public good (*Off.* 11.4–6), and a challenge that could bring honour to himself and to Rome. The challenge was to appropriate for Latin high culture yet another Greek creation, perhaps indeed the most difficult of all, given the resistance of the Roman outlook and the Latin language to abstract thought. The Romans had recognized from the start the superiority of Greek culture and had already had some success in creating a literature using Greek forms and Greek poetic metres, while Cicero himself had raised Roman oratory to a height that matched the best of Greek. Philosophy in Latin, however, had scarcely been attempted.

Between 46 and 44 BC, Cicero not only added to his works on rhetoric but created what amounted to an encyclopedia of Hellenistic philosophy, covering epistemology in the *Academica*, ethics in *De Finibus*, and natural philosophy in *De Natura Deorum*. These dialogues breathe the spirit of the sceptical Academy, for in them spokesmen for the major philosophical schools present their views and are subjected to exacting criticism. But Cicero also used the licence accorded by his sect to produce more dogmatic works on particular subjects, of which *De Officiis* is the last.

The political context of *De Officiis*

The great event that throws its shadow over *De Officiis* is the assassination of Caesar on the Ides of March 44 BC. Not only is Cicero at pains to justify the deed, over and over again, as tyrannicide (II.23–8, III.19, III.32, III.82–5), but he never misses an opportunity to castigate Caesar, by name or anonymously, for his unlawful ambitions (I.26, III.36, III.83), his demagoguery (I.64, II.21, II.78), his resultant rapacity towards men of property (I.43, II.29, II.83–4, III.36), and his harsh treatment of Rome's enemies and subjects (I.35, II.28, III.49). Though Cicero's intimate letters show that he sometimes took a more realistic view of the problems Caesar confronted and of his aims, they also show that at all times, before and during the dictatorship, as after, he believed that Caesar wanted tyrannical power (e.g. *Att.* X.I.3, X.4.2, X.8.6) and was bent on revolutionary social and economic measures. He also distrusted his much-advertised clemency (p. 19, n. 2; p. 71, n. 1).

The tragedy was that, in the view of Cicero and his friends, the Ides of March had not restored the Republic. The 'Liberators' had not thought any further steps necessary, not even convening the Senate as Cicero advised. With Antony in charge as consul, an amnesty was declared, and the office of dictatorship was abolished, but the dead Dictator's measures were maintained and his plans implemented. The two leading tyrannicides, Brutus and Cassius, held the office of praetor but were actually afraid to be in Rome. Then, in April, the Dictator's grand-nephew Octavian arrived in Italy, a formidable rival to Antony for the affections of Caesar's veterans and supporters. Antony, driven to more and more extreme measures of self-preservation, became in Cicero's eyes the real enemy whom the tyrannicides should have killed with Caesar, and whose killer would similarly deserve praise and glory.

The way in which Cicero expresses his uncertainty and anxiety about the fate of the Roman Republic in *De Officiis* fits into a pattern familiar from his letters and other works of the period. Cicero thought, at the time and afterwards, that peace bought with concessions to Caesar in 49 would have left the Republic alive, however debilitated (I.35, cf. *Fam.* VI.I.6); even during the civil war, he believed that a timely peace with the victorious Caesar could preserve the Republic, which had been weakened but was still strong enough to revive (*Fam.* XV.I5.I, IX.6.3, VI.I0.5); just after the Ides of March he could say that he had always believed that the period of rule by one man was merely a phase in a cycle of constitutions as described in Plato's *Republic* (*Div.* II.6–7). Yet, during the war between Pompey and Caesar and during the dictatorship, as indeed even earlier, he sometimes described the Republic as lost (e.g. *Att.* IX.5.2, IX.7.I, *Fam.* VI.2I.I) – an exaggerated way of expressing disappointment with its present condition. Similarly, in *De Officiis*, Cicero talks, on the one hand, of there being no *res publica* at all (I.35, II.3) or refers to the *res publica* as lost, fallen, overthrown or murdered (II.29, II.45, III.4, III.83). On the other hand, he exhorts his son Marcus to follow in his own footsteps (II.44, III.6, cf. I.4); he teaches him how to succeed within the Republican political system where military glory, forensic eloquence, legal expertise and public liberality could earn one fame, influence and power (I.II6, II.45–5I, II.58–60); and he enjoins it as a duty on those suited to public life to endure the labours and political risks involved (I.7I). When we find in *De Officiis* laments about the end of eloquence and jurisprudence (II.65–7), combined with assertions about the importance of mastering both (II.47, II.49, II.65 *fin.*), we are reminded of the *Brutus*, written under the dictatorship, where Cicero expressed gloomy resignation over the death of eloquence

(21–2) and jurisprudence (157), yet ended by hoping for a revival of the *res publica* and exhorting Brutus to strive to excel in oratory (332).

These contradictions are neither signs of irrationality in Cicero, nor simply the results of rhetorical exaggeration. In *De Officiis*, as in the *Brutus* (157), they reflect Cicero's view of the present political situation as temporary and transitional: he speaks of 'the *interruption* – not to say the destruction – of eloquence' (II.67) and he says, ostensibly of the period of Caesar's dictatorship, 'Freedom will bite back more fiercely when *suspended* than when she remains undisturbed' (II.24). Just as he knew in 46 that there was a villain, Caesar, who could be removed, so after his removal he blamed particular men, Antony and his adherents, for continuing Caesar's policies and confiscations (II.23, II.28), his autocratic and violent form of rule (II.22–3, II.65, III.1) and his mistreatment of Rome's subjects (III.49). They were engaged in destroying Rome, as others had been in the past (I.57). But the others had failed, and so might they. Although Cicero occasionally lets his mind dwell on how men come to subject themselves through fear and greed to the power of another (II.22) or on a way of life in which the patronage exercised by the upper classes would amount to seeking favours from those with the power to help (II.67), he continues to regard as the norm the situation in which people like himself and his son are the recipients, not the purveyors, of flattery (I.91), except when tempted to play the demagogue (II.63). For him the Republic was too vital a force to be extinguished so quickly.

The complexity of the political situation, as Cicero presents it in *De Officiis*, matches the complexity of his own position, as he portrays it in his letters. In April of 44 BC, before Octavian landed in Italy, Cicero felt there was no place for him in politics any more (*Att.* XIV.6.2). Even before the Ides of March he had planned to go to Greece to supervise his son's education; afterwards he had held back thinking he might be able to advise Brutus. He had moments of hope, such as the occasion when his son-in-law Dolabella repressed pro-Caesarian demonstrations (*Att.* XIV.19.1). But in July, after hoping to accompany Brutus and thus make his trip a dangerous and patriotic venture (*Att.* XVI.4.4), he finally set out alone. Then he returned, when the winds proved contrary and a compromise between Antony and the Liberators seemed imminent (*Att.* XVI.7, *Fam.* X.1.1). On the last day of August he entered Rome in triumph (*Fam.* XII.25.3) and two days later he delivered in the Senate the first of his attacks on Antony, the Philippic Orations, which were ultimately to lead to his proscription and death. Of the Fourth, delivered on 20 December of 44, Cicero later wrote that he had regained hope of liberty and laid the foundations of the Republic (*Fam.* XII.25.2). Despite moments of despondency, he never hesitated again or lacked courage to pursue his ill-conceived policy of defeating Antony at all costs. The man he thereby raised up was more competent and more dangerous. But even he, as Augustus the founder of the Principate, had to take account of Caesar's murder and of the passionate belief in the Republic for which Cicero and others had died, and dress his autocracy in its faded garments.

The political assumptions of *De Officiis* are not therefore unrealistic, for it was a time of genuine political ambiguity, and the concern of the work with the difficulty of moral decision exactly suits the corresponding moral ambiguity that individuals faced. Even his friend and confidant Atticus, more cautious and less volatile than Cicero, wavered in his political assessments, changed his mind about the right course for Cicero to take, and asked his advice about his own conduct (*Att.* XVI.7.3, XVI.13.4). As in 49, Cicero's personal letters at this time show him using in his deliberations the same concepts he treats in *De Officiis*: *honestum, decorum, turpe, utile, incommodum, officium* itself (see Notes on Translation). He rejects the Epicurean solution of staying out of politics, but cannot find a way to participate (*Att.* XIV.6.2, XIV.20.5). Both he and Atticus look for comfort to Cicero's discussion in the *Tusculan Disputations* of death as a refuge (*Att.* XV.2.4), but Cicero broods on the suitability of suicide, Cato's solution, in his own case (*Att.* XV.20.2). And when he writes to Atticus in August of 44 about firmness of purpose (*constantia*, which for him was a key Stoic concept), 'In all the many writings on the subject, no philosopher has ever equated a change of plan with lack of firmness' (XVI.7.3), we are reminded of what he says at *De Officiis* I.112 about the conduct of Cato and others in the civil war, or at I.120 about the correct way to make a necessary change of career.

The composition of *De Officiis*

The links between Cicero's surviving correspondence and *De Officiis* also reveal just why, when and how Cicero came to write the work.

In the first four chapters, at the end, and in the introduction to Book III (5–6), Cicero relates his choice of topic and his manner of treatment to the education of his twenty-one year old son to whom the essay is addressed. Letters to Atticus make it clear that Cicero planned the work with his son in mind: 'I am addressing the book to Marcus. From father to son what better theme?' (*Att.* XV.13a.2, cf. XVI.11.4). Young Marcus, Cicero's second child and only son, had been in Athens for a year studying both oratory and philosophy, and there is ample testimony in letters of the period to Cicero's concern with the progress of his education. He writes to Atticus about his son's well-written letters (*Att.* XIV. 7.2, XV.16.1, cf. Quint. 1.7.34); bombards his teachers with requests for reports (*Att.* XIV.16.3, XIV.18.4), and is clearly perceived by his friends, and by young Marcus himself, as expecting a great deal of him (*Fam.* XII.16.2, XVI.25). All of this accords very well with what Cicero says in *De Officiis*: Marcus will be able to practise his Latin by reading Cicero's philosophical discussion (I.1, I.2); he must satisfy the expectations created by his superior education and his illustrious parentage (III.6).

In the last chapter Cicero explains that *De Officiis* is a substitute for a visit to his son that he would have made had political reasons not prevented him. Seven years earlier, in 51 BC when Marcus was fourteen, he and his older cousin Quintus went out with Cicero to his province, Cilicia, and, under his careful supervision, the two boys pursued their studies with a tutor. Now, as he tells Atticus, he felt that a visit to Athens 'would do much to keep Marcus steady' (*Att.* XIV.13.4). There can be no doubt then that what Cicero says in *De Officiis* about its relevance to his son is true. In keeping with his sceptical beliefs, however, he represents himself as using sweet reason to cajole an independent person, entitled to his own views (I.2, III.33, III.121), rather than putting pressure on a rather ordinary, but docile, young man whom his older cousin regarded as bullied (*Att.* XIII.37.2).

Even the form of the work reflects something of the true relationship. The fact that young Cicero was studying with the Peripatetic philosopher Cratippus while Cicero bases himself here on the Stoics, might have pointed to dialogue form, with the son defending the

Peripatetic position against his father. But Cicero was always concerned that the roles he gave his speakers should seem appropriate to them, despite the freedom that the conventions of literary dialogue allowed. In the little work on oratory written some time before, the *Partitiones Oratoriae*, Marcus had been allowed to ask questions like a schoolboy; in *De Officiis* Cicero treats him as a student with his own ideas, but makes it clear that he was not yet ready to discuss philosophy with Cicero as well as listen to him (III.121).

The literary inspiration for this 'guidance and advice' that young Cicero is to keep with his notes on Cratippus' lectures (I.4, III.121) is, in fact, the Letter to a Son. Cicero cites several examples including letters of advice and reproof from King Philip to his son Alexander (II.48, II.53), and a letter of warning from the Elder Cato to his son (I.37). The tone of paternal guidance, encouraging but firm, is pervasive. Even in the midst of the argument, young Marcus has the lesson, that civil achievements are better than military ones, brought home to him by a slice of paternal autobiography, complete with an unashamed boast specifically addressed to him (I.77–8). On the philosophical level, while the relevance to the addressee is made clear in the deference paid to his Peripatetic leanings (e.g. I.2, I.89 (on The Mean), II.56–57, III.33), Cicero prefers to exhort him in Stoic terms, because that sets a higher standard (III.20).

De Officiis is, however, neither a general tract disguised as a personal address (like the *Pamphlet on Standing for Office* ostensibly addressed to Cicero by his brother Quintus), nor a piece of personal admonition disguised as a general essay (like the letter on how to govern a province addressed to Quintus by Cicero (*Qfr.* I.1)). It is both genuinely appropriate to Marcus Cicero and also directed at others, particularly young Romans of the governing class. In another philosophical work of this period, Cicero expresses the hope that he is helping to instruct the young of Rome (*Div.* II.4–5), and in *De Officiis* he often makes it clear that he has in mind those who have to decide on their way of life and need to learn from the advice and example of older men (e.g. I.117, I.121, I.147, II.44–51). It is important to bear in mind here the Roman belief in respect for age, imitation of ancestral achievement (II.44), and practical apprenticeship for public life (II.46). So Cicero has in mind, not only his son Marcus, but men like his son-in-law Dolabella (cf. *Att.* XIV.17a) and his nephew Quintus, clearly more gifted than his own son (*Att.* VI.1.12, X.11.3, X.12a.4) but easily seduced politically, first by Caesar and then by Antony (*Att.* X.7.3, XIV.17.3). Only months before Cicero composed *De Officiis*, he wrote of his nephew to Atticus, 'So complete has been the change in him produced by certain writings of mine which I have in mind and by constant talk and advice, that his political sentiments are likely in future to be just what we desire' (*Att.* XVI.5.2). The 'writings' are probably *De Gloria*, a lost work which, like *De Officiis* itself, combined what we would call moral and political instruction, and which actually overlapped in subject with the later work, as Cicero expressly indicates (II.31). It is clear that Cicero believed that such philosophical teaching could have a beneficial effect, particularly on the young.

It therefore seems natural not only that St Ambrose, in writing a work of moral advice for young priests whom he regards as his sons (*De Officiis* I.24), should choose Cicero's *De Officiis* as an appropriate model, but also that Machiavelli, in writing *The Prince*, a handbook of practical advice for the politically ambitious, should regard the same work as a rival worthy of attack (chaps. 16–18). For, as we shall see again, the young whom Cicero had particularly in mind were those whose place in society entitled them, and in his view obliged them, to attempt a career in politics.

It is possible to date the composition of *De Officiis* with reasonable precision. At the beginning of Book I we learn that young Marcus has already been in Athens for a year. Therefore Cicero is writing after 1 April, 44 BC, for a letter concerned with the vital matter of his son's annual allowance gives that as the date on which Marcus' first year of study came to an end (*Att.* XV.15.4). At the very end of the work Cicero alludes to his abortive journey to Athens to visit his son, and letters show that Cicero embarked for Greece on 17 July (*Att.* XVI.6.2, XVI.7.2). Finally, the letters enable us to date Cicero's situation, described at III. 1 as moving about from villa to villa because of the fear of violence from his enemies, to between mid-October and 9 December, after his first speeches attacking Antony (*Fam.* XII.23.4, *Att.* XV.13a.2, *Fam.* XI.5.1). Confirmation comes from two letters to Atticus about *De Officiis* itself. The first (*Att.* XV.13a.2) written from Cicero's villa at Puteoli (or possibly Cumae) about 28 October gives the subject of his work in Greek and promises that 'there will be work to show for this absence of mine'; the second sent from the same place on 5 November (XVI.11.4) reveals that he has been using a work of the philosopher Panaetius on that same subject to write and complete the first two books of his essay. Therefore Books I and II were completed between *c.* 28 October and 5 November of 44.

In the second letter Cicero tells Atticus that his work is being held up while he waits for Greek philosophical material that he expects to help him with the topic covered in Book III. One of the works that Cicero sent for had arrived by the middle of November (*Att.* XVI.14.4). He returned to Rome on 9 December and was soon deeply involved in politics. Even if we assume that Cicero started writing before October, that he polished Books I and II while waiting for his new material, and that he made revisions after his return to Rome, we cannot escape the conclusion that *De Officiis* was written quickly, given its size and complexity. A certain carelessness in structure and argument, a tendency to repetition and, occasionally, irrelevance can be connected with that fact. Some scholars have, however, gone further and tried to argue that, in so short a time, Cicero could not have done more than transcribe his Greek sources.

In *De Officiis* Cicero used his licence as a sceptical Academic to adopt the arguments that he found, at that time and on that subject, the most convincing, which were those of the Stoa (III.20). In making use of Stoic writings, he tells us, he retained the right to exercise his judgement and critical faculty: he was not merely translating or expounding them (see Notes on Translation, p. xlvii). The work he particularly followed (III.7) was the celebrated treatise *On Duty* (*Peri tou kathekontos*) by Panaetius, the Rhodian aristocrat who lived from about 180 to 109 BC, visited Rome, was the teacher and intellectual companion of Scipio Africanus Aemilianus, and became head of the Stoic school in Athens in about 129 BC. His treatise, written about thirty years before his death (III.8), hence in 140/39 BC, was now nearly a century old, but Cicero still preferred it to a later and fuller one by Panaetius' pupil Hecaton (III.63, III.89). Cicero could expect his friend Atticus and his readers in general to have heard of it, if we can judge from the abrupt way he refers to it, but not to know its structure in detail (*Att.* XVI.11.4, *Off.* I.7). Two centuries later it was still read and admired (Gell. *NA* XIII.28), but, sadly, it has not come down to us, and most of what we know about it comes from Cicero's treatise.

Panaetius apparently treated his subject in greater detail than Cicero, who condensed the subject matter of his model's three books into two (III.7, II.16 with n.I), but Panaetius' treatise was unfinished. Cicero may have known that from the start, for, in explaining to

Atticus his need for material for Book III, he says that he has already sent for a work on the subject by Posidonius, Panaetius' gifted pupil, and asked a contemporary Stoic philosopher for an abstract, apparently of the same work (*Att.* XVI.11.4).

This defect in Panaetius' work would have been outweighed for Cicero by the merits that had recommended it to Greek and Roman readers (see p. 99, n.1). Panaetius had a more agreeable style than most Stoics (*Fin.* IV.79), and he was interested in giving practical advice to the good man who was not a sage (*Fin.* IV.23, Seneca *Ep.* 116.5). In writing for the general educated public, as in this work, he was happy to use moral concepts like 'good' and 'virtuous' in their ordinary sense rather than in their more restricted and elevated Stoic sense (II.35). He also had no interest in the Cynic strain of Stoicism which ridiculed conventional euphemisms and institutions (1.128, 1.148).

For Cicero at least, there were other attractive features as well. Panaetius, though an orthodox Stoic, was influenced by Plato and Aristotle (*Fin.* IV.79), and Cicero wished in this work to minimize the difference between the Stoa, his own Academy, and the Peripatetic teaching to which his son was exposed. Moreover, Panaetius held up as a living model (II.76, cf. 1.90) Scipio Aemilianus, one of Cicero's heroes (*Off.* III.1–4) and the chief speaker in *De Re Publica*, where his opposition to Tiberius Gracchus, one of the villains of *De Officiis* (1.76, 1.109, II.43, II.80), is celebrated. But even more important than Panaetius' views were the interests he shared with Cicero. Panaetius treated the duties of men involved in public life, men who pleaded in the lawcourts (II.51) and endowed public buildings (II.60). He had anticipated Cicero in discussing exhaustively the means of winning repute and political support, while neglecting more commonly sought advantages like health and wealth (II.86, cf. II.16). Also suggestive is Atticus' response to Cicero's suggestion of translating the Greek word for duty as *officium*: he wondered if it would apply to public life as well as to private (*Att.* XVI.14.3). Atticus can only have asked that question on the basis of what he knew of Panaetius' work, for he had not yet seen a word of Cicero's.

As for the Posidonian material which Cicero had sent for (above, p. xix), that proved to be brief (III.8) and disappointing. Though it was useful, as Cicero had expected, for dealing with the subject of duties in particular circumstances relevant to Book III (see p. 62, n. 1), Cicero declares himself dissatisfied with all the material he found for that book and hence thrown back on his own resources (III.34).

Scholars have nonetheless asserted Cicero's dependence on Posidonius. Yet, even with regard to Books I and II, where we are on firmer ground, it is difficult to know how dependent Cicero is. On the one hand, he avows more often and more formally than in any of his other philosophical writings, his debt to one work in particular; on the other, the Elder Pliny (*NH* pref. 22–3), praising Cicero for his honesty in admitting dependence on Greek sources, compares the role of Panaetius in *De Officiis* with that of Plato in *De Re Publica*, where only the most general kind of inspiration is involved. Moreover, Cicero clearly expected his readers to accept his claim to be using Panaetius selectively and critically, for he feels it necessary to tell them occasionally that he has Panaetius' support for a controversial view (II.51, II.60). In fact, the similar philosophical terminology in his letters of the period, as well as his own allusions to his recent works on the principles of ethics (I.6, III.120), on glory (II.31), old age (I.151 and n. 2) and friendship (II.31), suggest that much of the thought in *De Officiis* antedates the actual time of composition. In any case, when we consider how marked the work is by contemporary events and how closely it mirrors Cicero's views elsewhere, we must conclude that Panaetius' work was too thoroughly digested and reworked by Cicero for us to separate the contributions of the two authors now. In an earlier work, Cicero had said that, in general, he did not simply translate the views of Greek philosophers but added his own judgement and arrangement of topics (*Fin.* I.5–6). The special dependence on his source that he avows here may lie in his decision to adopt and follow closely the structure of Panaetius' treatise, which he frequently mentions (e.g. I.9–10, II.9, II.88, III.7 ff., III.33–4). Even so, he added two supplementary topics to the three Panaetius adduced.

Themes and Perspectives

Each book of *De Officiis* deals with one of these three types of deliberation governing human conduct: honourable or the reverse; beneficial or the reverse; how to resolve apparent clashes between the two. The two supplementary topics, choosing between two honourable courses of action and choosing between two beneficial courses, form the conclusions to Books I and II respectively. (See the Synopsis, pp. xlviii–li.)

The modern reader may be struck at the outset by the inclusion, indeed the prominence, of the 'beneficial' or 'expedient' in a discussion of ethical conduct. This approach is not peculiar to Cicero but derives from the essential character of Greek and Roman ethical thinking. All the dogmatic schools of Greek philosophy held that the aim of life was the individual's *eudaimonia*, a word usually rendered as 'happiness' or 'well-being', and that the key to this blessed condition was provided by nature (including human nature). The schools offered different views on what constituted *eudaimonia* and hence on what the goal of life prescribed by nature was (see Summary, p. xxxv). But even for those that championed virtue, this pursuit was not opposed to, or even separate from, the pursuit of self-interest *properly understood*, for in pursuing the natural goal man fulfils his nature and achieves well-being. Cicero's readers would not then have been surprised to find him approaching the question of how one should behave by considering first 'the honourable', then 'the beneficial', and expecting the answers to agree in general, despite the existence of problematic areas in which the two appear to conflict.

One way to grasp the particular perspective of *De Officiis* is to consider what Cicero omits. The work is not a discussion of the nature of ethics or of the first principles of morality, such as Cicero had essayed in *De Finibus* (1.7, III.20). Cicero takes for granted the Stoic doctrine of the identity of the honourable and the beneficial, which he calls the 'rule' (III.81) and compares to the postulates of geometry (III.33); he states without argument that the Academic and Peripatetic moral principles would yield similar precepts (1.6) and be compatible with the *formula* for resolving apparent conflicts (III.20); he censures rather than rebuts the Epicurean doctrine of pleasure (1.5, III.39, III.117–20). Since even the basic principles of ethics are not examined, *a fortiori* there can be no treatment of the metaphysical foundations of ethics by which all these schools set considerable store.

De Officiis is concerned instead with practical ethics, with giving advice on the basis of the 'rule'. In Book I the 'honourable' is analyzed into four principal virtues to which our *officia*, defined as actions for which a persuasive justification can be given, are assigned (1.15, 1.8, cf. 1.101). These actions can be performed by 'good men' (in vulgar parlance), though when the wise man performs them, the understanding behind his choice and the consistency of his actions give them a higher moral value (III.14). Cicero is thinking primarily of those who wish to make moral progress and who will not choose the personally advantageous over the honourable, if they understand what really is honourable and advantageous on particular occasions (III.17–19). He cannot hope to set out a complete code of behaviour that will cater for every occasion. What he teaches is how to make moral decisions, how to analyze different possible courses of action: we should be, he says, 'good calculators of our duties' (I.59).

What has given this particular work of *practical ethics* an important place in the history of *political thought*, however, is its emphasis on social and political morality. Though at the outset (I.4) Cicero says that precepts about duty apply to the whole of life, what interests him is the behaviour of men in society, which is presented as the natural and best condition for human life (I.II, I.157–60, II.12–15). In Book I Cicero devotes much of his brief discussion of the first virtue, wisdom, to insisting that love of learning should not be allowed to draw us away from a life of action. The virtue that he regards as paramount is the second, justice, which governs social behaviour (III.28).

The extended discussion devoted to justice, however, reveals that Cicero is not equally concerned with *all* the social obligations of *all* men. Though he touches on our duty to mankind in general (I.50–3), later stating that the *formula* forbidding one to profit at another's expense applies there (III.30, III.42), he also makes it clear that no material sacrifices are required at this level (I.51–2). In discussing the different degrees of fellowship and the corresponding order of priority of our obligations (I.53–9), Cicero considers family relationships, friendships, duties to neighbours, to fellow-citizens and to those of the same race and language, giving priority in practical services to one's country and then to one's parents (I.58; see p. 62, n. 2). Of the relationships regularly included in Roman discussions of such priorities (e.g. Gell. *NA* V.13), guest-friendship (*hospitium*) and guardianship (*tutela*) receive only brief mention elsewhere (I.139, II.64, III.61, III.70), and clientship is only noted as a relationship regarded as so humiliating by those of any social standing that they would rather die than enjoy patronage or be called clients (II.69 with n. I). The omission of the last two is indicative of Cicero's general lack of interest in obligations towards recognized social inferiors. Though he notes that we have obligations even towards the lowest, i.e. slaves (I.41, cf. II.24), we hear nothing, not only of duties to clients (ties that may have been weakening in the late Republic), but of the relationship of patron to ex-slave. We hear only about patronage towards subjects of Rome and Italian towns (I.35, II.50, cf. II.27, III.74), just as the only hospitality that interests Cicero is that shown to illustrious foreigners on public business (II.64, cf. I.149): the liberality of Cimon to all those in his district is not furnished with a Roman parallel. Cicero only alludes vaguely to the advantages of favouring the poor in showing generosity (I.49, II.62–3, II.69–70). Of course, some of the relationships of mutual obligation he describes would be more unequal in reality than in theory, but Cicero, in presenting an ideal of conduct, respects their theoretical equality.

As the treatment of patronage and hospitality already suggest, Cicero is as selective about the subjects as about the objects of obligation. He is primarily interested in those who take part, or reasonably aspire to take part, in public life. This helps to explain the long passage about the just behaviour of states in war (I.34–40), which is to be followed up later with discussions of the inexpediency of founding an empire on fear and exploitation (II.26–9) and of the true expediency of generous and honourable conduct by states towards their enemies, subjects and citizens (III.46–9, III.86–8). This also explains why, in the treatment of the third virtue (courage or greatness of spirit), all but one of the twenty-three chapters (I.69–91) devoted to the performance of great and useful deeds are concerned with the civil and military activities of public life, including actually being in office (72–85). This is shown to be the best arena for demonstrating contempt for adversity and danger, though ambition must always be kept within the limits dictated by justice (86–7).

When Cicero comes to the fourth virtue (I.93–152), he is again concerned with his peers, though towards the end he mentions that foreigners, non-citizen residents and citizens generally have particular duties and alludes to professions honourable for the lower orders (I.151). The core of the discussion is the notion of *decorum*, 'seemliness', which dictates that we choose a form of life appropriate to our individual talents and our material and social position (see Notes on Translation p. xlvi). Cicero reverts often to those with illustrious ancestors to imitate (I.116) and his examples are drawn from the civic and military leaders of the past. He expects even elderly members of the governing class to serve the Republic (I.123). The emphasis on success goes with that on observing social norms and not giving offence (I.99, I.148). Cicero's detailed discussion of social conduct, including one's external appearance (1.130–1) and one's house (1.138–40), and of the art of civilized conversation (1.132–7) are clearly geared to aristocratic behaviour, and some of his advice, e.g. on the total avoidance of nudity (1.129), is severely restricted to Roman society. It may have been Cicero's awareness of the social disruption caused by the civil upheavals of his time that led him to codify the manners he wished to preserve. In any event, ethical teaching here becomes indistinguishable from tips on social expertise, particularly useful for those not necessarily born to it but ambitious to rise.

When Cicero comes to compare the obligations under the different virtues (1.152–61), he is again at pains to emphasize our duty to society, for the claims of each of the other three virtues are compared with those of justice, not of each other.

This emphasis is continued in Book II, where the support of one's fellow men is quickly identified as the most useful or beneficial thing an individual can acquire (II.11–19). But only one chapter (30) is devoted to friendship, the kind of support that is attainable by both outstanding men and ordinary men. It is to the outstanding men that Cicero offers his advice on winning glory through good will, faith and honour (31–51), and his precepts on liberality (52–85). The financial aspect of liberality (55–64) provides the occasion for a discussion of public entertainments and buildings, the key forms of aristocratic largesse in the ancient world. The other aspect is liberality in services, and here most of the discussion (72–85) concerns what those in office can do for all or particular groups of the citizenry. It would not seriously misrepresent *De Officiis* to describe it as a handbook for members of the governing class on their duties to their peers in private life and to their fellow-citizens in public life.

The third book deals with the topic that Posidonius pronounced the most essential in all of philosophy (8). Cicero first reconstructs the lines of Panaetius' missing argument, adopting as the *formula* for resolving apparent conflicts between the honourable and the beneficial the notion, already implicit in the discussion of justice in Book I (21, 42 *fin.*), that it is contrary to nature to secure a benefit for oneself at someone else's expense. He then proceeds to his own development, which he represents as compatible with either Stoic or Peripatetic premises (p. 112, n. 1). The word *formula* is borrowed from Roman civil law (p. 107, n. 3) which also supplies Cicero with some of his most interesting cases of conflict. These alone would have made the work more accessible to his Roman readers, more of whom would have had the traditional legal training for public life than would have probed the intricacies of Greek philosophy. But the legal material is not confined to illustration. Cicero found an analogy in Roman legal thinking for the casuistry or analysis of moral cases practised at a high level by the philosophical schools (III.91). The fascination that the category of duties in particular (i.e. exceptional) circumstances held for the Stoics (I.31, III.32, III.92–6) is symptomatic of this interest. In it Cicero found his justification for tyrannicide and, in particular, for the murder of Caesar by men who had been his friends. For if the *formula* prohibits individuals *and states* from benefiting at another's expense (p. 115, n. 1), it does not prohibit citizens who have a duty to their country, their friends, and mankind in general, from injuring someone who harms his community and places himself outside the pale of human society by his subhuman behaviour (III.32, cf. III.19).

Roman law and jurisprudence are relevant to Book III at a deeper level even than technique, for they have an obvious connection with justice, which here again, as the social virtue, is given priority. Though Cicero professes to be treating the apparent conflict of the beneficial with each of the four divisions of the honourable (III.96), the conflicts that occupy most of the book are those between justice and self-interest posing as wisdom or 'good sense' (40–96). Even the clash with courage (97–115) involves discussion of the justice of keeping oaths (102–110, III–115, cf. I.39), and the clash with temperance (116–120) turns into an attack on the Epicureans in which Cicero particularly condemns their adoption of the virtues as means to pleasure because, in his view, justice cannot be accommodated in this way. The attack on apparent 'good sense' brings Cicero into issues of fraud and good faith in which Roman law had made great progress in his own time through the use of the praetor's edict (p. 14, n. 1) to establish new types of legal action. Cicero describes the task of philosophy as raising human conduct to the standard set by natural law, but he also thought that human law codes should aspire to that standard (69–78). A man like Q. Mucius Scaevola the Pontifex, who set himself a higher standard of honesty than existing law required, also worked, as a judge, to raise legal standards (III.62, III.70). In Cicero's own lifetime legal actions offering protection against 'malicious fraud' were devised (60–1). Cicero also makes great play with the legal notion of the 'good man' (70, cf. p. 9, n. 1) and its relation to the higher philosophical conception (77).

This awareness and approval of recent legal developments combines uneasily with Cicero's equally strong conviction that the traditional Roman aristocratic code of behaviour exemplified the norms enunciated by the Greek philosophers, for he shared the conventional view of his contemporaries that they lived in an age of moral decline (III.III–112, cf. II.65–6) and should return to the *mos maiorum* ('the way of our ancestors'). Thus Cicero makes strenuous efforts to show that the wars through which Rome had acquired her empire were undertaken only as a last resort in seeking to establish peace (1.35, 1.38, II.26–7, cf. III.46) and that her ancestral procedures for declaring war instantiated the philosophical conception of a just war. Cicero planned from the start to use as the climax of Book III, and thus of the whole work, the extended example of M. Atilius Regulus, a patriotic martyr of the mid-third century BC (*Att.* XVI.II.4). His recital of how Regulus sacrificed himself in order to protect Roman interests while keeping faith with the enemy, concludes with a tribute to the seriousness with which Romans of the past regarded oaths (III–15). The Roman ancestors are shown to have practised by instinct what the Greeks could only preach.

That had already been the message of the works of political philosophy that Cicero had written a decade before, *De Re Publica* (now only partially preserved) and the unfinished *De Legibus*. *De Re Publica* is the Roman answer to Plato's *Republic*, presenting as the ideal, not a theoretical construct, but the ancestral Roman state, analyzed as the mixed constitution of Greek theory and restored to its idealized past condition. *De Legibus* presents a skeletal law code to go with the ideal state. Backed by a theory of natural law derived from Greek philosophy, the code itself is similar in most respects to existing Roman law or custom, except for certain innovations clearly inspired by Cicero's own political experiences. In *De Re Publica* Cicero makes it clear that only a governing class educated to a high standard of conduct can restore the Republic to a healthy condition: the evils that threaten this process are ruthless imperialism and self-seeking demagoguery (cf. *Off.* II.60), just the ones that, in the later work, are held responsible for the perilous condition of the Republic. In *De Legibus* natural law or *ius gentium* is the standard to which the Roman *ius civile* can and should conform, just as in *De Officiis*, the principle of not profiting at another's expense (III.23) particularly through fraud and cunning (III.68–72), a principle that belongs to *ius gentium*, is shown penetrating Roman legal procedures through the principle of 'good faith'. Together these three works present Cicero's formula for the regeneration of the Roman governing class, a fusion of Greek philosophical precepts with the traditional values of the great Roman statesmen of the past.

Throughout *De Officiis* Cicero's own political orientation is apparent. We have already noted how closely his view of Caesar and Antony here fits that in his personal letters. Other enemies including Clodius and Crassus are turned into negative moral examples (II.58, I.25, I.109, III.73, III.75). Cicero's own insistence on the *concordia ordinum* ('harmony of different classes') and the maintenance of financial credit, particularly during his consulship, are defended (II.84). The same lack of imagination with which he had confronted as a politician the social and economic problems of his day shows here in the one solution he offers in opposition to the *popularis* programmes for land distribution and debt relief (II.72–4, II.78–84). In place of his enemies' schemes for redistributing existing wealth, he suggests the acquisition of new wealth through imperialism (II.85). How was this to be reconciled with his demand for just wars and the equitable treatment of Rome's subjects?

Even if Cicero did not always succeed, he did at least try to use the tools of Greek philosophy, not only to analyze and raise Roman standards, but to live and act rationally. Even his partisan belief in the sanctity of private property, whose preservation he here suggests is the chief purpose of organized society (II.73), is grounded on a view of human nature as fundamentally social (I.158), on a theory of how society develops (I.11–12, I.54), and on a conception of how human law, which protects such institutions (I.21, I.51), is related to natural law (III.68–9, III.72). To this extent *De Officiis* transcends its particularity – its contemporary allusions, Roman prejudices, political bias. Very different societies at very different times have found in it, not only a repository of political experience, but an example of the sharpened insight that political crisis can inspire in a truly educated statesman.

Principal Dates

BC	Major Historical Events	Life of Cicero	Theoretical Works
106	Birth of Pompey	Birth of Cicero, 3 January	
104	C. Marius consul II triumphs over Jugurtha		
103–101	Marius consul III–V defeats the Cimbri and Teutones		
100	Marius consul VI. Birth of Julius Caesar		
95	L. Licinius Crassus and Q. Mucius Scaevola consuls pass Lex Licinia Mucia resented by Italian allies		
91–88	Murder of reformer M. Livius Drusus leads to Social War between Rome and her Italian allies who are defeated but offered Roman citizenship	Serves under Pompey's father in Social War Studying law with Q. Mucius Scaevola (Augur)	
88	L. Sulla marches on Rome and goes East to fight Mithridates. P. Sulpicius reformer killed	Hears Philo of Larissa in Rome Studying oratory	
87	Marius seizes Rome. Posidonius in Rome on embassy	Studying law with Q. Mucius Scaevola (Pontifex)	
86	Death of Marius		*De Inventione* (written after 91)

BC	Major Historical Events	Life of Cicero	Theoretical Works
83–81	Sulla returns to Rome, orders proscriptions, becomes Dictator		
80	Sulla consul	Defends Sextus Roscius, his first public case	
79–8	Sulla in retirement and dies	Travels and studies in Greece and Asia: hears Antiochus of Ascalon, Posidonius, Zeno and Phaedrus (Epicureans)	
75–4		Quaestor at Lilybaeum in Sicily	
73–1	Slave revolt led by Spartacus		
70	First consulship of Pompey and Crassus	Prosecutes Verres for extortion in Sicily	
69		Aedile: gives games	
67	Pompey clears the Mediterranean of pirates		
66	Pompey given command against Mithridates	Praetor. Speaks for Pompey's command	
65		Birth of his son Marcus. His brother Quintus is aedile	
63	Catilinarian conspiracy exposed	Consul with C. Antonius. Executes conspirators without trial	
62	Pompey returns to Rome in December	Quintus Cicero praetor	
61	Pompey triumphs over Mithridates	Testifies against P. Clodius on sacrilege charge	
		Quintus Cicero governs Asia (61–58)	

60	Pompey, Caesar and M. Crassus form 'First Triumvirate'		
59	C. Julius Caesar consul uses violence to legislate		
58	Caesar begins his conquest of Gaul	Measures of P. Clodius send Cicero into exile in March	
57	Pompey put in charge of the corn supply for five years	Q. Cicero serves under Pompey (57–6) Recalled from exile; returns to Rome in September	
56	Renewal of 'First Triumvirate' at Luca	Cicero warned and ceases to oppose them	*De Oratore*
55	Pompey and Crassus consuls II: both receive five-year commands; Caesar's command in Gaul renewed		
54	Crassus leaves for Syria to fight the Parthians; Pompey governs Spain from Italy through legates	Quintus Cicero serves under Caesar in Gaul (54–52)	*De Re Publica* begun
53	Defeat and death of M. Crassus		
52	Pompey elected sole consul after murder of P. Clodius and other violence	Elected augur in place of M. Crassus	
51	First attempts in the Senate to recall Caesar from Gaul before his command expires	Goes to govern Cilicia, arriving 31 July. Quintus serves under him.	*De Re Publica* published. *De Legibus* begun
50		Leaves Cilicia (30 July) and reaches Italy (24 November)	

BC	Major Historical Events	Life of Cicero	Theoretical Works
49	In January Caesar crosses the Rubicon into Italy, has himself named Dictator In March Pompey leaves Italy for the East	Cicero continues peace efforts, though assigned a command by Pompey In June leaves Italy to join Pompey	
48	In August: Pompey defeated by Caesar at Pharsalus In September: Pompey murdered in Egypt	Cicero returns to Italy and waits for Caesar's pardon at Brundisium	
47	Caesar makes Cleopatra queen of Egypt In September returns and begins legislation Leaves to fight Republicans in Africa	In July pardoned by Caesar along with Quintus and his nephew Quintus jr.	
46	In April Caesar defeats Republicans in Africa at Thapsus: suicide of Cato In November Caesar leaves Rome to fight the Republicans in Spain led by Pompey's sons	Divorces Terentia Delivers *Pro Marcello*, thanking Caesar for his clemency, in the Senate Marries Publilia	*Brutus* *Paradoxa Stoicorum* *Eulogy of Cato* *Orator*
45	In March Caesar defeats Republicans in Spain at Munda	In January Tullia gives birth to a son but dies in February In April young Marcus begins his studies in Athens	*Consolation to himself *Hortensius*: exhortation to philosophy *Academica* *De Finibus* *Tusculan Disputations* and *De Natura Deorum* begun

xxxii

44	Caesar named *dictator perpetuus*	Cato Maior de senectute
	Refuses offer of a crown from Antony	
	Caesar assassinated on 15 March	
	Antony takes control as consul	
	In April Octavian (later Augustus) lands in Italy	
	In July Senate assigns provinces to Brutus and Cassius	
	In April–June visiting his country villas in Italy	*De Divinatione* finished
	On 17 July leaves for Greece but quickly returns	*De Fato*
	On 31 August returns to Rome	**De Gloria*
	On 2 September delivers First Philippic Oration against Antony	*Topica*
	In October–December visiting his villas in Italy; writing Second Philippic	*Laelius de amicitia*
43	In April after Battle of Mutina, both consuls die	*De Officiis*
	In August Octavian seizes the consulship	
	In November the Triumvirate of Antony, Lepidus and Octavian established by Lex Titia	
	Proscriptions instituted: Cicero on list	
	Delivers Fifth–Fourteenth Philippic	
	On 7 December Cicero killed	

* = lost
Some minor undateable works have been omitted.

N.B. Some of the dates are only approximate.

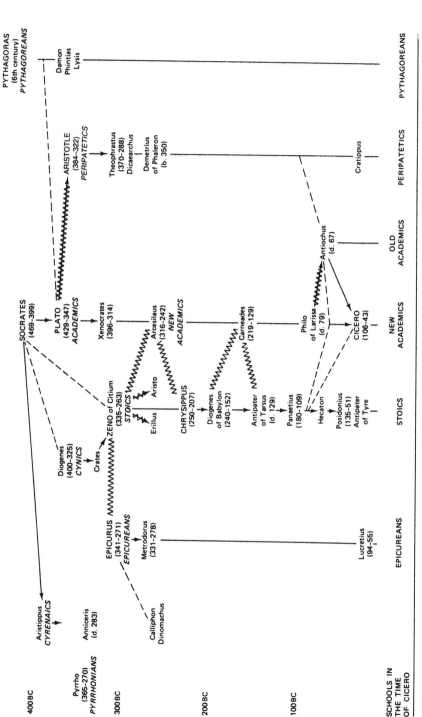

PYTHAGORAS
(6th century)
PYTHAGOREANS

Damon
Phintias
Lysis

PYTHAGOREANS

SOCRATES
(469–399)

ARISTOTLE
(384–322)
PERIPATETICS

PLATO
(429–347)
ACADEMICS

Theophrastus
(370–288)
Dicaearchus
Demetrius
of Phaleron
(b. 350)

Cratippus

PERIPATETICS

Xenocrates
(396–314)

Arcesilaus
(316–242)
NEW
ACADEMICS

Carneades
(219–129)

Philo
of Larissa
(d. 79)

Antiochus
(d. 67)

OLD
ACADEMICS

CICERO
(106–43)

NEW
ACADEMICS

Diogenes
(400–325)
CYNICS

Crates

ZENO of Citium
(335–263)
STOICS

Aristo

Erillus

CHRYSIPPUS
(250–207)

Diogenes
of Babylon
(240–152)

Antipater
of Tarsus
(d. 129)

Panaetius
(180–109)

Hecaton

Posidonius
(135–51)
Antipater
of Tyre

STOICS

Aristippus
CYRENAICS

Anniceris
(d. 283)

EPICURUS
(341–271)
EPICUREANS

Metrodorus
(331–278)

Calliphon
Dinomachus

Lucretius
(94–55)

EPICUREANS

Pyrrho
(365–270)
PYRRHONIANS

400BC

300BC

200BC

100BC

SCHOOLS IN
THE TIME
OF CICERO

KEY ——→ Direct teaching ——— School tradition – – – Influence VVVVVV Dispute

N.B. Some of the dates are only approximate

Summary of the Doctrines of the Hellenistic Schools

The brief accounts below are written from an unashamedly Ciceronian viewpoint, and with particular emphasis on ethical doctrines. (For references to more balanced accounts see Bibliography, pp. xl–xli.) Cicero saw the critical ethical difference between the schools as lying in the answer each gave to the question, 'What is the end of life?' (see especially *De Finibus* v.16–23).

The *Stoics* held that the end of life was virtue; virtue was the only thing that was good, and to live well was to live virtuously. Conversely, vice was the only evil. External advantages, health, wealth, and so on, were not good, but merely 'preferable'; sickness, poverty, even death, not bad, but 'unpreferable'. (Unorthodox Stoics such as Aristo and Erillus did not concede even that much, see p. 4, n. 1) Hence the premise that Cicero assumes throughout Book III: nothing is good except that which is honourable. In other words, the only thing that benefits us is virtue. Only the virtuous and wise man is truly happy, and he is happy whatever his external circumstances (see also Notes on Translation, pp. xliv–xlv).

The wise man lived in accordance with nature, with his own human nature and with the universal nature that was divine and providential. For the early Stoics one lived virtuously by choosing wisely and steadily 'the things in accordance with nature', as they described the preferable things. The wise man was compared to a good archer aiming at a target; it was not hitting the target that mattered, but aiming, that is choosing, well. In other words, virtue and happiness depended not on whether one achieved the preferable things, but on how one sought them.

Those things that the early Stoics had termed preferable, Panaetius called 'advantageous' or 'beneficial'. He discussed the virtuous and the beneficial separately; he thought we could ask independently of the same action both 'Is this virtuous?' and 'Is this beneficial?' (see p. 105, n. 2). For him, virtue was no longer simply aiming at the preferable things well. Virtues and benefits could, at first sight at least, be specified without reference to one another. However, Panaetius still believed that nothing was in the end good and beneficial unless it was virtuous; therefore when the two questions were asked about a single action, the answers should be the same. If an action appears to be both beneficial and dishonourable, one appearance must be misleading. It may seem to be beneficial for me to inherit this large legacy, or win that election; but it is in fact so only if I can acquire it without acting dishonourably.

The *Epicureans* took pleasure to be the end of life, and argued that the virtues should be valued because, and in so far as, they provided one with pleasure. The gods, they believed, had no interest or involvement in human affairs. Epicurus' wise man avoided public life except in an emergency.

The *Academy* that Plato founded in Athens continued in existence there at least until Philo of Larissa fled to Rome to escape the invasion of Mithridates of Pontus in 88 BC. At first its adherents interpreted Plato's teaching positively and dogmatically. However, under the leadership of Arcesilaus (mid-3rd century) the Academics took a sceptical turn. Interpreting Plato's writings as being open-ended and inquiring rather than dogmatic, they held no positive doctrines themselves, but criticised those of other schools, particularly the Stoics. Cicero's own teacher, Philo, held a modified scepticism: one could not seek certain knowledge, but should provisionally accept the view that, after examining the arguments, seems the most persuasive.

Philo's pupil Antiochus quarrelled with him over his scepticism. He held that the early Academy was in fact dogmatic, designating the school he himself founded the *Old Academy* and the heirs of Arcesilaus the *New Academy*. He seems in practice to have been strongly influenced by Stoicism.

In Cicero's eyes the ethics of the Old Academy and of the *Peripatetics* (Aristotelians) were practically the same: both held that virtue was the greatest good, but that external goods were also of real, though minor, value. Hence, while the Stoics thought that nothing was beneficial that was not honourable (III.20), the Academics and Peripatetics could consider something beneficial, and indeed good, which had no connection with honourableness and virtue. Thus if a dishonest action were to make someone rich, Panaetius would have described his wealth as only apparently beneficial, because the action was dishonest; the Peripatetics would say that his wealth was actually beneficial and good, but that its benefit was far outweighed by the badness of the action.

Bibliography

Ancient Works

There is a great deal of evidence for Cicero's life and intellectual milieu in his own works and in those of later Greek and Latin authors, all easily available in translation.

Cicero's works

The *Letters to Atticus* and *Letters to His Friends* are accessible in an excellent translation by D. R. Shackleton Bailey in the Penguin Classical Series, which also contains volumes of selected speeches and a volume of excerpts from the philosophical works called *On the Good Life*. The Loeb Classical Library contains all of Cicero's speeches and philosophical works in translation (with facing Latin text). A new series of translations of the philosophical works with facing Latin text, notes and introduction, published by Aris and Phillips, has made its debut with the excellent *Tusculan Disputations* I by A. E. Douglas. Still helpful is the translation with notes of *De Re Publica* in Sabine and Smith, *On the Commonwealth* (Ohio, 1929). An introduction and commentary on Book I of *On the Laws* is now available in *Cicero De Legibus* I, edited by N. Rudd and T. Wiedemann (Bristol, 1987).

In studying *De Officiis*, the reader will find particularly illuminating: Cicero's letters of the last years of his life; the speeches *In Defence of Sestius* (*Pro Sestio*) and *The Philippics* (especially I and II); his earlier works of political philosophy, *De Re Publica* (incompletely preserved) and *De Legibus* (unfinished); the works of moral philosophy *On the Ends of Good and Evil Things* (*De Finibus Bonorum et Malorum*) and, to a lesser extent, *The Elder Cato: on Old Age* (*Cato Maior de senectute*) and *Laelius: on Friendship* (*Laelius de amicitia*). The *Paradoxes of the Stoics* (*Paradoxa Stoicorum*), in which Cicero subjects the most extreme Stoic doctrines to rhetorical treatment, and the partially preserved books on Academic epistemology, *Academica*, in which he defends his own sceptical brand of Academic philosophy, will also be of interest.

Other ancient works

Plutarch's biography of Cicero is available in translation in the Penguin volume *Plutarch: the Fall of the Roman Republic*, and in an Aris and Phillips edition by J. L. Moles (1988). The Penguin Sallust volume offers an account of the Catilinarian conspiracy, which Cicero dealt with in his consulship, by a younger contemporary of Cicero's. Lucretius' Epicurean poem *On the Nature of Things* (*De Rerum Natura*), also in Penguin, illuminates Cicero's intellectual milieu, while the biography of his close friend Atticus by Cornelius Nepos, which is translated in the Loeb volume containing Florus and now, with full commentary, by N. Horsfall in the Clarendon Ancient History Series (Oxford, 1989), is very instructive for Cicero's life and the society in which he lived.

Modern Works

The second edition of the *Oxford Classical Dictionary* (1970) provides a brief introduction on most topics concerning ancient Greece and Rome.

Biography

D. L. Stockton, *Cicero, a Political Biography* (Oxford, 1971) is a readable account of his career and its political context; D. R. Shackleton Bailey, *Cicero* (London, 1971) uses the author's expert knowledge of the letters to evoke Cicero's personality; E. D. Rawson, *Cicero a Portrait* (London, 1975; paperback reprint, Bristol, 1983) is a sympathetic account, complete with a consideration of Cicero's intellectual contribution.

Different aspects of Cicero's life and work are covered by the essays,

including A. E. Douglas' 'Cicero the Philosopher', in *Cicero*, edited
by T. A. Dorey (London, 1965). The Introduction (pp. 1–28) in J. S.
Reid, *The Academica of Cicero* (Cambridge, 1885) is still worth reading
on Cicero and philosophy. See also P. L. Schmidt, 'Cicero's Place
in Roman Philosophy: a Study of his Prefaces', *Classical Journal* 74
(1979), 115–27. J. Glucker, 'Cicero's Philosophical Affiliations', *The
Question of 'Eclecticism': Studies in later Greek Philosophy*, ed. J. M.
Dillon and A. A. Long (Berkeley, 1988) is a valuable examination
of the evidence for Cicero's adherence to the sceptical Academy at
different periods of his life, but we are unconvinced by its thesis.

N. Wood, *Cicero's Social and Political Thought* (California, 1988)
aims to discuss Cicero's political thought as a whole in its historical
context, but both the treatment of the history and the analysis of
the Ciceronian texts are so oversimplified as to be seriously misleading.

Scholarship on Cicero is briefly summarized and perceptively criticized in A. E. Douglas, *Cicero*, Greece and Rome New Surveys in
the Classics, no. 2 (Oxford, 1968: with addenda, 1978).

Intellectual background

The most complete and up-to-date account of developments in
Cicero's time, including philosophy, law, historiography and anti-
quarianism, is E. D. Rawson, *Intellectual Life in the Late Roman Republic* (London, 1985), a highly learned work which does not deal with
Cicero directly but with his contemporaries. The forthcoming second
edition of *Cambridge Ancient History* vol. IX contains a chapter 'Intellectual Developments in the Late Republic' (a brief account including
Cicero) by M. Griffin. C. Wirszubski, *Libertas as a Political Idea at
Rome* (Cambridge, 1960) discusses some of the key concepts of Roman
political thought: see also D. C. Earl, *The Moral and Political Tradition
of Rome* (London, 1967) Chaps. 1–2. J. D. Minyard, *Lucretius and the
Late Republic*, Mnemosyne Supplement 90 (Leiden, 1985) contrasts
the different uses made of political and social concepts by Cicero
and some of his contemporaries in an oversimplified but suggestive
way.

The philosophical doctrines current in the period are clearly
summarized in J. Barnes, 'Hellenistic Philosophy and Science', *Oxford
History of the Classical World* (Oxford, 1986), 365 ff. and more fully
explained in A. A. Long, *Hellenistic Philosophy* (London, 1974). Volume I

of the source book by A. A. Long and D. N. Sedley, *The Hellenistic Philosophers* (Cambridge, 1987) gives the basic texts in translation with helpful philosophical commentary. J. Glucker, *Antiochus and the Later Academy* (Göttingen, 1978) is a very detailed and learned account of the vicissitudes of the philosophical schools as institutions, and of the Academy in particular, in Cicero's day and later. Essays on some of the philosophies and philosophers that were influential at Rome in the Late Republic are to be found in *Philosophia Togata* (Oxford, 1989), edited by M. Griffin and J. Barnes.

Political background

Aside from the biographies of Cicero already mentioned, which inevitably describe in detail the major political events of the period, there are many brief accounts of the history of the later Roman Republic, such as P. A. Brunt, *Social Conflicts in the Roman Republic* (London, 1971) and M. H. Crawford, *The Roman Republic* (London, 1978), and more detailed analyses in M. Gelzer, *Caesar, Politician and Statesman* (Oxford, 1968) and E. S. Gruen, *The Last Generation of the Roman Republic* (Berkeley, 1974). The second edition of the *Cambridge Ancient History* vol. IX, which deals with the late Republic, is about to appear. The classic work on the fall of the Republic is R. Syme, *The Roman Revolution* (Oxford, 1939), which treats the events of the period when *De Officiis* was written in fascinating detail.

The political, legal and social institutions of the Roman Republic are described in H. F. Jolowicz and B. Nicholas, *Historical Introduction to Roman Law* third edn. (Cambridge, 1972), C. Nicolet, *The World of the Citizen in Republican Rome* (London, 1980), and J. Crook, *Law and Life of Rome* (London, 1977), where the use of the law to uncover Roman social habits is very relevant to *De Officiis*.

The way Roman politics actually worked and its social context are analysed in different, often conflicting ways, in L. R. Taylor, *Party Politics in the Age of Caesar* (Berkeley, 1949), M. Gelzer, *The Roman Nobility* (Oxford, 1969), G. E. M. de Ste. Croix, *The Class Struggle in the Ancient Greek World* (London, 1981), pp. 327–72 (on Rome), and P. A. Brunt, *The Fall of the Roman Republic and Related Essays* (Oxford, 1988).

Roman imperialism in the Late Republic is examined in relation to Roman politics and economics in E. Badian, *Roman Imperialism in the Late Republic* (Oxford, 1968) and *Publicans and Sinners* (Oxford, 1972), and in K. Hopkins, *Conquerors and Slaves* (Cambridge, 1978), chaps. 1–2.

De Officiis

General treatments

A general introduction is to be found in the useful Latin edition of H. Holden, *M. Tulli Ciceronis De Officiis Libri Tres* which has been reissued many times: the introduction in the pre-1886 versions is superior but the notes (though many of them are concerned with points of Latin usage) are more helpful in the post-1886 versions. A brief introduction (particularly helpful on the later influence of the work) accompanies the translation with notes by J. Higginbotham, *Cicero on Moral Obligation* (California, 1967) and another (particularly useful on Cicero's historical examples) is provided by H. G. Edinger, *Cicero De Officiis/On Duties*, translated with notes (New York, 1974). A very perceptive discussion of the scope of the work, the circumstances of composition, the importance of the addressee and the 'source problem' is to be found in volume I of M. Testard, *Cicéron Les Devoirs* (Paris, 1965).

Specific aspects

Much of the work on *De Officiis* has been concerned with recovering the philosophical ideas of Panaetius, Cicero's avowed principal 'source' for most of Books I and II (see Introduction, pp. xix–xxi), or with separating Ciceronian elements from the views of Panaetius and other possible sources. Some recent examples include: A. Dyck, 'Notes on Composition, Text, and Sources of Cicero's *De Officiis*', *Hermes* 112 (1984), 215 ff.; P. A. Brunt, 'Aspects of the Social Thought of Dio Chrysostom and of the Stoics', *Proceedings of the Cambridge Philological Society* 1973, 8 ff. (which contains a valuable analysis of *Off.* I. 150 ff. on pp. 26 ff.); J. L. Ferrary, *Philhéllenisme et impérialisme* (Paris, 1988), pp. 395–424; 589–602; C. Gill, 'Personhood and Personality: The Four-*Personae* Theory in Cicero, *De Officiis* I', *Oxford Studies in Ancient Philosophy* 6 (1988), 169 ff.

A reaction against the notion of Cicero as a mere transcriber is now yielding studies that concentrate on Cicero's own ideas and methods. With reference to *De Officiis*, Testard's Introduction (mentioned above) already reflects that attitude. See also J. Annas, 'Cicero on Stoic Moral Philosophy and Private Property', *Philosophia Togata*, ed. M. Griffin and J. Barnes (Oxford, 1989); E. M. Atkins, *The Virtues of Cicero's De Officiis* (unpublished Cambridge Ph.D. thesis (1989)); '"Domina et Regina Virtutum": Justice and *Societas* in *De Officiis*', *Phronesis* (forthcoming).

The close links between *De Officiis* and other works of Cicero, notably the *The Philippics*, are well treated by P. MacKendrick, *The Philosophical Books of Cicero* (London, 1989), 249 ff., who also takes a balanced view of Cicero's contribution to philosophy.

Certain key concepts and attitudes, found in *De Officiis* and in other works of Cicero, have been helpfully analysed in their Roman context. On imperialism, see P. A. Brunt, 'Laus imperii: Conceptions of Empire Prevalent in Cicero's Day', in *Imperialism in the Ancient World*, ed. P. Garnsey and C. R. Whittaker (Cambridge, 1978) and E. S. Gruen, *The Hellenistic World and the Coming of Rome* (California, 1984), vol. I, chaps. 5–10. On private property, see J. M. Carter, 'Cicero: Politics and Philosophy', *Cicero and Vergil*, ed. J. R. C. Martyn (Amsterdam, 1972). On friendship, see P. A. Brunt, '"Amicitia" in the Late Roman Republic', *Proceedings of the Cambridge Philological Society* II (1965), 1–20, revised as chap. 7 of *The Fall of the Roman Republic and Related Essays* (Oxford, 1988). On *officium* (duty), see Brunt, 'Cicero's *Officium* in the Civil War', *Journal of Roman Studies* 76 (1986), 12 ff. On glory, F. A. Sullivan, 'Cicero and Gloria', *Transactions of the American Philological Association* 72 (1941), 382 ff. On *otium* (leisure), J. P. V. D. Balsdon, '*Auctoritas, Dignitas, Otium*', *Classical Quarterly* 1960, 43 ff.

Notes on Translation

Res publica (community, nation, political community, public affairs, public business, public life, republic, republican government)

Res publica means literally 'the public thing'. In his book *De Re Publica* (I.39) Cicero defines *res publica* as 'res populi', 'the thing of the people'. It can simply mean nation, community or political community. But it can also mean Republic: the Roman *res publica* is contrasted with the monarchy that preceded it. Hence Cicero can write of the present time 'we have lost the *res publica*' (II.29). Again, the phrase may refer to the public political activity that was for Cicero the essence of the free republic. Thus Cicero describes himself as having been completely devoted to *res publica*, that is to public life (II.4). Statesmen 'conduct the *res publica*', a usage which combines the senses of 'engage in public life' (as I have translated, eg 1.72) and 'run the nation'. It is extremely important to bear in mind when reading *De Officiis* that so many English words are required to translate the one Latin phrase. Cicero uses *res publica* to refer primarily to different aspects of one and the same thing: a type of political activity that constituted the political community at its best. In translation the unified focus of the term is necessarily obscured.

Honestas; honestus (honourableness; honourable)

Book I of *On Duties* is a guide to discovering whether an action is *honestus* or *turpis*. *Honestas* is analysed as consisting of the four primary virtues. But the nature of *honestas*, connected with *honor* (an honour or office) and reputation, is public. Our culture tends to internalize virtue and divorce it from social standing. The ethics of Cicero's class were, by contrast, avowedly public and competitive: the good man was the man who was well regarded. Cicero himself sought to reconcile the demands of public service with those of honour; the good man was for him in principle honour*able* and would actually be honoured by other good men. I have therefore used the translation 'honourable' for *honestus* and 'dishonourable' for its opposite *turpis*.

Utilitas; utilis; utor (benefit; beneficial; take benefit from, enjoy)

In Book II Cicero discusses whether an action is *utile* or not. The verb *utor* means both to use and to enjoy. Something *utile* may be both useful (a means to an end) and beneficial (an end in itself). The philosophical principles that Cicero adopts in *On Duties* (see pp. xxxvi–vii) mean that nothing can be beneficial that is dishonourable. But honourable actions may be beneficial not just because they are honourable, but also because they bring advantages such as glory and influence, which are discussed in Book II.

Officium; beneficium (duty, dutiful service; kind service)

Roman society was bound by a network of social relationships: families, friendships, patronage, political alliances. To a large extent such relationships were created and maintained by the exchange of services: my assisting someone else engendered an obligation on his part to assist me in future. The benefit given could be described as either *officium* or *beneficium*. Duties engendered by one's role were also called *officia*: sometimes the closest translation would be 'responsibilities'. Cicero chose the *officia* as the nearest Latin equivalent to the Stoic technical term *kathekon*, or 'appropriate action'. In doing so he enriched what he took from Stoic ethics with Roman associations; *De Officiis* interprets the virtues in terms of the obligations of role and relationships, obligations to other individuals or to the *res publica* as a whole. His use of the Latin plural to render the Greek singular reveals Cicero's Roman presuppositions.

Gratia; gratus (gratitude; grateful)

Gratia draws its meaning from the social network of friendships and other relationships bound by exchange of services. Someone who is in a position to grant benefits or give assistance has *gratia* in that he has influence or the potential to command gratitude. Someone who has already granted someone else a benefit has *gratia* in that, according to the public code, he deserves gratitude. *Gratus*, the adjective, may mean either 'welcome', 'gratifying', or else 'grateful'.

Fides (faith, faithfulness, keeping of faith)

Fides was so important a moral idea to the Romans that she was deified. Cicero tells us that harming *fides* disturbs the life of *societas (Pro Roscio Amerino* III). A relationship of *fides* between two parties meant that the one trusted and relied upon the other. Hence the word can mean either 'trustworthiness' or 'trust', 'faith'. It can be used of a wide variety of relationships. A patron is in a relationship of *fides* with his clients, a magistrate with those he serves. *Fides* can simply mean 'promise'. In war, an army might give itself up 'into the *fides*' of the conquering general (though it is disputed how much protection he was obliged to give them in consequence). In business, a contract *bonae fidei* ('of good faith') was contrasted with one of strict justice. Here a responsibility of fairness was placed upon the seller; he ought to make known any defects in what he was selling (see III.58–71).

Societas (fellowship)

A *socius* is an ally or partner. *Societas* is the relationship between individuals sharing a common project or a common way of life. The term can refer to any relationship from a business partnership between two people to civic society to the fellowship of the whole human race. Because of the range of uses, and because of Cicero's emphasis on the derivation of justice from man's natural sociability (1.12, 1.153–8), I have preferred 'fellowship' to 'society'.

Decorum, decet (seemliness, seemly)

Decorum is a moral concept of great importance for a life lived in the public eye. It embodies the notions of both fittingness and visibility. By observing *decorum* one will be seen to do the appropriate thing, taking into account the specific context and one's own status. The word is linked etymologically with *dignitas*.

Dignitas (standing, dignity)

Dignitas literally means 'worthiness'. In politics a man's *dignitas* was his reputation and standing. Roman senators competed for *dignitas*, and for some, such as Caesar, it became an overriding goal, driving their political ambition. Cicero himself criticized democracy on the grounds that it allowed no 'degrees of *dignitas*' (*De Re Publica* I.43).

Gravitas; gravis (seriousness, weightiness; serious, respected, weighty)

Gravitas was a Roman moral ideal. Matters that were *gravis* were weighty and important. Similarly a senator who possessed *gravitas* had authority and commanded respect; he was 'a man of weight'. *Gravitas* was contrasted with fickleness and changeability, and with frivolity. The *gravis* man was serious, showed seriousness of purpose, and was to be taken seriously.

Animus (spirit, mind, heart)

Cicero's psychology and our own are, of course, very different. For Cicero the *animus* was whatever animated the body; its functions included mental activity, the emotions, and other drives and instincts. In some cases 'soul' might be the best translation: philosophers argued over whether the *animus* survives after death. But *animus* can also mean 'heart' or 'spirit' in the sense of 'capacity to remain undaunted'. Hence *magnitudo animi* (greatness of spirit) is almost equivalent to *fortitudo* (courage). I have most often translated by 'spirit', in the hope that that important connection is not lost in translation.

Interpres, interpretor (expositor, expound)

At two points Cicero tells us that he is following, but not expounding, the Stoics or (specifically) Panaetius (I.6, II.60). Some translate as if he is contrasting his free rendering with a close translation. But that is misleading: *interpretor* commonly means 'interpret' or 'expound' rather than 'translate'. Cicero means that he is not writing as a Stoic explaining Stoic arguments, but rather as an independent Academic exploiting the Stoics as he wishes.

Synopsis

Book I

Book II

1

Book III

On Duties

Book I

(1) Marcus, my son, you have been a pupil of Cratippus' for a year already, and that in Athens. Consequently, you ought to be filled to overflowing with philosophical advice and instruction, through the great authority of both teacher and city: the former can improve you with his knowledge, the latter by her examples.[1] However, since I myself have always found it beneficial to combine things Latin with things Greek (something I have done not only in philosophy, but also in the practice of rhetoric), I think you should do the same, that you may be equally capable in either language.[2]

In this respect I have, it seems to me, provided a great service to my countrymen; as a result, not only those ignorant of the Greek language, but the learned also, think that they have found some assistance both in learning[3] and in making decisions.[4] (2) And you will certainly learn from the leading philosopher of our present generation, and you will go on doing so for as long as you like. (You

---

[1] On Cratippus (and all named persons), see Biographical Notes. Cf. *De Finibus* V.2–6 for the examples of the great men, including philosophers, whose monuments were in Athens.

[2] Despite initial hostility to teachers of Greek rhetoric, such study could, by the beginning of the first century BC, be defended as traditional against the new teaching in Latin, cf. *Brutus* 310.

[3] Some editors emend the manuscripts' *discendum* (learning) to *dicendum* (speaking).

[4] At II.2–9 C. addresses himself to these two groups in turn. He had already countered the aversion of the learned for philosophy in Latin in the *Academica* and *De Finibus*. In keeping with his own preference for Academic philosophy of the sceptical variety (see Summary, pp. xxxvi–xxxvii), C. throughout lays stress on helping his son and his readers generally to make their own moral choices (I.2, I.9, II.8, III.18, III.33).

ought, of course, to want to learn for as long as you are not dissatisfied
with your progress.) However, my writings do not differ greatly from
those of the Peripatetics (for we both want to be Socratics and Plato-
nists).[1] When you read them, therefore, though you must use your
own judgement about the content (for I shall not prevent that), you
will at least acquire a richer style of Latin prose by reading my work.
I would not like it to be thought that I say this arrogantly: for I
grant that many others surpass my knowledge of philosophy; and
if, when I have devoted the best part of my life to oratory, I then
claim for myself what is proper to an orator, that I speak suitably,
clearly and elegantly, I seem to have some right to lay such a claim.

(3) I strongly urge you, therefore, my dear Cicero, assiduously
to read not only my speeches, but also the philosophical works, which
are now almost equal to them.[2] The language is more forceful in
the former, but the calm and restrained style of the latter ought also
to be cultivated.[3] Furthermore, I see that it has not happened to
this day that the same Greek has laboured in both fields, pursuing
both forensic oratory and also the other, quieter, sort of debating.
Perhaps Demetrius of Phalerum can be counted as doing so, a man
of precise argument and an orator who, though not over-vigorous,
spoke so pleasantly that you can recognise him as a pupil of Theophrastus. My achievement in either field is for others to judge, but
there is no doubt that I have pursued them both. (4) I certainly think
that Plato, if he had wanted to try his hand at forensic oratory, would
have been able to speak weightily and expansively. Conversely, if
Demosthenes had held on to the things he learned from Plato, and
had wanted to articulate them, he could have done so elegantly and
with brilliance. I make the same judgement about Aristotle and

---

[1] See Plan of Hellenistic Schools, p. xxxiv and Biographical Notes under Socrates and
Plato. Cf. III.20 and pp. xxxvi–xxxvii.
[2] C. had published 17 philosophical works divided into 41 books by this date; he had
published 70 speeches (excluding The Philippic Orations, some of which were being
composed at this time): see J. Crawford, *M. Tullius Cicero: the Lost and Unpublished
Orations* (Gottingen, 1984), p. 12. C.'s exaggeration is perhaps excusable given the impressive speed with which he composed the philosophical works.
[3] For C.'s broad conception of oratory and oratorical training, see *De Oratore* II.4, III.70.
He contrasts the style suitable to philosophy with that suitable to forensic oratory in
Brutus 120–1. The former is characterized as the middle style of oratory in *Orator* 91–6,
where C. claims to be able to handle all three levels himself (100–5).

Isocrates; each, because he so enjoyed his own pursuit, despised the other one.[1]

Now when I had decided to write something for you at the present time (and much more in the future) I very much wanted to begin with something which was preeminently suitable to your age and my authority.[2] Many weighty and beneficial matters in philosophy have been discussed accurately and expansively by philosophers. However, it is their teachings and their advice on the question of duties that seem to have the widest application. For no part of life, neither public affairs nor private, neither in the forum nor at home, neither when acting on your own nor in dealings with another, can be free from duty. Everything that is honourable in a life depends upon its cultivation, and everything dishonourable upon its neglect.[3]

(5) The debate is one in which all philosophers share: for who would dare to call himself a philosopher if he had handed down no rules of duty? But there are some teachings that undermine all duty by the ends of good and evil things that they propound.[4] The man who defines the highest good in such a way that it has no connection with virtue, measuring it by his own advantages rather than by honourableness, cannot (if he is in agreement with himself and is not occasionally overcome by the goodness of his own nature) cultivate either friendship or justice or liberality. There can certainly be no brave man who judges that pain is the greatest evil, nor a man of restraint who defines pleasure as the highest good.

(6) All that is so obvious that the matter does not need to be debated, but I have in any case discussed it elsewhere.[5] If such systems of teaching were wanting to be consistent, they could say nothing about

---

[1] The rivalry with the Greeks was an important motive behind C.'s creation of a Latin philosophical literature. C. emphasizes forensic oratory as it had more prestige than the other two types, deliberative and display, and, in his view, required skill in all three levels of style.

[2] On the suitability of *De Officiis* to its addressee, see Introduction, pp. xvi–xvii.

[3] For the contrast between the broad scope of practical ethics here suggested and the very selective treatment offered in *De Officiis*, see Introduction, pp. xxiii–xxv.

[4] C. saw the ethical debate between the schools of philosophy as primarily one about the ends or goals of life, e.g. *De Finibus* v.15–23. See Summary, p. xxxv.

[5] Particularly in *De Finibus* Book II, where C. gives himself the role of criticizing Epicurean ethics propounded by his friend Manlius Torquatus. Cf. III.39 and 116–19 with n. 3 on 118. Members of this sect were the first to write philosophy in Latin, and their works, which C. regarded as crude, seem to have enjoyed some popularity. He alludes in (5) to the fact that many of his contemporaries who professed Epicureanism nonetheless entered public life and practised the traditional virtues, like Torquatus himself.

duty; nor can any advice on duty that is steady, stable, and joined to nature be handed down except by those who believe that what is to be sought for its own sake is honourableness alone (as some say) or honourableness above all (as others say). Therefore the giving of such advice is the peculiar province of the Stoics, Aristotelians and Peripatetics, since the opinions of Aristo, Pyrrho and Erillus have long since been driven out. They would have had the right to dispute about duty if they had left any means of choice between things, so that there might be a path to the discovering of duty.[1] I shall, therefore, for the present and on this question, follow the Stoics above all, not as an expositor, but, as is my custom, drawing from their fountains when and as it seems best, using my own judgement and discretion.[2]

(7) Since the whole discussion is going to be about duty, I propose first to define what duty is. I am surprised that Panaetius omitted to do this. For every piece of rational instruction upon any matter ought to begin with a definition, so that everyone understands what the subject of discussion is.[3]

The whole debate about duty is twofold. One kind of question relates to the end of good things; the other depends upon advice by which one ought to be fortified for all areas of life. The following are examples of the former: are all duties 'complete'? Is one duty more important than another? and other questions of that type. The duties for which advice has been offered do indeed relate to the end of good things, but here it is less obvious, because they appear rather to have in view instruction for a life that is shared. It is these that I must expound in these books.[4]

(8) There is also another division to be made concerning duty.

---

[1] All three of these philosophers, for different reasons, agreed that external things were indifferent; no one external condition (wealth, poverty, health, sickness etc.) was preferable to another. Therefore, C. thinks, they left no grounds for choosing to act in one way rather than in another (see also, Summary p. xxxv).

[2] C. insists on his independence in two respects: as his own philosophy allows him to adopt whatever seems the most persuasive case (see II.7–8, III.20), he has chosen to follow the Stoics at this time and on this subject. Second, he is not merely translating or expounding Stoic authorities but using them selectively and critically (see Introduction, pp. xix ff.).

[3] Cf. 1.101; *De Finibus* III.58.

[4] C. distinguishes here between, on the one hand, theoretical questions about the end of life and the concept of duty and, on the other hand, practical questions about how to choose and perform one's duties.

For a duty can be called either 'middle' or 'complete'. 'Complete' duty we may, I think, label 'right', as the Greeks call it *katorthoma*; while the duty that is shared they call *kathekon*.[1] They give their definitions in such a way as to define complete duty as what is right; while middle duty, they say, is that for which a persuasive reason can be given as to why it has been done.[2]

(9) There are in consequence, as it seems to Panaetius, three questions to deliberate when deciding upon a plan of action. In the first place, men may be uncertain whether the thing that falls under consideration is an honourable or a dishonourable thing to do; often, when they ponder this, their spirits are pulled between opposing opinions. Secondly, they investigate or debate whether or not the course they are considering is conducive to the advantageousness and pleasantness of life, to opportunities and resources for doing things, to wealth and to power, all of which enable them to benefit themselves and those dear to them. All such deliberation falls under reasoning about what is beneficial. The third type of uncertainty arises when something apparently beneficial appears to conflict with what is honourable: benefit seems to snatch you to its side and honourableness in its turn to call you back; consequently the spirit is pulled this way and that in its deliberation, and it arouses in its reflection a care that is double-edged.

(10) Although it is a very great fault to omit anything when categorising, this division leaves out two things. For one often deliberates not only whether a thing is honourable or dishonourable, but also which of two proposed courses that are honourable is the more honourable, or of two that are beneficial the more beneficial. Therefore the method that Panaetius thought should be threefold turns out to require division into five parts. First, therefore, we must discuss

---

[1] An alternative reading is 'while the shared one, they call duty'. 'Middle' (Latin *media*, Greek *mesa*) duties are so called because both the wise man and the ordinary man share in doing them (hence C. sometimes calls them 'shared duties'). However, only the wise man, who fully possesses every virtue, can perform a right action, one which, in itself, apart from its consequences, is perfect and complete (*Fin.* III.32). His 'complete' duty, as C. puts it (III.14) 'fulfils all the numbers'. C. explains the term 'middle' differently in *De Finibus* III.58–9.

[2] C. may choose the Latin word *probabile* ('persuasive') to translate the Greek for 'reasonable' (justification) because it suggests the sceptical Academic view that what is *probabile* can serve as a basis for action.

what is honourable, but asking of it two questions; then what is beneficial, by a parallel method; and then the comparison of the two.[1]

(11) From the beginning nature[2] has assigned to every type of creature the tendency to preserve itself, its life and body, and to reject anything that seems likely to harm them, seeking and procuring everything necessary for life, such as nourishment, shelter and so on. Common also to all animals is the impulse to unite for the purpose of procreation, and a certain care for those that are born. The great difference between man and beast, however, is this: the latter adapts itself only in responding to the senses, and only to something that is present and at hand, scarcely aware of the past or future. Man, however, is a sharer in reason; this enables him to perceive consequences, to comprehend the causes of things, their precursors and their antecedents, so to speak; to compare similarities and to link and combine future with present events; and by seeing with ease the whole course of life to prepare whatever is necessary for living it.

(12) The same nature, by the power of reason, unites one man to another for the fellowship both of common speech and of life, creating above all a particular love for his offspring. It drives him to desire that men should meet together and congregate, and that he should join them himself; and for the same reason to devote himself to providing whatever may contribute to the comfort and sustenance not only of himself, but also of his wife, his children, and others whom he holds dear and ought to protect.[3] Furthermore, such concern also arouses men's spirits, rendering them greater for achieving whatever they attempt.

★(13) The search for truth and its investigation are, above all, peculiar to man. Therefore, whenever we are free from necessary business and other concerns we are eager to see or to hear or to learn, considering that the discovery of obscure or wonderful things is necessary

---

[1] The three Panaetian topics are each assigned one of the three books of *De Officiis*. The two supplementary topics are treated at the end of Book I (152–61) and Book II (88–9). See Introduction, pp. xxi, xxv.

[2] In the next chapters C. describes the natural basis of the four cardinal virtues, justice (12), wisdom, greatness of spirit (13) and moderation (14), which are to provide the structure of Book I as a whole. C. starts from the natural impulses man shares with other animals and then shows how the possession of reason gives him in addition impulses that can develop into the four virtues. Cf. II.II.

[3] See I.158 and n. 1.

6

for a blessed life. Consequently, we understand that what is true, simple and pure is most fitted to the nature of man. In addition to this desire for seeing the truth, there is a kind of impulse towards pre-eminence, so that a spirit that is well trained by nature will not be willing to obey for its own benefit someone whose advice, teaching and commands are not just and lawful. Greatness of spirit and a disdain for human things arise as a result.

(14) The power of nature and reason is not insignificant in this too, that this one animal alone perceives what order there is, what seemliness, what limit to words and deeds. No other animal, therefore, perceives the beauty, the loveliness, and the congruence of the parts, of the things that sight perceives. Nature and reason transfer this by analogy from the eyes to the mind, thinking that beauty, constancy and order should be preserved, and much more so, in one's decisions and in one's deeds. They are careful also to do nothing in an unseemly or effeminate way, in all their opinions and actions thinking and doing nothing licentiously.

The honourableness that we seek is created from and accomplished by these things. Even if it is not accorded acclaim, it is still honourable, and, as we truly claim, even if no one praises it, it is by nature worthy of praise. (15) You are seeing, my son, the very face and form, so to speak, of the honourable; if it could be seen with the eyes, as Plato says, it would inspire an amazing love of wisdom.[1] Everything that is honourable arises from one of four parts: it is involved either with the perception of truth and with ingenuity; or with preserving fellowship among men, with assigning to each his own, and with faithfulness to agreements one has made; or with the greatness and strength of a lofty and unconquered spirit; or with order and limit in everything that is said and done (modesty and restraint are included here).

Although these four are bound together and interwoven,[2] certain kinds of duties have their origin in each individually. For example, in the part that we described as first, in which we placed wisdom and good sense,[3] there lie the investigation and discovery of what is true, and that is the peculiar function of that virtue. (16) For when

---

[1] *Phaedrus* 250d.
[2] See II.35.
[3] Wisdom and good sense, here treated together, are separated at I.153 (see n. 1), though their separate spheres are suggested at the end of I.19.

Wisdom - Percieving of truth

a man is extremely good at perceiving what is most true in each particular thing, and when he is able with great acuity and speed to see and to explain the reason, then he is rightly considered extremely sensible and wise. Therefore, the thing that underlies this virtue, the matter (as it were) that it handles and treats, is truth.

(17) As for the other three virtues, their aim is necessities: they are to procure and to conserve whatever is required for the activities of life, in order both to preserve the fellowship and bonding between men, and to allow excellence and greatness of spirit to shine out – both in increasing influence and in acquiring benefits for oneself and those dear to one, and also, and much more, in disdaining the very same things. Again, order, constancy, moderation, and the qualities similar to these are associated with the group that requires not only mental activity, but also some action. For we shall conserve honourableness and seemliness if we apply some limit and order to the things with which we deal in our life.

Wisdom Start

(18) We have divided the nature and power of that which is honourable under four headings. The first of these, that consisting of the learning of truth, most closely relates to human nature. For all of us feel the pull that leads us to desire to learn and to know; we think it a fine thing to excel in this, while considering it bad and dishonourable to stumble, to wander, to be ignorant, to be deceived.

In this category, which is both natural and honourable, one must avoid two faults: first, we should not take things that have not been ascertained for things that have, and rashly assent to them. Anyone who wants to avoid that fault (as everyone indeed should) will take time and care when he ponders any matter. (19) The second fault is that some men bestow excessive devotion and effort upon matters that are both abstruse and difficult, and unnecessary.[1]

When those faults are avoided, then the amount of effort and care that is given to things honourable and worth learning will rightly be praised; just as we have heard happened regarding Gaius Sulpicius in astronomy, and as we have learnt ourselves regarding Sextus Pompeius in geometry, many men in dialectical arguments, and yet

---

[1] Of the two faults mentioned, the first reflects C.'s profound dislike of dogmatism which made the sceptical Academic tradition so attractive to him (see Summary, p. xxxvi); the second reflects Roman priorities which also led C. to justify his philosophical writing in terms of his involuntary exclusion from public life and his hope of helping his countrymen in another way (II.2–6; cf. *Acad.* II.6; *Div.* II.6). See also I.71.

more in civil law (for these arts are all associated with the investigation of what is true). It is, however, contrary to duty to be drawn by such a devotion away from practical achievements: all the praise that belongs to virtue lies in action. On the other hand, there is often a break from it, and we are given many opportunities to return to our studies. Besides, the activity of the mind, which is never at rest, can maintain in us our pursuit of learning even without effort on our part. For reflective movements of the spirit occur in one of two ways: either when taking counsel about honourable matters, that pertain to living well and blessedly, or in the pursuit of knowledge and learning.

We have now discussed the first source of duty. (20) Of the three that remain the most wide-reaching one is the reasoning by which the fellowship of men with one another, and the communal life, are held together. There are two parts of this: justice, the most illustrious of the virtues, on account of which men are called 'good';[1] and the beneficence connected with it, which may be called either kindness or liberality.

Of justice, the first office is that no man should harm another unless he has been provoked by injustice; the next that one should treat common goods as common and private ones as one's own.[2] (21) Now no property is private by nature, but rather by long occupation (as when men moved into some empty property in the past), or by victory (when they acquired it in war), or by law, by settlement, by agreement, or by lot. The result is that the land of Arpinum is said to belong to the Arpinates, and that of Tusculum to the Tusculani.[3] The distribution of private property is of a similar kind. Consequently, since what becomes each man's own comes from what had in nature been common, each man should hold on to whatever has fallen to him. If anyone else should seek any of it for himself, he will be violating the law of human fellowship.

(22) We are not born for ourselves alone, to use Plato's splendid

---

[1] On the importance attributed to justice, see Introduction pp. xxiii ff. The remark that men are called 'good' for being just reflects not only common moral notions (II.38, III.75–6) but also the use of the phrase *vir bonus* in Roman law, e.g. *Digest* XIX.2.24 pr. 'satisfaction as a good man would judge' in a contract, to which C. also alludes in III.70 and 77.

[2] Justice in the narrow sense (the first part of C.'s second virtue) has a negative aspect – not to harm anyone unprovoked (21), and a positive one – to help our fellow men (22, cf. I.31). These correspond respectively to the positive and negative forms of injustice at I.23.

[3] C. uses as examples his home town and Tusculum where he had a villa.

words,[1] but our country claims for itself one part of our birth, and our friends another. Moreover, as the Stoics believe, everything produced on the earth is created for the use of mankind, and men are born for the sake of men, so that they may be able to assist one another. Consequently, we ought in this to follow nature as our leader, to contribute to the common stock the things that benefit everyone together, and, by the exchange of dutiful services, by giving and receiving expertise and effort and means, to bind fast the fellowship of men with each other.[2] (23) Moreover, the keeping of faith is fundamental to justice, that is constancy and truth in what is said and agreed. Therefore, though this will perhaps seem difficult to some, let us venture to imitate the Stoics, who hunt assiduously for the derivations of words, and let us trust that keeping faith (*fides*) is so called because what has been said is actually done (*fiat*).[3]

Of injustice there are two types: men may inflict injury; or else, when it is being inflicted upon others, they may fail to deflect it, even though they could. Anyone who makes an unjust attack on another, whether driven by anger or by some other agitation, seems to be laying hands, so to speak, upon a fellow. But also, the man who does not defend someone, or obstruct the injustice when he can, is at fault just as if he had abandoned his parents or his friends or his country.[4]

(24) Those injustices that are purposely inflicted for the sake of harming another often stem from fear; in such cases the one who is thinking of harming someone else is afraid that if he does not do so, he himself will be affected by some disadvantage. In most cases, however, men set about committing injustice in order to secure something that they desire: where this fault is concerned avarice is

[1] Letter IX 358a.
[2] C. in 21–2 has been trying to reconcile the natural sociability of man that is the root of the second virtue with the notion of private possession which he defends throughout (especially II.73, II.78). At I.51 the law of the community supplies the criteria for distinguishing what is communal and what is private.
[3] Stoic interest in etymology was connected with the belief that language had its basis in nature, not convention. The derivation of words also had a great vogue in Rome of this period and figures prominently in what remains of Varro's *On the Latin Language*, which he was writing about this time and dedicated in part to C.
[4] In the description of positive injustice (treated in 24–7) we must supply the absence of provocation noted at 20. Negative injustice is treated in 28–9.

extremely widespread. (25) Riches are sought both for the things that are necessary to life, and in order to enjoy pleasures. In men of greater spirit, however, the desire for wealth has as its goal influence and the opportunity to gratify others. Marcus Crassus, for example, recently said that no one who wanted to be pre-eminent in the republic would have wealth enough if he could not feed an army on its yield.[1] Magnificent accoutrements and an elegant and plentiful style of life give men further delight. The result of such things is that desire for money has become unlimited. Such expansion of one's personal wealth as harms no one is not, of course, to be disparaged; but committing injustice must always be avoided.[2]

(26) However, men are led most of all to being overwhelmed by forgetfulness of justice when they slip into desiring positions of command or honour or glory. That is why we find the observation of Ennius to be widely applicable:

> To kingship belongs neither sacred fellowship nor faith

For if there is any area in which is it impossible for many to be outstanding, there will generally be such competition there that it is extremely difficult to maintain a 'sacred fellowship'. The rash behaviour of Gaius Caesar has recently made that clear: he overturned all the laws of gods and men for the sake of the pre-eminence that he had imagined for himself in his mistaken fancy. There is something troubling in this type of case, in that the desire for honour, command, power and glory usually exist in men of the greatest spirit and most brilliant intellectual talent.[3] Therefore one must be all the more careful not to do wrong in this way.

(27) In every case of injustice it matters a great deal whether the

---

[1] This famous remark may be autobiographical: in 71 BC Crassus defeated the slave revolt led by Spartacus at a time when he held no regular command and the public treasury was low in funds.

[2] The first adumbration of what is to become the 'rule of procedure' at III.19–21: one cannot benefit oneself at the expense of another for that would violate the natural bond between men.

[3] On C.'s concern to justify Caesar's assassination earlier in the year, see Introduction, pp. xii; xxvi. C. had often praised in public Caesar's military and intellectual ability, and, despite serious political differences, there was much mutual respect: Caesar had dedicated a work on language to C.

injury was committed through some agitation of the spirit, which is generally brief and momentary, or purposefully and with fore-thought. For those things that happen because of some sudden impulse are less serious than those inflicted after reflection and preparation. But I have now said enough about actually committing injustice.

(28) As for neglecting to defend others and deserting one's duty, there tend to be several causes of this. For some men do not wish to incur enmities, or toil, or expense; others are hindered by indifference, laziness, inactivity or some pursuits or business of their own, to the extent that they allow the people whom they ought to protect to be abandoned. We must therefore watch out in case Plato's words about philosophers prove not to be sufficient. For he said that they are immersed in the investigation of the truth and that, disdaining the very things for which most men vigorously strive and even fight one another to the death, they count them as nothing. Because of that he calls them just. They observe one type of justice, indeed, that they should harm no one else by inflicting injury, but they fall into another; for hindered by their devotion to learning, they abandon those whom they ought to protect. And so, he thinks that they should not even embark upon public life unless they are forced to do so.[1] But that is something done more fairly when done voluntarily; for something that is done rightly is only just if it is voluntary. (29) There are also some who, whether through devotion to preserving their personal wealth or through some kind of dislike of mankind, claim to be attending to their own business, and appear to do no one any injustice. But though they are free from one type of injustice, they run into another: such men abandon the fellowship of life, because they contribute to it nothing of their devotion, nothing of their effort, nothing of their means.

Since we have set out the two types of injustice, and added the causes of each, and since we established previously what are the things that constitute justice, we shall now be able to judge with ease what is our duty on each occasion – that is, if we do not love ourselves too much. (30) For it is difficult to be concerned about another's affairs. Terence's Chremes, however, thinks 'nothing that is human

---

[1] For Plato's views see the *Republic*, especially VI 485b–87a, VII 520c–21b, VII 540d–e, I 347c, VII 519c–20d, 539e–40b.

is another's affair';[1] yet in fact we do tend to notice and feel our own good and bad fortune more than that of others, which we see as if a great distance intervenes; accordingly, we do not make the same judgements about them and about ourselves. It is good advice therefore that prevents you from doing anything if you are unsure whether it is fair or unfair. For fairness shines out by itself, and hesitation signifies that one is contemplating injustice.

(31) Occasions often arise when the actions that seem most worthy of a just man, of him whom we call good, undergo a change, and the opposite becomes the case. For example, from time to time it becomes just to set aside such requirements as the returning of a deposit, or the carrying out of a promise, or other things that relate to truth and to keeping faith, and not to observe them.[2] For it is seemly that they should be referred to those fundamentals of justice that I laid down at the beginning: first that one should harm no one; and secondly that one serve the common advantage. Such actions alter with the circumstances, and duty alters likewise, and is not invariable. (32) For it can happen that something that has been promised and agreed, if carried out, would be disadvantageous to the person to whom the promise has been made, or else to him who gave the promise. If Neptune in the myth had not done what he had promised to Theseus, Theseus would not have been deprived of his son Hippolytus. He made three wishes, as we read, and the third was this: he wished in his anger that Hippolytus should die. When it was granted he fell into the deepest grief. Therefore promises should not be kept if they are disadvantageous to those to whom you have made them. Nor, if they harm you more than they benefit the person whom you have promised, is it contrary to duty to prefer the greater good to the lesser. For example, if you had made an appointment to appear for someone as advocate in the near future, and in the meantime your son had fallen seriously ill, it would not be contrary to your duty not to do as you had said. Rather, the person to whom you had made the promise would be failing in *his* duty if he complained that he had been abandoned. Again, who does not see that if someone is forced to make a promise through fear, or deceived into it by trickery, the promise ought not to stand? One is released from such

---

[1] *The Self-Tormentor* 77.
[2] For the question of keeping promises, see also III.92–5.

promises in most cases by the praetor's code of justice, and sometimes by the laws.[1]

(33) Injustices can also arise from a kind of trickery, by an extremely cunning but ill intentioned interpretation of the law. In consequence the saying 'the more Justice, the more injustice' has by now become a proverb well worn in conversation. Many wrongs of this type are committed even in public affairs; and example is that of the man who, during a truce of thirty days which had been agreed with the enemy, laid waste the fields by night, on the grounds that the truce had been established for days, but not for nights. We should not approve the action even of our own countryman, if the story is true about Quintus Fabius Labeo (or some other person – for I know of it only from hearsay). He was assigned by the senate to arbitrate about the boundary between the Nolani and the Neapolitani. When he arrived at the place he spoke with each group separately, urging it to do nothing out of covetousness or greed, and to be prepared to retreat rather than to advance. When both of them did that, there was some land left in the middle. Therefore he set a limit to their boundaries exactly where they themselves had said; but he assigned the land that was left in the middle to the people of Rome. That was not arbitration, that was deception. Cleverness of such a king ought in every case to be avoided.

Moreover, certain duties must be observed even towards those at whose hands you may have received unjust treatment. There is a limit to revenge and to punishment. I am not even sure that it is not enough simply that the man who did the harm should repent of his injustice, so that he himself will do no such thing again, and others will be slower to act unjustly.

(34) Something else that must very much be preserved in public affairs is the justice of warfare. There are two types of conflict: the one proceeds by debate, the other by force. Since the former is the proper concern of a man, but the latter of beasts, one should only resort to the latter if one may not employ the former. (35) Wars,

---

[1] On promises and deposits, cf. III.92–5. C. finds an analogy for the category of 'duties in particular circumstances' (p. 62, n. 1) in Roman legal thinking (Introduction, p. xxvi), here in the allowances made by Roman law for agreements made under coercion or deception. Civil law in Rome comprised laws, those in the Twelve Tables or passed later, and *ius praetorium*, the *formulae* ('rules of procedure') set out by each successive city praetor (an annual magistrate) in his edict, through which important legal developments took place in the Late Republic (cf. p. 107, n. 3 and III.60–1 with nn.).

then, ought to be undertaken for this purpose, that we may live in peace, without injustice; and once victory has been secured, those who were not cruel or savage in warfare should be spared. Thus, our forefathers even received the Tusculani, the Aequi, the Volsci, the Sabini and the Hernici into citizenship. On the other hand they utterly destroyed Carthage and Numantia. I would prefer that they had not destroyed Corinth; but I believe that they had some specific purpose in doing so, in particular in view of its advantageous situation, to prevent the location itself from being some day an incitement to war.[1]

In my opinion, our concern should always be for a peace that will have nothing to do with treachery. If I had been followed in this we would still have some republican government (if perhaps not the very best); whereas now we have none.[2] And while you must have concern for those whom you have conquered by force, you must also take in those who have laid down their arms and seek refuge in the faith of generals, although a battering ram may have crashed against their wall.[3] In this matter, justice was respected so greatly among our countrymen that the very men who had received into their good faith cities or peoples conquered in war would, by the custom of our forefathers, become their patrons.

(36) Indeed, a fair code of warfare has been drawn up, in full accordance with religious scruple, in the fetial laws of the Roman people. From this we can grasp that no war is just unless it is waged after a formal demand for restoration, or unless it has been formally

---

[1] In 34–40 C. attempts to match Roman ancestral practice with philosophical ideas, going back to Plato (*Laws* 1 628d) and Aristotle (*Politics* 1333a35), about the correct purpose of war. He first mentions peoples of Italy conquered by Rome and later admitted to Roman citizenship in the fourth and third centuries BC (cf. II.75 for the Italian war in his own time). Carthage and Corinth were destroyed in 146 BC, Numantia in 133 BC. C.'s unease about the destruction of Corinth (condemned at III.46) shows in his sophistic attempt to bring it under the rule that wars should be undertaken only to ensure peace when diplomacy is inapplicable: he was reluctant to admit that the imperialism of 'our forefathers' was as ruthless as that of his own time (cf. II.26–7).

[2] C. had first tried to prevent the civil war between Caesar and Pompey and then to end it. For C.'s view of the state of the Republic, see Introduction, pp. xiii–xiv ff.

[3] C. here demands more generous behaviour than Roman traditional practice prescribed, probably because Caesar in his *Gallic War* II.32 recounted his strict application of the rule that only enemies who surrendered before the battering ram had touched their walls would be spared.

announced and declared beforehand.[1] When Popilius was general in charge of a province, Cato's son was serving as a novice soldier in his army. Popilius then decided to dismiss one of the legions, and included in the dismissal the young Cato, who was serving in that legion. But when, out of love of fighting, he remained in the army, Cato wrote to Popilius saying that if he allowed him to stay in the army he should bind him by a fresh military oath, since he could not in justice fight the enemy when his former oath had become void. Such was their extreme scrupulousness when making war. (37) There actually exists a letter of the Elder Marcus Cato to the younger Marcus, in which he writes that he has heard that his son, who was serving in Macedonia in the war against Perseus, had been discharged by the consul. He warns him therefore to be careful not to enter battle. For, he says, it is not lawful for one who is not a soldier to fight with the enemy.[2]

A further point is that the name given to someone who ought properly to have been called a foe (*perduellis*), is in fact *hostis*. I notice that the grimness of the fact is lessened by the gentleness of the word. For *hostis* meant to our forefathers he whom we now call a stranger. The Twelve Tables show this: for example, 'a day appointed for trial with a *hostis*'; and again, 'right of ownership cannot be alienated in favour of a *hostis*'. What greater courteousness could there be than to call him against whom you are waging war by so tender a name? Long usage, however, has made the name harsher; for the word has abandoned the stranger, and now makes its proper home with him who bears arms against you.[3]

(38) When, then, we are fighting for empire and seeking glory through warfare, those grounds that I mentioned a little above as

---

[1] The old Roman practice was for the priesthood of the *fetiales* to deliver an ultimatum to the enemy demanding compensation for his alleged oppression. If no satisfaction was forthcoming, a threat of war was announced and war was then formally declared by the Roman assembly. C.'s 'or' here is inexact: he means all three conditions to apply (cf. *Rep.* III.23 and 25).

[2] The similarity of the two incidents, as well as some awkwardness in the Latin, suggest that 'When Popilius ... making war' is a later interpolation. Unless, implausibly, the same fate befell the young Marcus Cato twice, one or another episode must be unhistorical. Popilius Laenas was consul in 172 BC; the consul in command against Perseus in 168 BC was Aemilius Paullus.

[3] The same point about the change in the meaning of *hostis* is made by C.'s contemporary Varro in *On the Latin Language* V.3.

just grounds for war should be wholly present.[1] But wars in which the goal is the glory of empire are waged less bitterly. For just as in civilian matters we may compete in one way with an enemy, in another with a rival (for the latter contest is for honour and standing, the former for one's civic life or reputation), similarly the wars against the Celtiberi and the Cimbri were waged with enemies:[2] the question was not who would rule, but who would exist. With the Latins, Sabini, Samnites, Carthaginians and Pyrrhus, on the other hand, the dispute was over empire. The Carthaginians were breakers of truces, and Hannibal was cruel, but the others were more just.[3] Indeed, Pyrrhus' words about the returning of the captives were splendid:

> My demand is not for gold; nor shall you give me a price. Let us each determine our lives by iron, not by gold, not by selling, but by fighting war. Let us test by our virtue whether Mistress Fortune wishes you or me to reign, or what she may bring. Hear these words too: if the fortune of war spares the virtue of any, take it as certain that I shall spare them their liberty. Take them as a gift, and I give them with the will of the great gods.

That is certainly the view of a king and one worthy of the race of the Aeacidae.[4]

(39) If any individuals have been constrained by circumstance to promise anything to an enemy, they must keep faith even in that.

---

[1] C. refers back to the just cause for war of 1.35 (see n. 1). He distinguishes wars for imperial dominance and glory from wars for the survival of Rome and demands that the former even be waged less bitterly. Yet even they are regarded here as fought in the interests of peace, in that they *defend* the empire against rivals, as in II.26, but cf. II.85 with n. 4.

[2] The Celtiberian war from 153 BC to the fall of Numantia in 133 BC could be called a war for survival only on the ground that Roman involvement in Spain went back to the third century BC when Carthage used it as a base for invading Italy. The Cimbri in 113–101 BC were threatening the northern borders of Italy and were finally defeated by C. Marius.

[3] Of the wars for empire, those for the conquest of Italy belong to the fifth to the third century BC, with the Samnite wars ending in 272. The wars with Carthage were in 264–241 (First Punic War), 218–201 (the Hannibalic war) and 149–146. By then Carthage, though prosperous again, could hardly be regarded as a serious imperial rival: hence C. adduces her treachery and cruelty to justify the destruction of the city.

[4] The verses are from Book VI of Ennius' epic poem *Annales*: King Pyrrhus of Epirus, who claimed descent from the son of Achilles, grandson of Aeacus, is addressing Roman envoys in 280 BC. They offered him a large bribe to surrender Roman prisoners of war but he handed them over without payment. See also III.86.

Indeed, Regulus did so when he was captured by the Carthaginians in the First Punic war and was sent to Rome for the purpose of arranging an exchange of captives, having vowed that he would return. For first of all, upon his arrival he proposed in the senate that the captives should not be returned; and then when his friends and relatives were trying to keep him, he preferred to go back to his punishment than to break the faith he had given to an enemy.[1]

(40) In the Second Punic war, after the battle of Cannae, Hannibal sent to Rome ten men, bound by a solemn oath that they would return if they did not succeed in arranging for those whom the Romans had captured to be ransomed. The censors disfranchised all of them for the rest of their lives, on the grounds that they had broken their oath. They treated similarly one of them who incurred blame by fraudulently evading his solemn oath. For after leaving the camp with Hannibal's permission, he returned a little later saying that he had forgotten something or other. He then considered that he had released himself from his oath on leaving the camp; but he had done so only in word and not in fact. For on the question of keeping faith, you must always think of what you meant, not of what you said.

Another very great example of justice towards an enemy was established by our forefathers when a deserter from Pyrrhus promised the senate that he would kill the king by giving him poison. Fabricius and the senate returned him to Pyrrhus. In this way, they did not give approval to the killing in a criminal way of even a powerful enemy, and one who was waging war unprovoked.[2] (41) Enough has been said about the duties of war.

Let us remember also that justice must be maintained even towards the lowliest. The lowliest condition and fortune is that of slaves; the instruction we are given to treat them as if they were employees is good advice: that one should require work from them, and grant to them just treatment.[3]

---

[1] The story of the capture of Regulus in 255 BC is elaborated in III.99–III.

[2] Most manuscripts omit the whole of 40 which reports two episodes of Roman history that C. recounts more fully in III.113–14 and 86.

[3] The Stoics, Roman lawyers and others held that there were no slaves by nature, only by fortune. Chrysippus is credited by Seneca (*On Benefits* III.22) with calling slaves 'permanent employees' and the Roman Stoic Rutilius Rufus is said to have paid his slaves for fish they caught, just as he did free men. On the other hand, paid employment was generally regarded as unsuitable for free men (I.150 with n. 1), while Roman law allowed the slave owner to punish, sell or kill his own slave with impunity.

There are two ways in which injustice may be done, either through force or through deceit; and deceit seems to belong to a little fox, force to a lion. Both of them seem most alien to a human being; but deceit deserves a greater hatred. And out of all injustice, nothing deserves punishment more than that of men who, just at the time when they are most betraying trust, act in such a way that they might appear to be good men.

I have now said enough about justice. (42) Next, I must do as I proposed and speak about beneficence and liberality. Nothing is more suited to human nature than this, but there are many caveats. For first one must see that kindness harms neither the very people whom one seems to be treating kindly, nor others; next, that one's kindness does not exceed one's capabilities; and then, that kindness is bestowed upon each person according to his standing.[1] Indeed, that is fundamental to justice, to which all these things ought to be referred. For those who do someone a favour in such a way that they harm him whom they appear to want to assist, should be judged neither beneficent nor liberal, but dangerous flatterers. Those who, in order to be liberal towards some, harm others, fall into the same injustice as if they had converted someone else's possessions to their own account.

(43) There are, though, many especially those greedy for renown and glory, who steal from one group the very money that they lavish upon another. They think that they will appear beneficent towards their friends if they enrich them by any method whatsoever. But that is so far from being a duty that in fact nothing could be more opposed to duty. We should therefore see that the liberality we exercise in assisting our friends does not harm anyone. Consequently, the transference of money by Lucius Sulla and Gaius Caesar from its lawful owners to others ought not to be seen as liberal: nothing is liberal if it is not also just.[2]

(44) The second need for caution is lest one's kindness exceeds one's capabilities. For those who want to be kinder than their possessions allow first go wrong by being unjust to those nearest

---

[1] The fundamental Stoic definition of justice was giving each his due, cf. 1.59 *fin*.

[2] See p. 10, n. 2. C. consistently condemns redistribution of property as unjust and ultimately inexpedient. At II.27 and 83, as in the contemporary *Philippic Orations* (II.108, v.17), c. treats as equally heinous Sulla's proscriptions and Caesar's sale of the property of those who died in the civil war, ignoring the cruelty of Sulla, whose cause he thought honourable (II.27), and the clemency of Caesar.

to them; they transfer to strangers resources which would more fairly be provided for, or left to, them. Usually there lurks within such liberality a greediness to plunder and deprive unjustly, so that resources may be available for lavish gifts. One can see that most men are not so much liberal by nature as drawn by a kind of glory; and in order to be seen to be beneficent they do many things that appear to stem not from goodwill, but from ostentation. Such pretence is closer to sham than to either liberality or honourableness.

(45) The third point I had laid down was that one should when exercising beneficence make choices according to standing. Here we should look both at the conduct of the man on whom we are conferring a kindness, and at the spirit in which he views us, at the association and fellowship of our lives together, and at the dutiful services that he has previously carried out for our benefit.[1] It is desirable that all such considerations should come together. If they do not, then the more numerous and more important grounds will carry more weight.

(46) Since we do not live with men who are perfect and clearly wise, but with those who are doing splendidly if they have in them mere images of virtue,[2] I think that we must understand this too: no one should be wholly neglected if any indication of virtue appears in him; moreover, one must particularly foster those who are most graced with the gentler virtues, modesty, restraint, and that very justice which I have now been discussing at length. For a brave and great spirit in a man who is not perfect nor wise is generally too impetuous; but those other virtues seem rather to attach themselves to a good man. That is all on the question of conduct.

(47) On the subject of the goodwill that each person has towards us, the first consideration of duty is that we should grant the most to the one who is most fond of us; but we should judge goodwill not as adolescents do, by the strength of its burning passion, but rather by its firmness and constancy. If services have already been rendered, that is if you have not to inspire gratitude, but rather to requite it, then you must take even greater care: for no duty is more necessary than that of requiting gratitude. (48) For if, as Hesiod

---

[1] C. discusses the conduct of the potential recipient in 46; his spirit towards us in 47; his services deserving our gratitude at 48–9 and the degree of his fellowship with us at 50 ff.

[2] Cf. III.13–16.

commands,[1] you should return in greater measure, provided that you can, anything that you have needed to borrow, what should we do when challenged by an unsought favour? Should we not take as our model the fertile fields, which bring forth much more than they have received? We do not hesitate to perform dutiful services for those whom we hope will assist us in the future; what, then, ought we to be like towards those who have already assisted us? There are two aspects of liberality: first, granting a kind service, and secondly, returning it. Whether we grant one or not is up to us. A good man, however, is not permitted to fail to return one (provided, of course, that he can do so without injustice).

(49) We must, moreover, discriminate between kind services we have received, and there is no doubt but that the greater the kindness, the more is owed to its bestower. Here we must first of all weigh up the spirit in which each man has acted, his devotion and his good-will. For many men do many things out of a certain rashness, failing to use their judgement, or maybe inspired by a frenzied or sudden impulse of the spirit towards everyone, like a gust of wind. Such favours should not be considered as important as those that are conferred through judgement, with forethought and constancy.

In granting favours, on the other hand, and in requiting gratitude, the most important function of duty (if all else is equal) is to enrich above all the person who is most in need of riches. But people generally do exactly the opposite; for they defer above all to him from whom they expect the most, even though he does not need them (50) Also, the fellowship between men and their common bonding will best be preserved if the closer someone is to you the more kindness you confer upon him.

Perhaps, though, we should examine more thoroughly what are the natural principles of human fellowship and community. First is something that is seen in the fellowship of the entire human race. For its bonding consists of reason and speech, which reconcile men to one another, through teaching, learning, communicating, debating and making judgements, and unite them in a kind of natural fellowship. It is this that most distances us from the nature of other animals. To them we often impute courage, as with horses or lions, but we

---

[1] *Works and Days* 349–51.

do not impute to them justice, fairness or goodness. For they have no share in reason and speech.

(51) The most widespread fellowship existing among men is that of all with all others. Here we must preserve the communal sharing of all the things that nature brings forth for the common use of mankind, in such a way that whatever is assigned by statutes and civil law should remain in such possession as those laws may have laid down,[1] but the rest should be regarded as the Greek proverb has it: everything is common among friends. The things that are common to all men seem to be of the kind that Ennius defines in one case, from which we can extrapolate to many cases:

> A man who kindly shows the path to someone who is
> lost lights another's light, so to speak, from his own.
> For his own shines no less because he has lit another's.

With this one instance, he advises us that if any assistance can be provided without detriment to oneself, it should be given even to a stranger. (52) Therefore such things as the following are to be shared: one should not keep others from fresh water, should allow them to take fire from your fire, should give trustworthy counsel to someone who is seeking advice; for they are useful to those who receive them and cause no trouble to the giver. We should therefore both make use of them and always be contributing something to the common benefit. Since, though, the resources of individuals are small, but the mass of those who are in need is infinitely great, general liberality must be measured according to the limit laid down by Ennius, that his own light shine no less; then we shall still be capable of being liberal to those close to us.[2]

(53) There are indeed several degrees of fellowship among men. To move from the one that is unlimited, next there is a closer one of the same race, tribe and tongue, through which men are bound strongly to one another. More intimate still is that of the same city, as citizens have many things that are shared with one another: the forum, temples, porticoes and roads, laws and legal rights, law-courts and political elections; and besides these acquaintances and com-

[1] Cf. p. 10, n. 2.
[2] The restriction on our obligation to mankind in general, that we do not harm our own interests, is balanced by that on our pursuit of those interests (1.25; III.21 ff.), that we should not damage anyone else's, as C. makes clear at III.42.

panionship, and those business and commercial transactions that many of them make with many others. A tie narrower still is that of the fellowship between relations: moving from that vast fellowship of the human race we end up with a confined and limited one.

(54) For since it is by nature common to all animals that they have a drive to procreate, the first fellowship exists within marriage itself, and the next with one's children. Then, there is the one house in which everything is shared. Indeed that is the principle of a city and the seed-bed, as it were, of a political community. Next there follow bonds between brothers, and then between first cousins and second cousins, who cannot be contained in one house and go out to other houses, as if to colonies. Finally there follow marriages and those connections of marriage from which even more relations arise. In such propagation and increase political communities have their origin. Moreover, the bonding of blood holds men together by good-will and by love; (55) for it is a great thing to have the same ancestral memorials, to practise the same religious rites, and to share common ancestral tombs.

Of all fellowships, however, none is more important, and none stronger, than when good men of similar conduct are bound by familiarity. For honourableness – the thing that I so often mention – moves us, even if we see it in someone else, and makes us friends of him in whom it seems to reside. (56) (All virtue indeed lures us to itself and leads us to love those in whom it seems to reside, but justice and liberality do so the most.) Moreover, nothing is more lovable and nothing more tightly binding than similarity in conduct that is good. For when men have similar pursuits and inclinations, it comes about that each one is as much delighted with the other as he is with himself; the result is what Pythagoras wanted in friend-ship, that several be united into one. Important also are the common bonds that are created by kindnesses reciprocally given and received, which, provided that they are mutual and gratefully received, bind together those concerned in an unshakeable fellowship.

(57) But when you have surveyed everything with reason and spirit, of all fellowships none is more serious, and none dearer, than that of each of us with the republic. Parents are dear, and children, relatives and acquaintances are dear, but our country has on its own embraced all the affections of all of us. What good man would hesitate to face death on her behalf, if it would do her a service? How much

more detestable, then, is the monstrousness of those who have savaged their country with all manner of crime and who have been, and are still, engaged in destroying her utterly?[1]

(58) Now were there a comparison, or competition, as to who ought most to receive our dutiful services, our country and our parents would be foremost; for we are obliged to them for the greatest kindnesses. Next would be our children and our whole household, which looks to us alone and can have no other refuge. Then our relations, who are congenial to us and with whom even our fortunes are generally shared. Therefore whatever is necessary to support life is most owed to those whom I have just mentioned; on the other hand a shared life and a shared living, counsel and conversation, encouragement, comfort, and sometimes even reproofs, flourish most of all in friendships; and friendship is most pleasing when it is cemented by similarity of conduct.[2]

(59) But, one ought when bestowing all these dutiful services to look at what each person most greatly needs, and what each would or would not be able to secure without our help. Thus the degrees of ties of relationship will not be the same as those of circumstance. Some duties are owed to one group of people rather than to another. You should, for example, assist your neighbour sooner than your brother or companion in gathering his harvest; but you should in a suit in the lawcourts defend a relative or friend rather than your neighbour.[3]

In every case of duty, therefore, considerations such as these ought to be examined, and we should adopt this habit and should practise so that we can become good calculators of our duties, and can see by adding and subtracting what is the sum that remains; from this you can understand how much is owed to each person. (60) But neither doctors nor generals nor orators are able, however much they

[1] One of C.'s many allusions to Antony and his followers as destroyers of the Republic, with which 'country' is here identified. See Introduction, pp. xii ff.

[2] In considering the degree of fellowship with us (see 1.45), C. first delimits our obligations to mankind in general (51–2) and then (57–8) ranks those to whom we owe support of a material kind – first country, then parents, then (in order of closeness) those related to us by blood or marriage. He goes on to note that social intercourse is owed primarily to friendship based on similarity of conduct. See 1.160 with n. 2.

[3] Even in the context of lawsuits, C. does not mention the distinctively Roman relationships of guardianship (*tutela*), clientship (*clientela*), and guest friendship (*hospitium*), which traditionally had a prior claim to legal support over blood relations, except parents (Introduction, pp. xxiii–xxiv).

have taken to heart advice about their art, to achieve anything very worthy of praise without experience and practice. Similarly, advice on observing duty certainly has been handed down, as I myself am now handing it down, but a matter of such importance also demands experience and practice. And now I have said enough on the question of how honourableness, upon which duty hangs, is derived from those things that constitute the justice of human fellowship.

(61) We have laid it down that the source of what is honourable and dutiful is of four kinds. But, we must realise, it is that which is done with a great and lofty spirit, one disdaining human affairs, which appears in the most brilliant light. For that reason, words such as these are so readily available as an insult:

greatness of spirit no girly men

> You, young men, show a womanly spirit, that maiden
> a man's.

or these:

> Son of Salmacis, neither sweat nor sacrifice secured
> you your spoils.[1]

When, however, it is a matter of praising, it is deeds done with a great spirit, courageously, outstandingly, which seem for some reason to wrest from us fulsome praise. Hence Marathon, Salamis, Plataea, Thermopylae, Leuctra have become battlefields for orators.[2] Hence also our own Horatius Cocles, the Decii, Cnaeus and Publius Scipio, Marcus Marcellus and countless others, and above all the Roman people itself, are notable for their greatness of spirit. The very fact that the statues we look upon are usually in military dress bears witness to our devotion to military glory.[3]

(62) However, if the loftiness of spirit that reveals itself amid danger

---

[1] Salmacis is a spring in Caria whose waters were thought to be enervating (Ovid, *Metamorphoses* IV.285 ff.). Both verses are by unknown poets.

[2] At Marathon (490 BC), Salamis (480), Plataea (479), the Greeks won notable victories over the Persians; at Thermopylae (480) the Spartans were defeated by the Persians and at Leuctra (471) by the Thebans. Orators frequently used these as historical illustrations.

[3] Traditionally statues of citizens in Rome showed them in civilian dress. The statue of Caesar in a breastplate placed in his forum (Pliny, *Natural History* XXXIV.18) is the first such statue attested in Rome, except for a statue of Horatius Cocles in armour in the first century BC (Dionysius of Halicarnassus V.25). C. may allude to equestrian statues which gained prominence when Sulla, Pompey and Caesar were so represented. Gilt equestrian statues of M. Aemilius Lepidus and Lucius Antonius were set up around the time that *De Officiis* was written (*Philippics* V.50, VI.12).

and toil is empty of justice, if it fights not for the common safety but for its own advantages, it is a vice. It is not merely unvirtuous; it is rather a savagery which repels all civilized feeling. Therefore the Stoics define courage well when they call it the virtue which fights on behalf of fairness. For that reason no one has won praise who has pursued the glory of courage by treachery and cunning; for nothing can be honourable from which justice is absent. (63) Therefore Plato's words are splendid: 'Knowledge,' he said, 'if separated from justice, should indeed be termed craftiness rather than wisdom.' But furthermore, a spirit which is ready to face danger, but is driven by selfish desire rather than the common benefit should be called not courage, but audacity.[1] Therefore we require men who are brave and of great spirit also to be good and straightforward, friends of truth and not in the least deceitful: such are the central qualities for which justice is praised.

(64) It is a hateful fact that loftiness and greatness of spirit all too easily give birth to wilfulness and an excessive desire for pre-eminence. We find in Plato that all the conduct of the Spartans was inflamed by desire for conquest.[2] Similarly, the more outstanding an individual is in greatness of spirit, the more he desires complete pre-eminence, or rather to be the sole ruler.[3] But when you desire to surpass all others, it is difficult to respect the fairness that is a special mark of justice. Consequently, such men allow themselves to be defeated neither by argument nor by any public or legal obligation. Only too often do they emerge in public life as bribers and agitators, seeking to acquire as much wealth as possible, preferring violent pre-eminence to equality through justice. The greater the difficulty, however, the greater the splendour: there is no occasion from which justice should be absent.

(65) It is not, therefore, those who inflict injury, but those who prevent it, whom we should consider the men of courage and great spirit. A true and wise greatness of spirit judges that deeds and not glory are the basis of the honourableness that nature most seeks.

[1] *Menexenus* 246c. Commentators extend the quotation as far as 'audacity'. The thought of the second sentence is not unPlatonic, but if C. is quoting Plato, he is quoting him very freely.
[2] *Laches* 182e.
[3] The allusion to Caesar's autocracy is clear, especially in the charges of demagoguery and rapacity (Introduction, p. xii), but C. also deplored Pompey's ambition (III.82), and Caesar complained that Pompey could not bear an equal (*Civil War* I.4.4).

It prefers not to seem pre-eminent but to be so: he who is carried by the foolishness of the ignorant mob should not be counted a great man. Furthermore, the loftier a man's spirit, the more easily he is driven by desire for glory to injustice. This is slippery ground indeed: scarcely a man can be found who, when he has undertaken toil and confronted dangers, does not yearn for glory as a kind of payment for his achievements.[1]

(66) A brave and great spirit is in general seen in two things. One lies in disdain for things external, in the conviction that a man should admire, should choose, should pursue nothing except what is honourable and seemly, and should yield to no man, nor to agitation of the spirit, nor to fortune.[2] The second thing is that you should, in the spirit I have described, do deeds which are great, certainly, but above all beneficial, and you should vigorously undertake difficult and laborious tasks which endanger both life itself and much that concerns life.

(67) All the splendour, the grandeur and I may add, the benefit, of the two lie in the latter; the cause of, the reason behind, the greatness of men, however, in the former. That is the factor that makes men outstanding in spirit and contemptuous of human things. And in fact this reveals itself in two ways: first, if you judge to be good only that which is honourable, and secondly if your spirit is free from every agitation. For it must be held that a brave and great spirit will little value things that appear to most men distinguished and even splendid, disdaining them with reason firm and steady; while a man of firm spirit and great constancy will endure circumstances that seem harsh, many and various as they are in the lives and fortunes of mankind, without departing from man's natural state, from the worthy standing of a wise man.

(68) It is not consistent for a man who is not broken by fear to be broken by desires, nor for one who has proved himself unconquered by toil to be conquered by pleasure. Therefore you must avoid these, and shun also the desire for money. Nothing is more the mark of a mean and petty spirit than to love riches; nothing more

[1] C. had recently written a treatise *On Glory* (II.31). Cf. II.43 for the distinction between true and false glory.
[2] The Stoics thought happiness could be achieved by becoming independent of external circumstances through the realization that nothing is really good but virtue which is in our control.

honourable and more magnificent than to despise money if you are without it, but if you have it to devote it to liberality and beneficence. Beware also the desire for glory, as I have said. For it destroys the liberty for which men of great spirit ought to be in competition. Nor should you seek military commands. In fact sometimes these should be refused and sometimes even resigned. (69) We must empty ourselves of every agitation of the spirit – desire and fear, of course, but also sorrow and excessive pleasure and anger – in order to gain that tranquillity of spirit, that freedom from care, which ensures both constancy and standing.[1]

There have been many, and there still are, who have sought that kind of tranquillity by abandoning public business and fleeing to a life of leisure. These include the noblest and foremost philosophers,[2] and also certain strict and serious men who could not endure the behaviour of the populace or its leaders. Some of these have spent their lives on their estates finding their delight in their family wealth.[3] (70) Their aim was the aim of kings: that needing nothing, and obeying no one, they might enjoy liberty, the mark of which is to live just as one pleases. That aim, then, is common both to those who desire power and to such men of leisure. The former, however, think that they can achieve it by acquiring great wealth, the latter if they are satisfied with the little that is already theirs. Neither view should be utterly despised. Note, though, that the life of leisure is easier and safer, less troublesome to oneself or to others. Those, on the other hand, who have adapted themselves to great achievements in the service of the political community, lead lives more profitable to mankind and more suited to grandeur and fame.

(71) Men of outstanding ability who have devoted themselves to learning rather than choose public life, or those who have retired from public life hampered by ill health or some quite serious cause,

---

[1] The Stoics aimed to rid themselves of the passions, two of which, desire and fear, involved accepting false notions about future good and evil, the other two, pleasure and pain, false notions about present good and evil. Anger was a subdivision of desire (*Tusculan Disputations* IV.21).

[2] Plato in *Republic* 516d–517e described how philosophers, having glimpsed truth, would be unwilling to return to the half-truths of political life and might be rejected. The founders of the Stoa, Zeno, Cleanthes and Chrysippus had not entered public life but advocated participation in it. Panaetius, though belonging to the governing class at Rhodes, could have justified his abstention by his outstanding intellectual gifts, as in I.71.

[3] C. may be thinking of his friend Atticus (Nepos, *Atticus* 6.1–2).

should therefore perhaps be excused when they yield to others the power and the praise of governing.[1] When, however, those without a reason claim to despise the commands and magistracies which most men admire, I do not think that should be counted as praiseworthy – indeed no, but rather as a vice. It is a difficult thing not to approve their view insofar as they disdain glory and think it worthless. But they appear to be afraid of hard work and trouble, and also, or so it seems, the humiliation and disrepute which results from failure and defeat. For there are those who are so inconsistent in opposite circumstances that they despise pleasure with the utmost rigour, but are weak when faced with pain; glory they ignore, but they are broken by humiliation. And they are not very constant even in this.

Civic life better than military life.

Better to get things through Debate than war / reasonable methods

(72) But those who are equipped by nature to administer affairs must abandon any hesitation over winning office and engage in public life. For only in this way can either the city be ruled or greatness of spirit be displayed. No less than philosophers, and I suspect even more so, must those who choose public life acquire the magnificent disdain for human affairs that I stress, and tranquillity of mind and freedom from care. Otherwise, how will they live without anxiety, with seriousness and with constancy? (73) This is easier for philosophers in that there is less in their life which is vulnerable to the blows of fortune, and their needs are fewer; and if they do meet with misfortune, their fall can not be so severe. It is with good reason, therefore, that greater impulses to achieve greater things are aroused in the spirits of those engaged in public life than of those who live quietly; therefore they need greatness of spirit and freedom from anguish all the more.

When anyone does undertake public business, he should remember to reflect not only on how honourable that is, but also on whether he has the capacity to succeed. Here he must take thought so that indolence does not make him despair prematurely, nor greed spur him to over-confidence. Before you approach any business, thorough preparations must be made.

(74) Most men consider that military affairs are of greater significance than civic; I must deflate that opinion. For men have not infrequently sought war out of desire for glory. This has most often been true of men of great spirit and talent, and all the more so if military

---

[1] C. is here less uncompromising than in I.19.

service suits them and they love the business of warfare. However, if we are prepared to judge the matter correctly, many achievements of civic life have proved greater and more famous than those of war.[1]

(75) Themistocles may rightly be praised, and his name possess greater renown than Solon's, Salamis may be summoned as a witness to a famous victory, which may indeed be ranked above the counsel that Solon showed when he instituted the Areopagus; in fact, however, the latter should be judged no less splendid than the former. For the former benefit was a single one; the latter will serve the city for ever: by that counsel the very laws of the Athenians and their ancestral institutions are preserved. Themistocles could claim to have helped the Areopagus in nothing; the Areopagus, however, might truly claim to have assisted him: the very war was waged according to the counsel of the senate that Solon had established.[2] (76) The same may be said about Pausanias and Lysander. It may be thought that their achievements won for Sparta imperial rule. But they cannot begin to be compared with the laws and discipline instituted by Lycurgus, which were, rather, the very causes of their having armies so well trained and courageous. I did not consider that Marcus Scaurus in my boyhood[3] yielded anything to Gaius Marius; nor Catulus to Pompey when I myself was involved in public life. Arms have little effect abroad if there is no counsel at home. Africanus was outstanding as a man and as a general. But when he destroyed Numantia he benefited the republic no more than did Publius Nasica at the same time, when, though a civilian, he killed Tiberius Gracchus. The deed, it is true, was not a matter merely of civilian methods: effected as it was by physical force, it involved methods appropriate to war.

---

[1] C. himself aspired to a triumph (p. 31, n. 2), while knowing he could never match his illustrious contemporaries. The whole discussion of public life from 69 on is leading up to 78 where C. urges his son to follow in his footsteps. Cf. II.45 for his son's own military bent.

[2] C. appears to subscribe to the tradition that Solon first established the Areopagus, which Plutarch says he found in 'most writers' (*Solon* 19). Plutarch and Aristotle, however, held that the Areopagus already existed and that Solon created a new Council of 400. This version, perhaps based on a confusion of the two councils, suited C.'s point here that civil achievements are the basis of military, for it was the Areopagus that contributed naval pay at the time of the Athenian victory at Salamis.

[3] C. indicates the time (the end of the second century BC) when this comparison was being made, and the place, for both men were important to his home town of Arpinum. Marius was a native son and M. Aemilius Scaurus, who took an interest in the town, congratulated C.'s grandfather on his opposition to the introduction of the secret ballot.

However, it was civic counsel that prompted it, and no army was involved.

(77)· The best expression of all this is the verse which, I gather, is often attacked by shameless and envious men:

Let arms yield to the toga, and laurels to laudation.[1]

To mention no others, when I held the helm of the republic, did not arms then yield to the toga? Never was there more serious danger to the republic than then, and never was there greater quiet. Through my vigilance and my counsel the very arms swiftly slipped and fell from the hands of the most audacious citizens. Was any achievement of war ever so great? What military triumph can stand comparison?[2] (78) I am allowed to boast to you, Marcus my son. For yours it is both to inherit my glory and to imitate my deeds. Pompey himself, indeed, whose military exploits won lavish praise, paid me the tribute of saying in the hearing of many that he would have won his third triumph in vain had my service to the republic not ensured that he had somewhere to celebrate it.[3] Therefore the courageous deeds of civilians are not inferior to those of soldiers. Indeed the former should be given even more effort and devotion than the latter.

(79) That honourableness that we seek from a lofty and magnificent spirit is in general produced not by bodily strength, but by strength of spirit. However, we must exercise the body, training it so that when it has to attend to business or endure hard work it is able to obey counsel and reason. The honourableness that we seek depends entirely upon the concern and reflection of the spirit. In this field the civilians who are in charge of public affairs provide no less a benefit than those who wage war. And so it is by often their counsel that a war may be avoided or terminated, and sometimes declared;

---

[1] The verse, 'Cedant arma togae, concedat laurea laudi' comes from Book III of C.'s poem *On His Own Times*. From the time of its composition in 60 BC, it was derided for its assonance and its conceit. At this time C. defended it against the gibes of Antony (*Philippic* II.20). See Introduction, pp. xi, xv, xviii.

[2] The triumph involved a great procession of soldiers, captives and spoils led by the victorious commander in regal dress, C. moved heaven and earth to try to secure one after he was hailed Imperator (the necessary preliminary) by his soldiers for his victory in Cilicia in 51.

[3] In the Greek examples of 75–6, Solon and Lycurgus provide the necessary institutions long before Themistocles, Pausanias and Lysander achieve their military successes; the Roman examples are pairs of contemporaries in which the statesman excels the general. The two themes come together in the comparison of Pompey and C. in 78.

it was through Marcus Cato's counsel that the Third Punic war was declared, and his authority had effect even after his death.[1] **(80)** We must therefore value the reason which makes decisions above the courage which makes battle; yet we must be careful to do that because we have reasoned about what is beneficial, and not merely for the sake of avoiding war. Moreover, war should always be undertaken in such a way that one is seen to be aiming only at peace.

It is the mark of a truly brave and constant spirit that one remain unperturbed in difficult times, and when agitated not be thrown, as the saying goes, off one's feet, but rather hold fast to reason, with one's spirit and counsel ready to hand.

(81) That is the mark of a great spirit; but this is the mark also of great intellectual talent: to anticipate the future by reflection, deciding somewhat beforehand how things could go in either direction, and what should be done in either event, never acting so that one will need to say, 'I had not thought of that'. Such is the work of a spirit not only great and lofty but also relying on good sense and good counsel. To charge rashly into battle and engage the enemy hand to hand is monstrous and beastlike. But if the necessity of the occasion demands, one must fight hand to hand, preferring death to slavery or dishonourableness. **(82)** (In the case of destroying and plundering cities it is particularly important to take care that nothing is done with recklessness or cruelty.)

It is also the mark of a great man in times of unrest to punish the guilty but to preserve the mass of people, holding fast to what is upright and honourable, whatever fortune may bring. For just as some, as I have mentioned above, put war before civic affairs, so you will find many to whom dangerously hot-headed counsels seem greater and more brilliant than calm and considered ones. **(83)** We must never purposefully avoid danger so as to appear cowardly and fearful, yet we must avoid exposing ourselves pointlessly to risk. Nothing can be stupider than that. When confronting danger, therefore, we should copy the doctor, whose custom it is to treat mild illnesses mildly, though he is forced to apply riskier, double-edged, remedies to more serious illnesses. Only a madman would pray for a facing storm during a calm; but when a storm does arise the wise man meets it using all his reason. That is particularly so when a

---

[1] Up until his death in 149 BC, the Elder Cato ended every speech in the Senate with 'Carthage must be destroyed'. He had his way posthumously in 146.

successful outcome may bring more good than the period of uncertainty evil. The dangers attending great undertakings fall sometimes
upon their authors and sometimes upon the nation. Again, some are
called to put their lives at risk, others their glory and the goodwill
of their fellow-citizens. We must, therefore, be more eager to risk
our own than the common welfare, and readier to fight when honour
and glory, than when other advantages, are at stake.

Pub. Serv. should do only what is good for citizens. Dont help your self.

(84) However, many have been found who were willing to pour
out on their country's behalf not only money, but even life itself,
yet they would not make the slightest sacrifice of glory, not even
when the nation was crying out for it. Callicratidas, for example,
had as the Spartan general in the Peloponnesian war performed many
notable deeds. At the last, however, he undermined them all by disobeying the counsel of those who thought the fleet should have left
Arginusae rather than engage the Athenians. His reply was that if
the Spartans lost their fleet they could build another, whereas for
him, flight was impossible without disgrace. That blow was a moderate
one to the Spartans. But this was ruinous: when Cleombrotus reck-
lessly engaged Epaminondas because he feared unpopularity, all
Sparta's resources were destroyed. How much better Quintus
Maximus! Ennius writes of him:

> One man alone restored our affairs by delaying; our
> safety he preferred to all thought of his fame. Therefore
> the hero's glory now shines, and ever more brightly.[1]

We must avoid that type of error even in civic affairs. For there
are those who do not dare to say what they think, however excellent
it may be, through fear of unpopularity.

(85) In general those who are about to take charge of public affairs
should hold fast to Plato's two pieces of advice: first to fix their gaze
so firmly on what is beneficial to the citizens that whatever they do,
they do with that in mind, forgetful of their own advantage. Secondly,
let them care for the whole body of the republic rather than protect
one part and neglect the rest.[2] The management of the republic
is like a guardianship, and must be conducted in the light of what
is beneficial not to the guardians, but to those who are put in their

---

[1] From Book xii of the *Annales*.
[2] See *Republic* i 342e, v 465d–6c, vii 519e, iv 420b.

[handwritten margin notes: electioneering is a wretched practice. two sides shouldn't be enemies. pertinant to today]

charge.[1] By consulting the interests of some of the citizens and neglecting others, they bring upon the city the ruinous condition of unrest and strife. Consequently some appear as *populares*, and others as devotees of the best men, but few as champions of everyone.[2] (86) That was the reason for serious strife in Athens. In our republic it has caused not merely unrest but even disastrous civil war.[3] That is something which any serious, courageous, citizen who is worthy of pre-eminence in the republic will shun with hatred. He will devote himself entirely to the republic, pursuing neither wealth nor power, and will protect the whole in such a way that the interest of none is disregarded. He will expose no one to hatred or unpopularity by making false accusations. He will, in sum, so adhere to justice and what is honourable that in preserving them he will endure any reverse, however serious, and face death rather than abandon those things I have mentioned.

(87) Electioneering and the struggle for positions of honour is an altogether wretched practice. Again Plato's words on the subject are splendid: those who compete between themselves over who should administer the republic act as if sailors were to fight over which of them should be principal helmsman. Similarly he advises that we should consider as enemies those who take up arms against us, not those who want to protect the republic in the way each judges best.[4]

---

[1] 'Management' translates *procuratio* and 'guardianship' *tutela*, both terms of civil law for relationships in private life based on faith (*fides*). *Tutela* is the relationship of a guardian to a person legally unable to manage his own affairs, notably minors and women; *procuratio* is the supervision of another man's business interests, in theory without payment, such as Atticus undertook for C. and other friends (Nepos, *Atticus* 15.3).

[2] The contrast is between two types of politics, not two parties. *Popularis* was usually applied to individuals claiming to represent the interests of the people, as opposed to the Senate and the upper orders generally: they stressed the sovereignty of the popular assemblies and the importance of the office of tribune of the plebs, and advocated economic and social reforms to help the poor. The *optimates* favoured the interests of the *optimi* or 'best men' (their own flattering term) and upheld the authority of the Senate, resisting distributions of wealth and property. C. liked to think of himself as promoting the harmony of all the orders but his sympathy with the Senate and his defence of private property mark him as an Optimate, though a moderate one.

[3] C. points to the political conflicts at Athens between oligarchs and democrats at the end of the fifth century BC. In Rome he thinks of the conflicts of his own time, involving actual armies, between Marius and Sulla, then Caesar and Pompey. That between the tyrannicides and Antony and Octavian lay ahead.

[4] C. exploits, in a rather misleading way, the famous ship analogy of *Republic* VI 488. It is not clear where he found the second piece of Platonic advice.

It was in that way that Publius Africanus and Quintus Metellus used to disagree with one another, without bitterness.[1]

(88) Furthermore we should not listen to those who think we should be deeply angry with our opponents, and consider that that is what a great-spirited and courageous man does. For nothing is more to be praised, nothing more worthy of a great and splendid man than to be easily appeased and forgiving. Among free peoples who possess equality before the law we must cultivate an affable temper and what is called loftiness of spirit. Otherwise, if we are angry with those who approach us when it is inconvenient or make over-bold demands on us, we shall become unhelpfully and hatefully sour. We must, however, recommend gentleness and forgiveness on the understanding that we may exercise severity for the sake of the republic; for without that the city cannot be governed. Punishment and correction should never be insulting. It should be undertaken in accordance with what is useful to the republic, not to the one who administers the punishment or reprimand. (89) We must be careful that the punishment should not be heavier than the offence, and that we do not have some beaten when others charged with the same offence are not even summoned. It is particularly when punishing that one should restrain one's anger: a man who is angry when he goes to punish will never maintain that intermediate course between too much and too little that the Peripatetics approve. They are in fact right to approve if only they did not praise angriness, calling it a beneficial gift of nature. For surely anger should be denied on all occasions.[2] Our prayer should be that those in charge of the republic be like the laws, which are led to punish not through anger, but through fairness.[3]

---

[1] In C.'s *Laelius de amicitia* 77, Laelius claims that Scipio Aemilianus disagreed with Q. Metellus Macedonicus without bitterness, but in the *De Re Publica* 1.31 he calls Metellus a leader of the 'slanderers and enemies' of Scipio.

[2] Aristotle described the virtues as middle states between two extremes. Thus mildness was intermediate between irascibility and 'angerlessness'; the mild man would be angry on appropriate occasions and to the appropriate degree (*Nichomachean Ethics* IV.5). C. here follows the Stoics in thinking the wise man should be free of all passions (p. 28, n. 1), but, in deference to his son's current instructor, notes the Peripatetic view (see Introduction, p. xvii) that appropriate anger was useful (*Tusculan Disputations* IV.43). C. also uses the standard of 'the middle way' in his discussions of seemliness (1.130, 1.140) and political liberality (II.59, II.60).

[3] Aristotle himself compares the rule of law to that of passionless reason in *Politics* III.16, *Rhetoric* I.1.7.

(90) When things are going well and as we would wish, we should make a great effort to avoid haughtiness, scorn and arrogance. Unreliability is revealed as much in reacting excessively to success as to adversity. It is a splendid achievement to face all of life with equanimity, never altering the expression of one's face, as we hear that Socrates and Gaius Laelius did. Philip, king of Macedon, may have been surpassed in deeds and glory by his son, but I note that he was both more affable and more humane. Philip, therefore, was always a great man, while Alexander often acted most dishonourably. They seem to give us good advice, then, who warn that the more we excel, the more humbly we should behave. According to Panaetius, his pupil and friend Africanus used to say that when frequent skirmishing has made horses fierce and high-spirited, men are accustomed to give them to trainers so that they may have gentler mounts to ride. Similarly, men whom success has made unbridled and over-confident should be led into the training-ring of reason and learning, so that they perceive the frailty of human affairs and the variability of fortune.

(91) Even in times of extreme good fortune we very much need to make use of our friends' counsel, and it is then more than previously that we should attribute to them authority. At this time too must we beware of giving ear to flatterers or of allowing ourselves to be fawned upon. It is easy to be fooled in this, for we think that we are the kind of people who ought to be praised. Consequently countless blunders arise, when such opinions so inflate men that they become the objects of dishonourable mockery and fall into serious errors.

So much for that subject.

(92) Our judgement should be that the achievements which are greatest and show the greatest spirit are those of the men who rule the republic. For their government reaches extremely widely and affects the greatest number. Many men of great spirit, however, have lived and still live lives of leisure. Some, limiting themselves to their own business, investigate and examine great matters of some kind. Others have taken a middle course between philosophy and the administration of the republic: enjoying their own personal wealth, they neither increase this by every possible method nor prevent those close to them from making use of it, sharing it rather with friends and the republic too if the need arise. Their wealth should in the first place be well won, and not dishonourably or invidiously acquired.

Secondly, it should be increased by reason, industriousness, thrift. Thirdly, it should be available for the benefit of as many as possible, provided they are worthy of it, and be at the command not of lust and luxury but of liberality and beneficence.[1]

A man who observes these rules may live not only in a grand, impressive, and spirited manner, but also with simplicity and trustworthiness, a true friend of other men.

| (93) Next we must discuss the one remaining element of honourableness. Under this appear a sense of shame and what one might call the ordered beauty of a life, restraint and modesty, a calming of all the agitations of the spirit, and due measure in all things.[2] Under this heading is included what in Latin may be called *decorum* (seemliness); the Greek for it is *prepon*. The essence of this is that it cannot be separated from what is honourable: for what is seemly is honourable, and what is honourable is seemly. It is easier to grasp than to explain what the difference is between 'honourable' and 'seemly'. (94) For whatever it may be, what is seemly is manifested then, when the honourable precedes it. For this reason, what is seemly appears not only in the part of the honourable that we must discuss here, but also in the first three parts: it is seemly to use reason and speech sensibly, to do what one does with forethought, in everything to see and to gaze on what is true. On the other hand, mistakes, errors, lapses, misjudgements are as unseemly as delirious insanity. Seemly, too, is everything that is just, but what is unjust, being dishonourable, is unseemly. There is a similar story to tell about courage: what is done in a great and manly spirit seems worthy of a human being and seemly, as for the opposite, being dishonourable, it is unseemly.

(95) Therefore this seemliness of which I speak relates to the whole

---

[1] C. may have been thinking of his friend Atticus who took a great interest in politics and, according to his biographer Nepos (*Atticus* 2.4–6), observed high standards in acquiring and using his wealth.

[2] What these apparently disparate virtues, here grouped together, have in common are first, limit and appropriateness to context, and secondly, concern with appearance and not offending others. Thus impulse must obey the limit set by reason so that the passions are moderated (102); the sense of shame must respect the conventions of society (99, 128, 148); one's life must be appropriate to one's 'roles' (107, 115); and behaviour must fit one's age and civic status (122–5). Immoderate passions are visible and offend (102); but one must also regulate aspects of living such as jokes and conversation (103–4, 132–6), gait and dress (128–31) and houses (138–40), all of which are in the public eye.

of honourableness; and it is related in such a way that it is not seen by esoteric reasoning, but springs ready to view. For there is indeed such a thing as the seemly, and one grasps that it is in every virtue. It is, however, more easily separated from virtue in thought than in fact. Just as bodily loveliness and beauty cannot be separated from healthiness, similarly the seemliness that we are discussing is indeed completely blended with virtue, but is distinguished by thought and reflection.[1]

(96) But furthermore this has two senses: first, we understand a seemliness of a general kind, involved with honourable behaviour as a whole, and secondly, something subordinate to this, which relates to an individual element of what is honourable.[2] The former is customarily defined something like this: what is seemly is that which agrees with the excellence of man just where his nature differs from that of other creatures. Their definition of the part subordinate to this takes the seemly to be that which agrees with nature in such a way that moderation and restraint appear in it, along with the appearance of a gentleman.

(97) We are able to infer that it is grasped in this way from that seemliness to which poets aspire. (This is often discussed more fully in a different context.)[3] We say that poets 'observe what is seemly' when what is said and done is worthy of the role. If Aeacus or Minos were to say, 'Let them hate provided that they fear', or, 'The father himself is his children's tomb,' it would seem unseemly, because we believe them to have been just men. When Atreus says it, however, there is loud applause: the words are worthy of his role. The poets, though, will judge what is seemly for each by his role; but nature

---

[1] Seemliness is found particularly in the fourth group of virtues which concern what is appropriate and how one appears to others. However, C. argues, all virtuous behaviour is in fact seemly; as soon as one grasps that an act is just, one sees it also as seemly, just as one cannot see a body as healthy without seeing it as beautiful. Virtue in general is seemly because it is appropriate for a man (96) and wins approval when others recognize it as virtue.

[2] The manuscripts say 'individual elements'; however, C. is clearly contrasting the seemliness of honourableness as a whole (that is of all the four virtues together) with the special seemliness of the fourth group of virtues. Similarly in 96, where the manuscripts read 'in each one part of virtue', the emended reading 'in one part of virtue' is given.

[3] The notion of what is appropriate was common in treatises on poetry and rhetoric. C. has a brief discussion in *Orator* 70–4.

has imposed on us a role that greatly excels and surpasses that of other creatures.

(98) Poets, therefore, will look to what is suitable and seemly for a huge variety of roles, even wicked ones. But our parts have been given to us by nature: since they are ones of constancy, of moderation, of restraint, of a sense of shame, and since the same nature teaches us to be mindful of the way we behave towards other men, it becomes apparent how widespread is not only that seemliness which extends over all that is honourable, but also that which is seen in one part of virtue.[1] For just as the eye is aroused by the beauty of a body, because of the appropriate arrangement of the limbs, and is delighted just because all its parts are in graceful harmony, so this seemliness, shining out in one's life, arouses the approval of one's fellows, because of the order and constancy and moderation of every word and action.

(99) Thus we must exercise a respectfulness towards men, both towards the best of them and also towards the rest. To neglect what others think about oneself is the mark not only of arrogance, but also of utter laxity. There is a difference between justice and shame when reasoning about humans. The part of justice is not to harm a man, that of a sense of shame not to outrage him. Here is seen most clearly the essence of seemliness. I think it will be understood from this explanation what kind of thing it is that we call 'being seemly'.

(100) The duty which is derived from this follows above all the road that leads to agreeing with and preserving nature. If we follow her as our guide we will never go astray; we will follow that which is by nature discriminating and clear-sighted, that which is suited to bonding men together, that too which is vigorous and courageous. Seemliness, however, appears to the greatest effect in the element that we are discussing at present.

Nor is it only the movements of the body that should be commended when they are suited to nature, but also those of the spirit when they too are adapted to her. (101) For the power of the spirit, that is its nature, is twofold: one part of it consists of impulse, called in Greek *horme*, which snatches a man this way and that; the other of reason, which teaches and explains what should be done and what

---

[1] See p. 38, n. 2.

avoided. Reason therefore commands, and impulse obeys.[1] All action should be free from rashness and carelessness; nor should anyone do anything for which he cannot give a persuasive justification: that is practically a definition of duty.

(102) One must ensure, therefore, that the impulses obey reason, and neither run ahead of it, nor through laziness or cowardice abandon it, and that they are calm and free from every agitation of spirit. As a result there will shine forth in their fullness both constancy and moderation. If impulses overstep their bounds, if, leaping away, so to speak, whether attracted by something or repelled, they are not adequately restrained by reason, then indeed they transgress due measure and limit. They abandon, they cast off, obedience, they do not submit to reason, to whom they are subject by the law of nature. The body too, as well as the spirit, is then agitated by them. One can see the faces of angry men, of men aroused by some passion or fear, of men exulting in excessive pleasure: the faces, the voices, the gestures, the postures of them all are transformed.[2]

(103) To return to our delineation of duty: from all this we realize that all impulses should be controlled and calmed, that our attention and forethought should be aroused in such a way that we do nothing rashly or at random, without consideration or care. Furthermore, we have not been created by nature to seem as if we were made for jesting and play, but rather for earnestness, for greater and weightier pursuits. We may of course joke and play, but in the way that we sleep and otherwise rest, that is when we have given time enough to weighty and serious matters. The humour itself should be of a well bred and witty type, neither extravagant nor excessive. We do not allow boys complete freedom, in their play, but only as much as is compatible with acting honourably; similarly, the light of an upright character should shine forth even from our jokes.

---

[1] C. uses Stoic terminology, though orthodox Stoics, unlike Plato and Aristotle, did not divide the soul into potentially conflicting parts (cf. *Tusculan Disputations* IV.10–11). For them, to act incorrectly or to experience passions (see p. 28, n. 1) is the result of an error of judgement about what is desirable, impulse automatically follows the judgement of reason, and virtue is a matter of knowledge, not of ruling obedient impulses.

[2] The contrast between the spirit and the body here, as in 100 *fin.*, is not between thought and action (which, as the result of impulse, has been treated under spirit in 101–2) but between the conduct (actions and passions) of men and their physical appearance (gestures, expressions). Cf. 1.126 where 'deed and word' are contrasted with 'bodily movement and state'.

(104) There are in general two brands of humour, the one ungentlemanly, insolent, outrageous, indecent, the other refined, sophisticated, clever, witty. Not only our own Plautus and Attic Old Comedy,
but also the books of the Socratic philosophers,[1] are packed with
the latter sort. Many things said by many other men are also witty,
as for example in the collection made by the Elder Cato, known as
the *Apophthegms*.[2] It is easy to make the distinction between a well
bred and an ungentlemanly joke. the former, provided the time is
right, as when one is relaxing, is worthy of even the most serious
man;[3] the latter, if the words are indecent and the subject dishonourable, are unworthy of any free man. A certain proportion must be
maintained in play lest we lose ourselves altogether and lapse into
behaviour that is dishonourable, carried away by pleasure. Examples
of honourable play are provided by the Campus Martius[4] and the
pursuit of hunting.

(105) It is a part of every enquiry about duty always to keep in
view how greatly the nature of a man surpasses domestic animals
and other beasts. They perceive nothing except pleasure, and their
every instinct carries them to it. A man's mind, however, is nourished
by learning and reasoning; he is always enquiring or acting, he is
led by a delight in seeing and hearing. And furthermore, even if
anyone is a little too susceptible to pleasure (provided that he is not
actually one of the beasts – for some are men not in fact, but in
name only – but if he is a little more upright than that) although
captivated by pleasure he will deceitfully conceal his impulse for it
because of a sense of shame.

(106) From this we understand that bodily pleasure is not sufficiently worthy of the superiority of man and that it should be scorned
and rejected. But if there is anyone who assigns some worth to pleasure
he must take care to keep his enjoyment of it in proportion. The
nourishment and care we give our bodies should therefore be
measured by the needs of healthiness and strength, not of pleasure.
If we wish to reflect on the excellence and worthiness of our nature,

[1] C. appears to mean Plato, Xenophon and Aeschines in whose works Socrates' irony
was displayed (cf. *Brutus* 292).
[2] A collection of *bons mots* by the Elder Cato (cf. *De Oratore* II.271).
[3] 'Most serious' is added by editors to fill an obvious gap.
[4] The area northwest of the centre of Rome and east of the Tiber that was used as
an exercise ground even after extensive building there in the Augustan period (Strabo
Geography, V.3.8).

we shall realize how dishonourable it is to sink into luxury and to live a soft and effeminate lifestyle, but how honourable to live thriftily, strictly, with self-restraint, and soberly.

(107) Furthermore, one must understand that we have been dressed, as it were, by nature for two roles:[1] one is common, arising from the fact that we all have a share in reason and in the superiority by which we surpass the brute creatures. Everything honourable and seemly is derived from this, and from it we discover a method of finding out our duty. The other, however, is that assigned specifically to individuals.[2] For just as there are enormous bodily differences (for some, as we see, their strength is the speed that they can run, for others the might with which they wrestle; again, some have figures that are dignified, others that are graceful), similarly there are still greater differences in men's spirits. (108) Lucius Crassus and Lucius Philippus had plenty of wit; Gaius Caesar, the son of Lucius, still more, though it was more studied; but in the same period Marcus Scaurus and the youthful Marcus Drusus were showing exceptional seriousness, Gaius Laelius was extremely jolly, his intimate friend Scipio had greater ambition and a more earnest style of life. Of the Greeks, we are told that a pleasant and humorous and genial conversationalist, who put up a pretence whenever he spoke, was Socrates (the Greeks called him an *eiron*).[3] On the other hand, Pythagoras and Pericles acquired great authoritativeness without any jollity. We hear that Hannibal the Carthaginian was crafty, as was, of our leaders, Quintus Maximus, who found it easy to conceal or to keep silent, to dissemble, to set traps, and to anticipate the enemy's plans. The Greeks place Themistocles and Jason of Pherae before all others in this class; and Solon did something outstandingly cunning and crafty: for in order both to make his own life safer, and the more to assist the republic, he pretended that he was mad.[4]

(109) Others are very different from these, being straightforward

---

[1] The word translated as 'role', *persona*, is taken from the theatre (cf. 1.97) where it can mean a mask, a role, or the actor playing the role.

[2] The Stoic aim of living in accordance with nature, that is fulfilling the nature of man, is here expanded to accommodate the personal traits and talents of individual men.

[3] The Greek word from which 'irony' comes.

[4] Solon, in order to evade the consequences of an Athenian law forbidding anyone to advocate the resumption of the struggle with Megara, in which Athens had met with defeat, pretended madness and recited verses urging the recovery of the island of Salamis.

and open; they think that nothing should be done through secrecy or trickery, they cultivate the truth and they are hostile to deceit. There are others again who would endure anything you like, devote themselves to anyone you like, provided they acquire what they want; we saw that in the case of Sulla and Marcus Crassus. We are told that the craftiest and most patient of this type was the Spartan Lysander, while Callicratidas, the next commander of the fleet after Lysander, was the opposite; and that another man again, although he has great power, manages to appear in conversation to be one among many. We saw that in Catulus, both father and son, and we see it also in Quintus Mucius and in Mancia.[1] I have heard from my elders that it was true also of Publius Scipio Nasica; but that his father, on the other hand, the man who punished the desperate ventures of Tiberius Gracchus, was not at all affable in conversation, and for that very reason became great and famous.[2] There are countless other dissimilarities of nature and conduct, which do not in the least deserve censure.

(110) Each person should hold on to what is his as far as it is not vicious, but is peculiar to him, so that the seemliness that we are seeking might more easily be maintained. For we must act in such a way that we attempt nothing contrary to universal nature; but while conserving that, let us follow our own nature, so that even if other pursuits may be weightier and better, we should measure our own by the rule of our own nature. For it is appropriate neither to fight against nature nor to pursue anything that you cannot attain. Consequently, it becomes clearer what that seemliness is like, precisely because nothing is seemly 'against Minerva's will', as they say, that is, when your nature opposes and fights against it.

(111) If anything at all is seemly, nothing, surely, is more so than an evenness both of one's whole life and of one's individual actions. You cannot preserve that if you copy someone else's nature and ignore your own. For just as we ought to use the language that is familiar to us so that we do not draw well justified ridicule upon ourselves

---

[1] The easiest textual correction suggested is to insert 'in' before 'Mancia' (translated 'and in Mancia'), making C. refer here, as in *De Oratore* II.274, to the wit of Helvius Mancia. See the Biographical Note on Mancia.

[2] The manuscripts include in this sentence a reference to 'Xenocrates, that severest of philosophers'; however, it is obscure and editors delete it.

(like some, who cram Greek words into their speech),[1] so we ought not to introduce any discordancy into our actions and into the whole of our lives.

(112) Indeed, such differences of natures have so great a force that sometimes one man ought to choose death for himself, while another ought not. For surely the case of Marcus Cato was different from that of the others who gave themselves up to Caesar in Africa? Indeed it would perhaps have been counted as a fault if they had killed themselves, for the very reason that they had been more gentle in their lives, and more easy-going in their behaviour. But since nature had assigned to Cato an extraordinary seriousness, which he himself had consolidated by his unfailing constancy, abiding always by his adopted purpose and policy, he had to die rather than look upon the face of a tyrant.[2]

(113) How many things Ulysses suffered during his lengthy wanderings! He both was a slave to women (if Circe and Calypso ought to be called women) and was willing to be accommodating and pleasant to everyone in everything that he said. Indeed, even when home he endured the insults of slaves and maidservants in order at last to attain what he desired. On the other hand Ajax's spirit was such, we are told, that he would have preferred to seek death a thousand times than to endure such things. Reflecting on such matters, everyone ought to weigh the characteristics that are his own, and to regulate them, not wanting to see how someone else's might become him; for what is most seemly for a man is the thing that is most his own.

(114) Everyone, therefore, should acquire knowledge of his own talents, and show himself a sharp judge of his own good qualities and faults; else it will seem that actors have more good sense than us. For they do not choose the best plays, but those that are most

---

[1] Though C. sometimes gives the Greek equivalents of technical terms in his philosophical works, he does not otherwise, except in his letters to intimates, mix Greek words with his Latin.

[2] Suicide was, in Stoic terms, an *officium ex tempore*, that is a duty imposed by particular circumstances (see I.31–2), for one's normal duty was to preserve one's life in accordance with the natural instincts. Cato himself felt that what he did was not appropriate for his companions in the same external situation of being defeated by Caesar at Utica (Plutarch, *Younger Cato* 65.4; 66.4), but that, as accepting pardon would be dishonourable *for him*, death would secure his moral freedom. His death made C. himself feel the need of a justification for staying alive (*Fam.* IX.18.2; IV.13.2), and this unease is reflected in the emphasis he gives this example.

suited to themselves. Those who rely on their voice choose the *Epigoni* and the *Medus*, those who rely on gesture, *Melanippa* and *Clytemnestra*; Rupilius, whom I remember, was always doing *Antiope*, while Aesopus did not often take part in the *Ajax*.[1] If an actor, then, will observe this on the stage, will not a wise man observe it in his life?

We shall, therefore, exert ourselves above all in those things to which we are most suited, if necessity has on occasion pushed us towards things that are beyond our natural talents, we shall have to apply all possible care, preparation and diligence so that we can perform them, if not in a seemly fashion, still with as little unseemliness as possible. Nor ought we so much to strive to acquire good qualities that have not been granted us, as to avoid faults.

(115) To the two roles of which I spoke above, a third is added: this is imposed by some chance or circumstance. There is also a fourth, which we assume for ourselves by our own decision. Kingdoms, military powers, nobility, political honours, wealth and influence, as well as the opposites of these, are in the gift of chance and governed by circumstances. In addition, assuming a role that we want ourselves is something that proceeds from our own will; as a consequence, some people apply themselves to philosophy, others to civil law, and others again to oratory, while even in the case of the virtues, different men prefer to excel in different of them.

(116) Those whose fathers or ancestors won glory by outstanding performance in a particular field generally devote themselves to excelling in the same way themselves; Quintus Mucius, the son of Publius, did so in civil law, and Paullus' son Africanus in military matters. Some, indeed, add to that inherited from their fathers praise that is all their own. Africanus, again, is an example: through his oratory he increased the glory he had gained in war. Conon's son Timotheus did the same: he was his father's equal in military praise, and he added to that praise glory for his learning and intellectual talent.

Sometimes, though, it turns out that some people decline to imitate their ancestors and pursue some course of their own. Those who

---

[1] These are all names of lost tragedies on Greek themes by Roman playwrights. The *Epigoni* were the descendants and avengers of the seven chieftains who died in battle before Thebes. Medus was a son of Medea rescued from death by his mother. Melanippa was freed by two sons she bore to the god Neptune. Clytemnestra was the wife of Agamemnon. Antiope was saved by her sons from her lover's wife.

exert themselves the most in this way are, on the whole, men born of unknown ancestors who aim for great things themselves.

(117) We ought therefore, when we seek what is seemly, to grasp all these things with heart and mind. First of all, though, we must decide who and what we wish to be, and what kind of life we want. That deliberation is the most difficult thing of all; for it is as adulthood is approaching, just when his counsel is at its very weakest, that each person decides that the way of leading a life that he most admires should be his own. The result is that he becomes engaged upon a fixed manner and course of life before he is able to judge what might be best. (118) Prodicus, as we find in Xenophon,[1] told the story of Hercules, who when he was just becoming a young man (which is the time given by nature for each to choose the path of life that he will take) went out to a lonely place; he sat there for a long time while he pondered by himself which path it was better to take. For he could see two: the one of pleasure and the other of virtue.

That could perhaps have happened to Hercules 'sprung from the seed of Jupiter', but it is not the same for us; we imitate those whom each of us thinks he should, and we are drawn to their pursuits and practices. Moreover, we are generally imbued with our parents' advice and led towards their customs and manners. Others are swayed by the judgement of the masses, and long especially for the things that seem most glittering to the majority. Some, however, have followed the right path of life, whether by good fortune or by the goodness of their own nature, or through parental guidance.

(119) It is, however, an extremely rare type of person who is endowed with outstanding intellectual ability or a splendidly learned education, or both, and who has also had time to deliberate over which course of life he wants above all to follow. In such deliberation all counsel ought to be referred to the individual's own nature. For just as in each specific thing that we do we seek what is seemly according to what and how each of us has been born (as I said above), we must exercise much more care when establishing our whole way of life, so that we can be constant to ourselves for the whole length of our life, not wavering in any of our duties.

---

[1] The story is told in *Memoirs of Socrates* II.1.21–34 where the choice is presented by two women, one of voluptuous appearance who shows him a short easy road, the other modest and beautiful who shows him a longer difficult one, which he chooses.

(120) Nature carries the greatest weight in such reasoning, and after that fortune. We should generally take account of both in choosing a type of life, but of nature more;[1] for it is far steadier and more constant. Consequently it sometimes appears that fortune, like some mortal, is struggling with immortal nature. When, therefore, someone has adopted a plan of life entirely in accordance with his nature (if it is not a vicious one) let him then maintain constancy – for that, most of all, is seemly – unless perhaps he comes to realize that he has made a mistake in choosing his type of life. If that happens (and it can indeed happen) he ought to change his behaviour and his plans. If circumstances assist such a change we shall effect it more easily and advantageously. If not, it must be made gradually and tentatively, just as wise men consider it more seemly gradually to loosen one's ties of friendship if they become less pleasurable or creditable, than suddenly to break them off. (121) If we do change our way of life, every care must be taken so that we appear to have done so with good judgement.

I said a little earlier that we should imitate our ancestors, but I must make some exceptions: first, so that we do not imitate them in their faults; and secondly, if our nature is not strong enough to be able to imitate them in certain respects. Thus, for example, the son of the elder Africanus, who adopted the son of Paullus, could not, because of his poor health, be as like his father as the younger Africanus was like his. If someone can neither defend men in lawsuits, nor grip the people with his speeches, nor wage war, he ought still, however, to show such qualities as are in his power, justice, keeping faith, liberality, modesty and restraint, so that fewer demands are made upon him where he is deficient. The best inheritance, however, is that passed down to children by their fathers, that glory of virtue and of worthy achievements that is more excellent than any patrimony; to disgrace that must be judged wicked and vicious.

(122) A further point is that the same duties are not assigned to those of different ages: some are for youths and others for older men. We must also, therefore, say something about this difference.

---

[1] That is, the second role (our natural talents and temperament) and, to a lesser extent, the third (the social circumstances which fortune has given us) should determine the fourth (our way of life).

It befits a youth to respect his elders and to choose from them the best and most upright, upon whose counsel and authority he might depend. For the inexperience of early life ought to be ordered and guided by the good sense of the old. It is especially at this age, moreover, that one must guard against passions, and train one's mind and body in toil and endurance, so that they might flourish when working hard at military and civil duties. Even when they wish to relax their minds and surrender themselves to enjoyment, young men should be wary of lack of restraint and mindful of a sense of shame. That will be easier if they are willing for their elders to associate with them even in activities of this kind.

(123) As for old men, it seems that their bodily labours ought to be reduced, but the exercise of their minds actually increased. They ought indeed to make an effort to assist as much as they can their friends and the young, and most of all the republic, with their counsel and good sense. There is nothing of which old age should be more wary than yielding itself to idleness and inactivity. Again, luxurious living is dishonourable for any age, but particularly disreputable for the old. Indeed, if unrestrained passions are added also, the evil is doubled; old age not only draws disgrace upon itself, but also causes the young, with their lack of restraint, to become still more shameless.

(124) It would not go beyond my brief to say something also of the duties of magistrates, of private individuals, of citizens and of foreigners. It is, then, the particular function of a magistrate to realize that he assumes the role of the city and ought to sustain its standing and its seemliness, to preserve the laws, to administer justice, and to be mindful of the things that have been entrusted to his good faith.

A private person, on the other hand, ought first to live on fair and equal terms with the other citizens, neither behaving submissively and abjectly nor giving himself airs; and secondly to want public affairs to be peaceful and honourable. For we are accustomed to think and say that such a man is a good citizen. (125) It is the duty of a foreigner or resident alien to do nothing except his own business, asking no questions about anyone else, and never to meddle in public affairs, which are not his own.

We have thus pretty well discovered what our duties are when the questions are 'What is seemly?' and 'What suits different roles, circumstances, or ages?"[1] Nothing, however, is so seemly as preserving constancy in everything that you do and in every plan that you adopt.

(126) This seemliness can be seen in every deed and word, and indeed in every bodily movement or state, and the latter depend upon three things, beauty, order and embellishment that is suited to action. (Such things are difficult to express, but it will be enough if they are grasped.) Furthermore, also contained in these three things is a concern to win the approval of those with and among whom we live. Let us, therefore, say a few words about them as well.

From the beginning nature itself seems to have been thoroughly rational concerning our bodies: she has placed in sight those parts of our form and features that have an honourable appearance, but has covered and hidden the parts of the body that are devoted to the necessities of nature and would have an ugly and dishonourable look. (127) Nature's very careful craftmanship is mirrored in men's sense of shame. For everyone of sound mind keeps out of sight the very parts that nature has hidden, and makes an effort to obey necessity itself as secretly as possible. Again, concerning those parts of the body that are used out of necessity, they refer by their own names neither to the parts themselves, nor to their uses. It is not dishonourable to do such things, provided one does them in secret, but it is indecent to speak of them. Therefore, neither such activity, if it is public, nor indecency of speech, is free from scurrility.

(128) We must certainly not listen to the Cynics,[2] or to those Stoics that were almost Cynics, who critize and mock us because we think that, though some things are not themselves dishonourable, the words for them are shameful, while we call by their own names

---

[1] The classification of duties in 107 ff. perhaps combines new Panaetian notions about the roles (107–21) that determine one's style of life as a whole, under the fourth virtue, with older Stoic teaching assigning various duties to a man according to his various social roles in the family and society (Seneca *Letter* 94), under the virtue of justice. 'Ages' refers to 122–3; 'circumstances' to 124–5 and 'roles' either to 107–21 or to 124–5 again.

[2] The Cynics rejected social convention. The name comes from the Greek word for 'dog' and was attached to them because of their shameless habits. Zeno, the founder of the Stoa, was a pupil of the Cynic Crates, and his *Republic* was said to have been written 'on the dog's tail' because it argued that various social conventions were unnatural. In an entertaining letter to his friend Papirius Paetus (*Fam.* IX.22), C. attributes the view that one should call a spade a spade to Zeno and advocates instead the modesty of Plato and his Academy.

those things that are dishonourable. It is actually dishonourable to rob, to deceive, or to commit adultery, but to speak of them is not indecent. To attend to the matter of children is actually honourable, but the word for it is indecent. They have many arguments to the same conclusion, contrary to a sense of shame. For ourselves, however, let us follow nature and avoid anything that shrinks from the approval of eyes and ears. Let our standing, our walking, our sitting and our reclining, our countenances, our eyes and the movements of our hands all maintain what I have called seemliness.

(129) In these matters we must avoid two things in particular: we should do nothing effeminate or soft, and nothing harsh or uncouth. Surely, we should not concede to actors and orators that such considerations are appropriate for them, but unconnected with us. Indeed, the customs of theatre people are, thanks to a discipline of long-standing, characterized by so great a sense of shame that no one may step on to the stage without a breech-cloth. For they fear that if an accident occurred, parts of the body might be revealed that it is not seemly to see. According to our own custom, indeed, adult sons do not bathe with their fathers, nor sons-in-law with their fathers-in-law. We ought therefore to preserve a sense of shame of this sort, especially as nature herself is our mistress and guide.[1]

(130) There are two types of beauty; one includes gracefulness, and the other dignity. We ought to think gracefulness a feminine quality and dignity a masculine one. Therefore a man should both remove from his person every unworthy adornment, and also be wary of comparable faults in his gestures and movements. For the movements taught in the palaestra[2] are often somewhat distasteful, and some of the gestures used by actors are not free from affectation. In either case what is upright and straightforward is praised. Furthermore, the dignity of one's appearance must be preserved by fine colouring, and colouring by exercising the body. One should also

[1] Not only the prohibition here noted as Roman (cf. Plutarch, *Elder Cato* 20), but also the adverse view of nudity in 127 are unlikely to derive from the Greek Panaetius. No explanation is given of how the observance of social conventions, fundamental to the notion of 'seemliness' (1.99 and 148), and the adoption of nature as a guide are to be reconciled, given the different (often conflicting) social customs of different societies.

[2] A Greek word meaning 'place of exercise'. There the correct movements and stance for various physical activities were taught. C. distinguishes gestures appropriate there and on the stage from those suitable to ordinary life.

add a neatness that is neither distasteful nor over-fussy, but just enough to avoid boorish and uncivilized neglectfulness. A similar rationale should be applied in the matter of dress: here, as in most things, the intermediate course is the best.

(131) We must also beware of adopting too effeminate a languidness in our gait, so that we look like carriages in solemn procession, or of making excessive haste when we are in a hurry. If we do that, we begin to puff and pant, our expressions change, and we distort our faces. Such things are a strong sign that we do not possess constancy.

Much more, however, we ought to strive to ensure that the movements of our spirit do not abandon nature. We shall achieve that if we are wary of becoming excited or of falling into dispiritedness and if we keep our spirits intent upon the preservation of seemliness. (132) The spirit can be moved in two ways: by thought or by impulse. Thought is for the most part occupied with seeking what is true, while impulse drives one to act. We must therefore take care to exercise our thought on the best possible subjects, and to render our impulses obedient to reason.[1]

Speech also has great power, and that in two areas: in oratory and in conversation. Oratory should be employed for speeches in lawcourts, to public assemblies or in the senate, while conversation should be found in social groups, in philosophical discussions and among gatherings of friends – and may it also attend dinners! Guidance about oratory is available, provided by the rhetoricians, but none about conversation, although I do not see why that could not also exist. But teachers are found wherever there are devoted pupils, and no one is devoted to learning about conversation, while everywhere is packed by the crowds around the rhetoricians. However, such advice as there is about words and opinions will be relevant also to conversation.

(133) It is our voice that gives expression to our speech; we should, therefore, have two aims for our voices: they should be clear and they should be attractive. We must, of course, look to nature for each of these, but the one quality will be improved by practice, and the other by imitating those who speak distinctly and gently. The two Catuli had nothing to make you think they possessed a refined

[1] See p. 40, n. 1.

judgement in the matter of language. They were, it is true, men of letters, but so were others.[1] However, they are thought of as the finest exponents of the Latin tongue: their pronunciation was pleasant, their enunciation neither over-nice nor muffled, so avoiding both offensiveness and lack of clarity, their delivery without oratory, yet neither feeble nor sonorous. The speech of Lucius Crassus was more expansive and no less humorous, but the reputation of the Catuli for speaking well is just as great. Caesar, the brother of Catulus the father, so far surpassed everyone else in witticisms and humour that even in speeches of the forensic type his conversational style defeated the oratory of others.

We must work at all these things, if we are in everything seeking that which is seemly.

(134) Conversation, in which the Socratics[2] particularly excel, ought therefore to be gentle and without a trace of intransigence; it should also be witty. Nor should any one speaker exclude all others as if he were taking over occupancy of his own estate. He should think it fair in shared conversation, just as in other things, for everyone to have a turn. Above all, let him have regard for the subject of discussion; if it is serious, he should treat it with gravity, if light-hearted, with wit. He should take care above all that his speech does not reveal that there is some fault in his behaviour; in general that happens particularly when someone speaks quite deliberately about people who are absent in an abusive or insulting manner in order to disparage them, whether he does so to raise a laugh or with severity. (135) Conversations are for the most part about domestic business or public affairs or else the study and teaching of the arts. We should, then, even if the discussion begins to drift to other matters, make an effort to call it back to the subject; but we should do so according to the company: for we do not all at all times enjoy the same subjects in the same way. We must also be aware of the extent to which conversation is being enjoyed; and just as there was a reason for beginning it, so let a limit be set for its conclusion. (136) Again, just as in the whole of our lives we are very rightly advised to avoid agitation

---

[1] The play on words is impossible to reproduce: 'judgement in the matter of language' translates *iudicio litterarum* and 'men of letters' *litterati*. In the next sentence 'enunciation' glosses *litterae*.

[2] See p. 41, n. 1. Plato's Socrates is recommended in *De Oratore* II.270 as a guide to refined conversation. This is the style C. aimed to follow in his philosophical dialogues (I.3).

(that is, excessive movements of the spirit that do not obey reason) similarly, our conversation should be free from movements of this type, so that anger is not aroused, and no greediness reveals itself, nor slovenliness, nor idleness, nor any other such thing. We must take particular care to be seen to respect and have affection for those with whom we share conversations.

A further point: sometimes it happens that it is necessary to reprove someone. In that case we may perhaps need to use a more rhetorical tone of voice, or sharper and serious language, and even to behave so that we seem to be acting in anger. However, we should have recourse to this sort of rebuke in the way that we do to surgery and cautery, rarely and unwillingly; never unless it is necessary, if no other medicine can be found. However, anger itself should be far from us; for nothing can be done rightly or thoughtfully when done in anger. (137) One ought for the most part to resort only to mild criticism, though combined with a certain seriousness so as to show severity while avoiding abusiveness. We must furthermore make it clear that any sharpness there may be in the reproof has been adopted for the sake of the person who is being reproved. It is right, moreover, even in disputes that arise with our greatest enemies, and even if we hear unworthy things said against us, still to maintain our seriousness and to dispel our anger. For things that are done with some degree of agitation cannot be done with constancy, nor be approved by those who are present. It is also unattractive to commend yourself, particularly if you do so untruthfully, or to imitate the 'boastful soldier',[1] arousing the ridicule of your listeners.

(138) Since I am covering everything here (or at least that is my wish) I must also speak about the kind of house of which I would approve for a man of the first rank who has achieved political honours. Its purpose is its use: the design of its buildings should be adapted to this, though one must attend carefully to the requirements of comfort and of standing. Gnaeus Octavius, who was the first of his family to be made a consul, was honoured, we are told, for having built a splendid home, such as gives one great standing, upon the Palatine. That house, open as it was to the public gaze, is thought to have

---

[1] A favourite character in Greek and Roman comedy and the actual title of a play by Plautus.

won for its master, a new man,[1] votes for his consulship. Scaurus demolished it and built an annexe to his own dwelling. The one, then, was the first to bring the consulship to his house, while the other, the son of a fine and most notable man, brought back to the house he had extended not just rejection, but humiliation and disgrace. (139) One's standing ought to be enhanced by one's house, but not won entirely because of it; the master should not be made honourable by the house, but the house by the master. Just as in other matters one should take account not only of one's own affairs but also of others', so a notable man ought to be concerned that his house is spacious; for he will have to receive many guests there and admit to it a multitude of men of all sorts. On the other hand, a grand dwelling can, if there is emptiness there, often bring disgrace upon its master, and very much so if once upon a time, with a different master, it had usually been thronging with people. It is indeed unpleasant when passers by can say:

> Ancient house, you are governed, alas, by a master who
> is not your equal.

There are many cases at the moment where one might well say that.[2]

(140) You must also be careful, particularly if you are building yourself, not to overstep the limit in expense and magnificence. Indeed, in this area much harm lies even in the example set. For most men eagerly imitate the actions of their leaders in this matter in particular. Take the excellent Lucius Lucullus: who imitated his virtue? But how many imitated the magnificence of his country houses! But a limit to these certainly ought to be set, and brought back to an intermediate level. The same intermediate standard should be applied also to all questions of one's needs and style of life.[3]

I have said enough now on this subject.

(141) To sum up: when undertaking any action, we must hold fast to three things. First, impulse must obey reason; nothing is more suited to ensuring the observance of one's duties than that. Secondly,

[1] 'New man' was a technical term for someone from a non-senatorial family who reached the consulship, like C. himself. After his consulship in 63, C. actually bought a house on the Palatine.
[2] One notorious case was Antony's acquisition of the house of the dead Pompey, similarly derided in the *Second Philippic* (104).
[3] See I.89 with n. 2.

we must keep in mind the importance of the thing we wish to achieve, so that we employ neither more nor less care and effort than the case requires. The third thing is that we should be careful to moderate all things that may affect our appearance and standing as a gentleman. The best limit, moreover, is to maintain seemliness itself, which we have discussed already, and not to step beyond it. However, of these three things, the most important is for impulse to obey reason.

(142) Now I must say something about the orderliness of things, and the opportuneness of occasions. These are included under the knowledge that the Greeks call *eutaxia*, and not under that that we translate as 'moderateness'.[1] The latter word contains the element 'moderate', while *eutaxia* is that in which we understand the maintenance of orderliness. Therefore (if we may call this too moderateness) it is defined by the Stoics as follows: moderateness is the knowledge of putting in their proper place things that one says or does. (Thus the significance of orderliness and that of proper placing seem to be the same; for they also define orderliness thus: the arrangement of things in appropriate and suitable places: and they say that the 'place' of an action is the opportuneness of the occasion.) The opportune time for acting is called in Greek *eukairia*, and in Latin *occasio*. Consequently this type of moderateness, which we interpret as I have explained, is the knowledge of opportuneness, that is, of the fitting occasions for doing something.

(143) 'But the same definition could be given for good sense, which we discussed at the beginning.'

Here, however, we are enquiring about moderation, restraint and such virtues. We talked in their proper place of the things appropriate to good sense; now we must discuss the things appropriate to the virtues of which we have for some time now been speaking, the things that concern a sense of shame and the approval of those with whom we live.

(144) Orderliness must, then, be imposed upon our actions in such

---

[1] The Latin is awkward and ambiguous. Others translate as if C. means that the Greek *eutaxia* had two senses, 'moderateness' and 'orderliness', both of which he proposes to translate with *modestia* ('moderateness'). As there seems to be no evidence of *eutaxia* meaning moderateness, C. is probably thinking of another Greek word, possibly *metriotes*, corresponding to *modestia*. Elsewhere *modestia* has been translated by 'modesty' rather than 'moderateness'.

a way that all the parts of our life, as of a speech that has constancy, are fitted to one another and in agreement. For it is dishonourable and a great failing to introduce into a serious matter something worthy of a dinner party, or some frivolous conversation. Pericles and the poet Sophocles were colleagues as praetor[1] and had met about some shared duty. By chance, a beautiful boy went past and Sophocles said, 'Pericles, what a lovely boy!' His answer was a good one: 'It is seemly for a praetor, Sophocles, to abstain not only from touching, but even from looking.' But if Sophocles had said the same thing at an athletes' trial, it would not have been just to criticize him; so great is the significance of place and time. Similarly, if someone who was about to conduct a lawsuit were to practise to himself while on a journey or a walk, or were to reflect deeply on some other matter, he would not be criticized. If, however, he were to do the same at a dinner party, his lack of awareness of the occasion would make him appear uncivilized.

(145) Actions that are strongly discordant with civilized behaviour, such as singing in the forum, or any other instance of extreme waywardness, are readily apparent and do not call for very much admonition or advice. However, greater care is required to avoid failings that seem to be minor and cannot be recognized by many people. If a lyre or a flute is only slightly out of tune a knowledgeable person will still usually notice it. We ought to see that nothing in our lives happens to be discordant, in just the same way – or, rather, as much more so as the harmony of actions is greater than that of sounds. (146) The ears of musicians can perceive that lyres are even the smallest bit out of tune; similarly if we ourselves are willing to notice faults keenly and carefully, we shall often grasp important things from small indications. We shall readily be able to judge what is done fittingly, and what discords with duty and nature, from a glance of the eyes, from the relaxation or contraction of an eyebrow, from sadness, cheerfulness or laughter, from speech or from silence, from a raising or lowering of the voice, and so on. Here it can be advantageous to judge by looking at others the nature of each of these things, so that we ourselves may avoid anything that is unseemly about them.

---

[1] C. uses the Latin term *praetor* which the Greeks translated as *strategos* ('general'). The occasion belongs to 440 BC.

For somehow it is the case that we can detect failings better in others than in ourselves. Consequently a very easy way for pupils to be corrected is if their teachers imitate their faults in order to remove them.

(147) It is not an inappropriate thing, when making choices that cause you to hesitate, to summon men who are learned, or experienced also, and to discover what they would approve in the case of each sort of duty. For the majority tend to be carried along to where they are led by nature herself. In such matters we must see not only what each person says, but also what he thinks, and indeed why he thinks it. Painters and makers of statues, and even poets indeed, each want the public to inspect their own work, so that they may correct anything that most people criticize; they ask not only themselves, but others too, what is wrong with it. In the same way, there are very many occasions when we ought to rely on the judgement of others in choosing or rejecting, or altering and correcting, our actions.

(148) We need give no advice about things done in accordance with custom and civic codes of behaviour, as they themselves constitute pieces of advice. No one should be led into the error of thinking that because Socrates or Aristippus did or said something contrary to custom and civic practice, that is something he may do himself. For those men acquired such freedom on account of great, indeed divine, goodness. But the reasoning of the Cynics must be entirely rejected; for it is hostile to a sense of shame, and without that nothing can be upright, and nothing honourable.[1]

(149) Furthermore, we ought to respect and revere those whose life has been conspicuous for its great and honourable deeds, who have held sound views about the republic, and have deserved, or still deserve, well of her – just as if they had achieved a specific honour or command. We ought also to grant a great deal to old age; to yield to those who exercise magistracies; and to discriminate between citizen and foreigner, and in the case of a foreigner as to whether he has come in a private or a public capacity. In short, so as not to go into details, we ought to revere, to guard and to preserve the common affection and fellowship of the whole of humankind.

(150) Now as for crafts and other means of livelihood, the following

[1] See p. 49, n. 2 and p. 50, n. 1.

is roughly what we have been told[1] as to which should be thought fit for a free man,[2] and which demeaning. First, those means of livelihood that incur the dislike of other men are not approved, for example collecting harbour dues, or usury. Again, all those workers who are paid for their labour and not for their skill have servile and demeaning employment; for in their case the very wage is a contract to servitude. Those who buy from merchants and sell again immediately should also be thought of as demeaning themselves. For they would make no profit unless they told sufficient lies, and nothing is more dishonourable than falsehood. All handcraftsmen are engaged in a demeaning trade; for there can be nothing well bred about the workshop. The crafts that are least worthy of approval are those that minister to the pleasures:

> fishmongers, butchers, cooks, poulterers, fishermen

as Terence puts it;[3] add to this, if you like, perfumers, dancers, and the whole variety show.

(151) Other arts either require greater good sense or else procure substantial benefit, for example medicine, architecture or teaching things that are honourable. They are honourable for those who belong to the class that they befit.[4] Trade, if it is on a small scale, should be considered demeaning. If, however, men trade on a large and expansive scale, importing many things from all over, and distributing them to many people without misrepresentation, that is not entirely to be criticized. Indeed, if ever such men are satiated, or rather satisfied, with what they have gained, and just as they have often left the high seas for the harbour, now leave the harbour itself for land in the country, it seems that we have every right to praise their occupation. However, there is no kind of gainful employment that is better, more fruitful, more pleasant and more worthy of a free man than

---

[1] As P. A. Brunt (Bibliography, p. xlii) argues, C. may appeal here not only to Roman traditions but to the Greek ones that influenced Panaetius. The inclusion of prescriptions for men of the lower classes suggests that the account goes back to more general discussions of how to earn a livelihood such as Chrysippus' *On Lives*, while the stress on a life of leisure and independence conforms to standard Greek ideas shared by Plato and Aristotle.

[2] See p. 18, n. 3.

[3] *Eunuch* 257.

[4] Not suitable to the upper classes, C.'s primary concern (Introduction, pp. xvii, xxiv–xxv). As the subject is ways of earning money, not choice of occupation, the teaching that is frowned upon is teaching for pay, (not the sort that Panaetius or C. did).

agriculture.[1] As I have said plenty about this in my book *The Elder Cato*, you may find there everything relevant to the subject.[2]

(152) I think that I have explained well enough how duties have their roots in the different elements of what is honourable. However, there can often be a conflict and one may need to compare possibilities, each of which is honourable, to determine which is the more honourable of two honourable courses.[3] (Panaetius omitted to discuss this topic.) Everything that is honourable has its source in the four elements: the first learning, the second sociability, the third greatness of spirit and the fourth moderation. It is often necessary in selecting one's duty to compare these one with another.

(153) In my view those duties that have their roots in sociability conform more to nature than those drawn from learning. This can be confirmed by the following argument: suppose that a wise man were granted a life plentifully supplied with everything he needed so that he could, by himself and completely at leisure, reflect and meditate upon everything worth learning. But suppose also that he were so alone that he never saw another man: would he not then depart from life?

The foremost of all the virtues is the wisdom that the Greeks call *sophia*. (Good sense, which they call *phronesis*, we realize is something distinct, that is the knowledge of things that one should pursue and avoid.) But the wisdom that I declared to be the foremost is the knowledge of all things human and divine; and it includes the sociability and fellowship of gods and men with each other. If, as is certain, that is something of the greatest importance, then necessarily the duty that is based upon sociability is also of the greatest importance. Moreover, learning about and reflecting upon nature is somewhat truncated and incomplete if it results in no action. Such action is seen most clearly in the protection of men's interests and therefore

---

[1] C. is not thinking of the small working farmer but of the large landowner like himself, for whom the Elder Cato wrote (see n. 2). Digging and ploughing for him were menial occupations (*Fin.* 1.3). Landowning had the highest social status in a world without bankruptcy laws or social security, where land was normally the only safe form of investment.

[2] In the *Cato Maior de senectute*, written earlier in this year, the principal speaker celebrates the pleasures of agriculture at 51–60, alluding to his own treatise on the subject.

[3] Justice and wisdom are compared at 153–8 and 160, justice and greatness of spirit at 157, and justice and temperance at 159 (see Introduction, pp. xxi, xxv).

is concerned with the fellowship of the human race. For that reason this should be ranked above mere learning.[1]

(154) Any good man will agree with that, and will show it in practice. For there is no one, surely, however greedy he is to examine and understand the nature of things, who, though contemplating in his studies the highest objects of learning, would not cast them all aside, if his country were suddenly and critically endangered and he could come to its aid or relief. Would he not do so even if he thought he could number the stars or measure the size of the earth? And he would do the same if the interests or safety of a parent or friend were at stake. (155) From all this we realize that the duties of justice must be given precedence over the pursuit of knowledge and the duties imposed by that. For the former look to the benefit of mankind, and a man should hold nothing more sacred than that.

But note that those who have devoted their entire life to learning things have, after all, managed to contribute to the benefits and advantages of mankind. They have educated many to be better citizens and more beneficial to their countries. So, for example, Lysis the Pythagorean taught the Theban Epaminondas, Plato taught Dion of Syracuse, and there are many similar cases; I myself, whatever assistance I have given the republic, if I have indeed given any, came to public life trained and equipped by my teachers and their teachings.[2] (156) Not only when they are alive and present do such men educate and instruct their assiduous students; they continue the same task after their death by means of their writings, which they leave as memorials. There is no theme relevant to the laws of our country, to its customs, to its education, that they have overlooked; they seem to have devoted their leisure to our business. The very men, then, who have given their lives to the pursuit of teaching and wisdom, provide above all good sense and understanding for the benefit of

---

[1] The translation takes the subject of the sentence beginning 'If, as is certain' to be not wisdom but 'sociability and fellowship'; that seems the only way of finding an intelligible argument here (see Miller's Loeb edition for an attempt to make sense of the orthodox translation). Another puzzle is that C. calls wisdom rather than justice the foremost of the virtues (see p. 7, n. 3). His aim may be to subordinate pure enquiry to practical. Wisdom is foremost in the sense that it is basic and directive; it includes the understanding of the cosmic community that is a prerequisite for action. But if that is the most important part of wisdom the duties following from it are the most important duties. Hence the most valuable part of wisdom turns out to be that with practical consequences (cf. 1.18–19).

[2] See Introduction p. x and 11.4 with n.2.

mankind. Therefore it is better to speak at length, provided one does so wisely, than to think, however penetratingly, without eloquence. For speculation turns in on itself, but eloquence embraces those to whom we are joined by social life.

(157) Now it is not in order to make honeycombs that swarms of bees gather together, but it is because they are gregarious by nature that they make honeycombs. In the same way, but to a much greater extent, men, living naturally in groups, exercise their ingenuity in action and in reflection. Therefore unless learning is accompanied by the virtue that consists in protecting men, that is to say in the fellowship of the human race, it would seem solitary and barren. In the same way, if greatness of spirit were detached from sociability, and from the bonding between humans, it would become a kind of brutal savagery. And so it turns out that the bonds between and the sociability of men take precedence over any devotion to learning.

(158) It is not true, as some claim, that men embarked upon communal life and fellowship in order to provide for life's necessities just because we could not manage, without others, to provide ourselves with our natural requirements.[1] In that case, if everything needed for sustenance and comfort were provided by a magic wand, so to speak, then any talented man would drop all his business and immerse himself completely in learning and knowledge. But it would not be like that: he would flee from loneliness, seeking a companion for his studies; he would want both to learn and to teach, both to listen and to speak. Therefore every duty whose effect lies in preserving the bonding between men and their fellowship must be preferred to the duty that is limited to learning and knowledge.

(159) It should perhaps be asked whether this sociability, which conforms so greatly to nature, should always be given precedence even over moderation and modesty. I do not think so: for some things are so disgraceful, or so outrageous, that a wise man would not do them even to protect his country. Posidonius has collected many such examples, but some are so repellent, so disgusting, that it seems dis-

---

[1] C. does not deny that social life makes it easier to secure one's own needs (cf. I.12, II.12–15, II.73). He rejects, however, the view that men first formed societies in order to satisfy these needs. That notion in Plato's *Republic* II.369b and Aristotle's *Politics* I.2 was given particular theoretical weight by the Epicureans and had recently been exploited by Lucretius (*On the Nature of Things* V.1005 ff.). The Stoics held that man was sociable by nature.

honourable even to mention them.[1] And so a wise man will not undertake such things for the sake of the republic, and indeed the republic will not want him to undertake them for its sake. But in fact it turns out conveniently that a situation could not arise where it would benefit the republic for such a man to perform any such deed.

(160) Let the following, then, be regarded as settled: when choosing between duties, the chief place is accorded to the class of duties grounded in human fellowship. Moreover, since well considered action will be the consequence of learning and good sense, acting with forethought is in fact more worthwhile than merely thinking sensibly.

So much for that subject. The topic has now been explained, so that it should not be difficult for any one asking a question about duties to see which should take precedence over another. Further, there are degrees of duties within social life itself; consequently, we can understand which takes precedence over which, that duties are owed first to the immortal gods, secondly to one's country, thirdly to one's parents and then down the scale to others.[2]

(161) From this brief discussion you may realize that men are often uncertain not only over whether something is honourable or dishonourable, but also over which is the more honourable of two honourable possibilities. Panaetius passed over this theme, as I said above. But now let us go on to the questions that still remain.

---

[1] C. may allude here (from memory or in a later insertion) to the work of Posidonius he ordered to help him with Book III: it contained a treatment of duties in particular circumstances (see Introduction, pp. xx–xxi). Posidonius could have considered there if some actions, usually shameful, could be correct where they would help one's country or mankind in general (cf. III.19, 30, 40, 90, 93, 95). III.90 provides an argument that would justify the view taken here, i.e. the long-term interests of one's country are *not* served by having citizens behave like this.

[2] The degrees of duty given here differ from the account in 53–8 in that they include the gods and omit specific mention of mankind in general. In 53 C. lists the degrees of fellowship in logical order, starting with the widest (mankind) and ending with the narrowest (marriage); in 54 he reverses the order to explain the origins of states. The degrees of duty in 58 follow neither the logical nor historical order, as they reflect benefits received and extent of dependence on us (58): in 52 and 58 it is strongly implied that country comes first and general humanity last. Here the gods are given priority over country, but the gods, though the source of the greatest benefits (II.11), cannot be repaid in 'whatever is necessary to support life' (58), only in piety (II.11) and observance of the social order they have ordained (III.28).

Book II

(1) Marcus my son, I think that in the preceding book I have explained well enough the way in which duties are based on what is honourable and on each particular type of virtue. Next I must pursue the classes of duties that relate to civilized living and to the availability of the influence and wealth that men find beneficial. As I said before, we must ask both what is beneficial and what is the opposite, and then what is more or most beneficial of several beneficial possibilities. That is what I shall go on to discuss, but first let me say a few words both about my overall project and about my own view of philosophy.

(2) My books have inspired in some men a devotion not only to reading but also to writing. Occasionally, though, I still fear that some good men despise the very name of philosophy, and are amazed that I spend so much time and effort on it.[1] For my part, when the republic was being run by the men to whom it had entrusted itself, I devoted all my concern and all my thoughts to it. But then a single man came to dominate everything,[2] there was no longer any room for consultation or for personal authority, and finally I lost my allies in preserving the republic, excellent men as they were. Then I did not surrender to the grief that would have overwhelmed me had I not fought it, nor to pleasures unworthy of an educated man.

(3) I only wish that the republic had remained in its original con-

---

[1] C.'s apology is directed at the 'good men' in 2–6 and at the 'learned' in 7–8. See 1.1 with n. 4. Of those inspired to *write*, the most notable was Marcus Terentius Varro, the greatest scholar of the time.

[2] One of the many allusions to Caesar's dictatorship (see Introduction, p. xii).

[handwritten margin note: Devoted self to Action rather than writing]

dition, rather than fall into the hands of men greedy not merely for change, but for revolution.[1] For first I would be devoting myself to action rather than writing, as I used to when the republic was standing. Secondly, it would be my own speeches rather than my present subject matter that I would be putting on paper, as I have often done before. All my care, all my thought, all my effort, used to be directed towards the republic; when that ceased completely to exist, then inevitably legal and senatorial speeches ceased to flow from my pen.

(4) But my mind could not be entirely inactive. Therefore, as I was versed in such studies from my youth, I thought that I could most honourably set aside my troubles by turning to philosophy. I had spent much time on this as a young man for the sake of education.[2] Later I began to take up the honourable burden of public office, and gave myself completely to public life. Now the only time I had for philosophy was that which I could spare after seeing to the needs of my friends and of the republic. All of that was used up in reading; I had no leisure for writing.

(5) From the greatest of evils I seem still to have salvaged a little good: I now have the chance to put into writing ideas that were not familiar enough to my countrymen, but most worthy of knowing. In heaven's name, what is more desirable, what more distinguished than wisdom? What is better for a man, what more worthy of a man? Those who seek it are called philosophers, and philosophy, if you want to translate it, is nothing other than the pursuit of wisdom.[3] Wisdom, according to the definition of the philosophers of old, is the knowledge of everything divine and human, and of the causes which regulate them. If anyone despises the pursuit of that, it is difficult to see what on earth he would see fit to praise.

(6) Perhaps it is mental entertainment that you want, and a break from your worries? Philosophers are constantly investigating anything that strives to promote a good and happy life; what pursuit could you compare with theirs? Or maybe your concern is constancy and virtue – if any discipline can attain those for us, it is this one. But

[1] C. refers to Antony and his supporters who implemented Caesar's policies after his death.
[2] C.'s study of philosophy began before he was twenty (see Introduction, p. x). Cf. 1.155 for the value of philosophy to statesmen.
[3] Greek *philosophia*, from *philos*, a friend or lover, and *sophia*, wisdom.

perhaps, for such very great matters, there is no such discipline? That suggestion, when even the most trivial of matters have their method, is the suggestion of a man who speaks without reflection, a man mistaken in the things that matter most. If, on the other hand, there is a way of learning about virtue, where could you find it if you rejected this field of study? When I am advocating the study of philosophy, as I have done in another book,[1] I usually discuss these things in more detail. Now, though, I only needed to explain why, deprived as I am of the obligations of public life, I have devoted myself primarily to this pursuit.[2]

(7) An objection is brought against me, and by educated men at that, who ask whether I seem to be acting quite consistently. For although I say that nothing can be securely grasped, I am still ready to discourse on various matters; and now indeed I am engaged in advising about duty. I should like them to learn my views satisfactorily. We are not the ones whose minds wander in uncertainty and who have nothing by which to direct themselves.[3] If we took away our grounds not only for arguing, but also for living, what would reason, indeed what would life be like? No, what we do is this: where other men say that some things are certain and others uncertain, we disagree with them and say rather that some things are persuasive and others not. (8) What, therefore, should prevent me from accepting what seems persuasive to me and rejecting the opposite, so avoiding the presumption of assertion and escaping the recklessness that is so far removed from wisdom? We argue against every opinion on the grounds that what is in fact persuasive could not be revealed unless the two competing sides of each case had been heard. I explained all this well enough, or so I think, in my *Academica.*[4]

My dear Cicero, although you are now studying so old and so distinguished a philosophy under Cratippus, who is not unworthy

---

[1] The *Hortensius,* now lost. Its impact on St Augustine is movingly described in his *Confessions* III.4.

[2] C. argues at e.g. 1.19, 1.28, 1.70–3 that those suited to public life have an obligation to participate and at 1.121 that we must be seen to have a good reason for changing our way of life: hence his *apologia* (see p. 8, n. 1).

[3] See p. 4, n. 1. C.'s target here is the Pyrrhonists (see Biographical Note under Pyrrho).

[4] C. was proud of this rather technical dialogue about the theory of knowledge, of which we have only the first book of the second edition and the second book of the first edition.

of that noble tradition's founders, I still wanted you to know something of the very similar tradition that I prefer.

But now let me proceed to my proposed topic.

(9) I laid down then,[1] you may recall, five methods for the accomplishment of duty, of which two related to seemliness and honourableness, and two to things advantageous for life – resources, wealth, power. The fifth was concerned with deciding what to choose in case those already mentioned seemed to conflict with one another. I have now completed the section with which I want you to be most familiar, that on honourableness. What I am going next to address is that which is labelled 'beneficial'. Custom has stumbled over this word and strayed from the path, gradually sinking to the point where she has severed honourableness from benefit, decreeing that something can be honourable which is not beneficial, and beneficial which is not honourable. Nothing more destructive than this custom could have been introduced into human life.

(10) It is indeed true that philosophers of the greatest authority make a distinction in thought between these two[2] kinds, combined though they are, and doubtless they do so honourably and strictly. For they hold that whatever is just is also beneficial, and again, whatever is honourable is also just. Therefore it follows that whatever is honourable is also beneficial. Those who do not see this clearly often admire shrewd and crafty men and mistake wickedness for wisdom. Theirs is an error that must be uprooted; and their fancy must be wholly converted to that hope which consists of the understanding that they will achieve what they want by honourable policies and just deeds, and not by deceit and wickedness.

(11) Of the things which concern the preservation of human life, some are inanimate, gold and silver, for example, the produce of the earth, and so forth, and some are animate, having their own drives and impulses. Of the latter, some do not share in reason, but others do use it. Horses, cattle and other herd animals, and bees, all of whose efforts contribute something to the needs of human life, are without reason. There are two groups which use reason: gods

---

[1] In I.9–10.

[2] The manuscripts read 'these three kinds, combined' or 'these three things, combined in kind'. Holden explains that the three things are (i) the honourable, (ii) the beneficial, and (iii) the honourable and beneficial. But C. is talking about only two things, the honourable and the beneficial: better then to emend 'three' to 'two'.

and men.[1] The gods are placated by devoutness and sacred observance. Next to the gods, however, and close after them, it is men who can bring most benefit to other men.

(12) Things that are harmful or disadvantageous can be divided in the same way. But here the gods are excepted because they are not thought to do harm. Therefore, it is reckoned, the greatest source of disadvantage to mankind is other men. The things we have called inanimate are generally produced by man's efforts; we should not have them without the application of craft and manipulative skills, nor should we enjoy them without human organization.[2] Neither medical care, nor navigation, nor agriculture, nor the harvest and storage of fruits and other crops could have existed without the effort of man. (13) Then, there would surely be no exporting of that which we have in excess, nor importing of that which we need, if these services were not performed by men. Nor, by the same reasoning, would the stones required for our needs be quarried from the earth, nor

the iron, copper, gold and silver hidden deep within

be dug out unless by the labour of men's hands. Consider our houses, which repel the biting frosts and abate the oppressive heat: how could they have been provided for the human race in the first place? And how afterwards, if they collapsed through storm, through earthquake, or through age, could they have been repaired, had not a common way of life taught us in such cases to seek assistance from other men? (14) You may add aqueducts, diversions of rivers, the irrigation of fields, breakwaters, artificial harbours: how could we have those without the work of man?

From these and many other instances, it is clear that without the labour of men's hands we could not in any way have acquired the fruits and benefits that are culled from inanimate objects. Finally, what fruit or advantage could be culled from animals, unless men gave us assistance? For those who were foremost in discovering what use we could make of each beast were, without doubt, men; and

---

[1] The argument ascends the 'ladder of nature'. Plants are 'inanimate' in not having the power of locomotion (cf. I.II).

[2] See p. 61, n. 1. That the arts of civilization could be abused, leading to luxury and political turmoil, was often argued in antiquity and had recently been by Lucretius, *On the Nature of Things* v.1106 ff.

even now we could not feed them nor tame them nor protect them nor take from them their fruits in due season without human labour. By man too, are harmful animals killed and those which can be of use captured.

(15) Why do I need to enumerate the multitude of arts without which there could be no life at all? What assistance would be given to the sick, what delights would there be for the healthy, what sustenance or comfort, if there were not so many arts to minister to us? It is because of these that the civilized life of men differs so greatly from the sustenance and the comforts that animals have. Nor indeed could cities have been built or populated if men did not gather together. As a result, laws and customs were established, and a fair system of justice and a regular training for the business of life. These led to a softening of men's spirits and a sense of shame; the result was that life became less vulnerable, and through giving and receiving, through sharing our abilities and advantages, we came to lack nothing.

(16) I have dwelt longer on this point than is necessary. But is there anyone to whom the facts that Panaetius related at great length are not obvious[1] – that no one, whether a general in war or a leading statesman at home, could have accomplished deeds of great service without the support of his fellow-men? He recalls Themistocles, Pericles, Cyrus, Agesilaus, and Alexander, denying that their great achievements would have been possible without other men's co-operation. He calls unnecessary witnesses, although the matter is not in doubt. On the other hand, just as we secure great benefits because men collaborate and agree, conversely there is no truly pernicious curse that is not brought upon man by man. Dicaearchus, that great and prolific Peripatetic, has written a book about the destruction of mankind. In this he gathers together the other causes of death such as floods, epidemics, devastation, sudden stampedes of wild creatures whose onslaught, as he teaches us, has wiped out whole tribes of men. Then he shows by comparison how many more men have been destroyed by attacks by other men, that is in war or uprisings, than by every other type of disaster.

(17) Thus there can be no doubt on this question, that it is men who inflict on their fellow-men both the greatest benefit and the great-

---

[1] See Introduction, p. xix for C.'s condensation of Panaetius' work. Aulus Gellius (*Attic Nights*, 13.28) preserves a passage of Panaetius' book that is represented by only a brief reference in *De Officiis* 1.81.

est harm. Therefore I count it as the special property of virtue to make its own the hearts of other men and to enlist them in its own service. Consequently, whatever benefit to human life arises from inanimate things or from the use and management of animals is attributed to the manual arts; it is the wisdom and virtue of outstanding persons, however, that inspire other men to be prompt, ready and devoted in assisting our advancement.

(18) Indeed, virtue as a whole may be said practically to depend upon three things. One is perceiving what is true and clear in each case, what agrees with, or what follows from, what, what gives rise to each thing, what is the cause of each thing. The second is restraining the disturbed movements of the spirit (which the Greeks call *pathe*) and making the impulses (which they call *hormai*) obedient to reason.[1] The third is treating those with whom we associate knowledgeably and with moderation in order that their support may secure for us the requirements of nature in full and ample measure; and that if any disadvantage threatens to afflict us, we may, through the same men, avert it, and avenge ourselves on those who have attempted to harm us, inflicting such punishment as fairness and humanity allow.

(19) Shortly, I will discuss the methods by which we can acquire the ability to embrace and retain the support of other men, but before that I must briefly mention something else. Can anyone be unaware of the great power of fortune, which impels one in either direction, towards success or towards adversity? Whenever we enjoy her prospering breezes we are carried to the haven for which we long; when she blows in our face we are wrecked. To fortune again belong such occasional mishaps as squalls, storms, shipwrecks, collapse of buildings and conflagrations which have inanimate causes, and then the blows, bites and attacks of animals. But these, as I said, are comparatively rare. (20) Then on the one hand take the destruction of armies (three lately,[2] and often, on other occasions, many) and the downfall of generals (recently of an excellent and exceptional man)[3] and take also that resentment from the masses which has often led to the exile, ruin or flight of deserving citizens.[4] Take on the other hand success,

---

[1] See I.101 with n. 1.
[2] The three armies are those of Pompey at Pharsalus (9 August 48), of his eldest son at Munda in Spain (6 April 46) and of Metellus Scipio at Thapsus in Africa (17 March 45), all defeated by Julius Caesar.
[3] Pompey (see Biographical Note).
[4] C. may have in mind his own 18 months' exile in 58–7 BC.

civil honours, military commands and victories: though all these are indeed subject to fortune, in neither case can they be effected without the resources and assiduous support of other men.

Now that that point has been understood, I must discuss how we can entice and arouse other men to support what is beneficial to us. If my lecture is overlong, let it be compared with the greatness of the benefit in question; then perhaps it will seem all too brief.

(21) Insofar as men assist another in promoting his position or honour, they may do so either out of good will, when for some reason they are fond of him; or for honour, if they look up to his virtue and consider him to be worthy of the most magnificent fortune; or because they have faith in him, and judge that they are taking good care of their own interests; or because they fear his power; or on the other hand if they have expectations of someone, as happens when kings or *populares*[1] propose lavish distributions; or finally they are attracted by financial reward.[2] That is the most sordid and impure of reasons both for those who are held in its grip and for those who try to resort to it; (22) for things are in a bad way when what ought to be achieved through virtue is attempted by means of money. Since, however, there are times when such assistance is necessary, I shall talk about how it should be used. But first I shall discuss those matters that are closer to virtue.

There are a variety of reasons also why men submit themselves to the command or power of another. For they may be attracted either by goodwill or by the greatness of his previous kind services; or because the man has a very high standing; or perhaps by the hope that such a choice will be beneficial for them; or by fear that they may be compelled by force to obey; or else they may be won over by the hope or promise of lavish distributions; or finally, as we often see in this republic of ours, they may be hired for pay.[3]

(23) But there is nothing at all more suited to protecting and retain-

---

[1] See p. 34, n. 2. On demagoguery in kings, see II.53 and 80. C. objects to such politically motivated handouts at I.42–3, II.72–3, II.78–85.

[2] Goodwill is discussed at 32, honour at 36–8, faith at 33–4; fear at 23–9, distributions and financial reward at 52–85. The six factors recur in a more sinister form in 22 as reasons for giving not just support but submission to non-Republican political domination.

[3] See Introduction, pp. xii–xiii on Caesar's acts as dictator and on Antony's and Octavian's appeal to Caesar's veterans and other beneficiaries of Caesar's liberality.

ing influence than to be loved, and nothing less suited than to be feared. For, as Ennius splendidly puts it:

> They hate the men they fear; and whom one hates one
> would have dead.

Indeed no amount of influence can withstand the hatred of a large number of men. That, if it was unrecognized before, is certainly recognized now.[1] It is not only the death of that tyrant, whom the city endured under force of arms (and still obeys to a great extent though he is dead), that declares the power of men's hatred to destroy. Many tyrants have met a similar end; indeed hardly one has escaped such a death. Fear is a poor guardian over any length of time; but goodwill keeps faithful guard for ever.

(24) Admittedly those who exercise a command over men constrained only by force may need to employ severity, just as a master must towards his servants if he cannot otherwise control them.[2] But that those who live in a free city should contrive to be feared – could anyone be more insane? For however swamped the laws may be by some individual's influence, however freedom herself may cower, still the time comes when they rise up, through silent judgements or in the secret elections to positions of honour. Freedom will bite back more fiercely when suspended than when she remains undisturbed. Let us therefore embrace the course that extends the most widely; and that is the strongest to secure not only safety, but also influence and power, so that fear may be absent but love preserved. That is how we will most easily achieve what we want both in private matters and in public affairs. For those who wish to be feared cannot but themselves be afraid of the very men who fear them.

(25) The elder Dionysius had his hair singed with coals because he feared the barber's knife. What tormenting fears do we imagine must continually have racked him? In what spirit do we imagine Alexander of Pherae must have spent his life? He, as we read, though he loved his wife Thebe greatly, even so when he came to her in

---

[1] See Introduction, p. xii on the references to Caesar's murder. C. implicitly denies Caesar's famous clemency which C. himself had praised in *Pro Marcello*.

[2] This passage might seem to conflict with 1.41 (see n. 3) and reflect instead the Peripatetic view that there are natural slaves who need to be controlled by force, not ruled by consent as citizens are. But, in contrast with C.'s exploration of that view in *De Re Publica* III.37–8, he says here that force is to be used *only if necessary*, and he limits his comparison to rulers of free states.

her room from the feast used to order a barbarian (indeed one marked with Thracian tattoos, so it is said!) to precede him with drawn sword, and used to send attendants before him to search the lady's caskets and to check that no weapon be hidden in her clothes. Wretched man, to hold a barbarian, a tattooed slave, more faithful than your wife! Nor was he deceived. She herself did indeed kill him, suspecting that he had a mistress.

Nor is there any military power so great that it can last for long under the weight of fear. (26) Phalaris is a witness to that. His cruelty is notorious beyond all others, and he died not by ambush (as Alexander did, whom I have just mentioned) nor at the hands of a few men (as our own friend);[1] instead the entire population of Agrigentum assailed him as one. What then of Demetrius? Did not all the Macedonians abandon him and transfer themselves to Pyrrhus? And what of Sparta's allies, who almost universally deserted her unjust command, playing at the disaster of Leuctra the role of spectators and men of leisure?[2]

In such a matter it gives me more pleasure to recall foreign examples than ones from home. But as long as the empire of the Roman people was maintained through acts of kind service and not through injustices, wars were waged either on behalf of allies or about imperial rule; wars were ended with mercy or through necessity;[3] the senate was a haven and refuge for kings, for peoples and for nations; moreover, our magistrates and generals yearned to acquire the greatest praise from one thing alone, the fair and faithful defence of our provinces and of our allies. (27) In this way we could more truly have been titled a protectorate[4] than an empire of the world.

We had already begun gradually to erode this custom and practice; but after the victory of Sulla we rejected it entirely. For when our citizens had suffered such great cruelty, there then ceased to be anything that seemed unjust towards allies. In Sulla's case, dishonourable

---

[1] Julius Caesar, of course. There were more than 60 conspirators in the assassination plot. We know the names of 16 including Brutus and Cassius.

[2] The Thebans under Epaminondas defeated Sparta in 371 BC, liberating the Arcadians and the Messenians who had endured prolonged subjection working as slaves (known as Helots) on their confiscated lands. See p. 95, n. 1.

[3] See p. 17, n. 1. The defensive aspect of wars for empire is brought out by linking them with wars to defend Rome's allies. But C. knew that Rome had often expanded its empire by defending allies it had chosen to acquire (*Rep.* III.35).

[4] 'Protectorate' here translates *patrocinium*, the abstract noun for the relationship of patron to client or ex-slave, used here metaphorically for the relation of ruling state to subject.

victory succeeded an honourable cause: for he planted his spear in the forum[1] and sold the property of good men and rich men, and men who were at the very least citizens, daring to proclaim that he was selling his own booty. There followed a man whose cause was unrighteous and whose victory fouler still; he did not confiscate the property of individual citizens, but embraced entire countries and provinces under a single law of ruin. (28) That is why we see Massilia being carried around in a triumphal procession as an example to oppressed and devastated nations abroad of the empire we have forfeited.[2] That is why we see a triumph being celebrated over the very city without which our generals themselves could never have achieved a triumph for their wars beyond the Alps. I should relate many other iniquities inflicted upon our allies, had ever the sun seen anything unworthier than that particular one. Our present sufferings are, therefore, just. For if we had not tolerated the crimes of many men going unpunished, such extreme licence would never have come into the hands of one. His estate indeed was inherited by only a few; but there were many wicked heirs to his greedy desires.[3]

(29) The seed and occasion of civil wars will be present for as long as desperate men remember and hope for that bloody spear. Publius Sulla shook it when his kinsman was dictator; and again thirty-six years later he did not withdraw from a still more criminal spear. Yet another, who was a clerk in that former dictatorship, was urban quaestor in the next.[4] From this it ought to be understood

---

[1] A reference to the proscriptions in which Sulla outlawed his enemies in the civil war and confiscated their property, either giving it to supporters or selling it. Sales by auction took place near a spear stuck in the ground.

[2] Massilia, the modern Marseilles, was a Greek colony which had become an ally of Rome even before Gaul became a Roman province. It was captured by Caesar in the civil war because it favoured Pompey's cause. Models of captured towns were carried in the triumphal procession (see p. 31, n. 2). Cf. *Att.* XIV.14.6 for C.'s reaction at the time.

[3] The principal of the three heirs to his estate was C. Octavius his grand-nephew (the later Emperor Augustus). The 'heirs to his desires' are probably Antony and his friends in particular.

[4] See I.43 with n. 2. Publius Cornelius Sulla presided over the sale of confiscated property in 82 BC and 36 years later in 46 BC. 'Another' is Cornelius Sulla, an ex-slave of the dictator who served him as secretary and held the quaestorship (a largely financial office and the first on the ladder of senatorial magistracies) under Caesar. Cf. *Philippics* II.64 for the auctioning of Pompey's property.

that when such prizes are offered there will never be a lack of civil wars. And so only the walls of the city remain standing – and they themselves now fear the excesses of crime. The republic we have utterly lost. And we have fallen into this disaster – for I must return to my proposition – because we prefer to be feared than to be held dear and loved.[1] If these things could have happened to the Roman people when they ruled unjustly, what ought individuals to think? Since, then, it is obvious that the power of goodwill is great, and that of fear feeble, we must next discuss the ways in which we can most easily acquire, with honour and faithfulness, the love that we desire.

(30) But we do not all need these equally. For whether a man needs to be loved by many, or whether a few will be enough, must be determined by the life he has adopted. Let this be taken as fixed and primary and most necessary, that one should have faithful companionships with friends who love us and who esteem our qualities. For this is one thing in which there is no great difference between outstanding and ordinary men, and it must be acquired almost equally by both of them. (31) All men, perhaps, do not equally need honour, glory, the citizens' goodwill. However, if these do fall to anyone's lot, they are quite helpful (among other things) in acquiring friendships.[2]

But I have spoken about friendship in another book, which is entitled *Laelius*. Now let me discuss glory. There are indeed two books of mine on this subject also, but let us touch upon it as it is of the greatest assistance in conducting matters of importance.[3] The peak and perfection of glory lies in the following three things: if the masses love you, if they have faith in you, if they think you worthy of some honour combined with admiration. These, if I must speak simply and briefly, are brought forth from the masses by almost the same things as they are from individuals. But there is also another approach

---

[1] Since C. cannot actually claim that Rome's misrule, like Sparta's, lost her the control or allegiance of her subjects (cf. II.75), he argues that her misrule encouraged misconduct at home, resulting in civil war and the loss of the Republic.

[2] Goodwill, faith and honour are about to be discussed as means to glory, which is only relevant to 'outstanding men'. C. pauses to mention the form of support from their fellows that all men can achieve, friendship.

[3] The *De Gloria*, written earlier than the *Laelius* in this year, is lost.

to the masses, which enables us to infiltrate, so to speak, into the hearts of everyone together.[1]

(32) First, then, of the three I have listed, let us look at advice concerning goodwill. This is secured most of all by kind services; but secondly, goodwill is aroused by the willingness to provide kind service, even if ones's resources are not, perhaps, adequate for it. A vigorous love is aroused in the masses, however, by the very reputation and rumour of liberality, of beneficence, of justice, of keeping faith, and of all the virtues that are associated with gentleness and easiness of conduct. For, because the very thing we call honourable and seemly pleases us in itself, and moves the hearts of all by its nature and appearance, shining out brightly, so to speak, from the virtues that I have mentioned – because of that, when we think people possess these virtues, we are compelled by nature to love them. These indeed are the weightiest causes of loving; for there may be a few more trivial ones besides.

(33) We can bring it about in two ways that others have faith in us: if we are deemed to possess both good sense and justice combined with it. For we have faith in those whom we judge to understand more than us, whom we believe can foresee the future, able when the issue arises and the crisis arrives, to settle the matter, adopting the counsel that suits the circumstance. For men reckon that such good sense as that is useful and genuine. As for just and faithful men, however, that is good men,[2] one has such faith in them that no suspicion of deceit or injustice arises. That is why we think that we are absolutely right to entrust to them our safety, our fortunes, and our children. (34) Of the two, justice has more power to win faith; indeed although it has authority enough even without good sense, good sense without justice is of no avail in inspiring faith. The more cunning and clever a man is, the more he is hated and suspected if deprived of the reputation of integrity. The result is that justice combined with intelligence will have as much power as it wishes to win faith. Justice without good sense will be able to do much; without justice, good sense will avail not at all.

(35) Someone may be wondering why, although it is argued by all philosophers, and I myself have frequently argued it, that whoever

---

[1] Cf. 44–51 on how to bring our qualities to general notice.
[2] See I.20 with n. 1.

has one virtue has them all, I now separate them, as if someone who has no sense could at the same time be just.[1] One degree of precision is required when truth herself is debated and refined, but another when speech is entirely adapted to common opinion. For this reason we speak here just as ordinary men do, calling some men brave, others good, others sensible. For when we discuss popular opinion we must use popular and familiar words, in the very way that Panaetius did.[2]

But let us return to our subject.

(36) Of the three things that related to glory, the third was that other men should judge us worthy of both their honour and their admiration. In general men admire everything they notice that is great and beyond their expectation; in particular, if they see in individuals any good things that take them by surprise. Therefore they look up to and lavish great praise upon those men in whom they think they see outstanding and exceptional virtues; but they look down upon and despise those whom they think have no virtue, nor spirit, nor vigour. (For they do not despise everyone of whom they think ill. They do not despise those they think wicked, slanderous, deceitful, or equipped to commit injury; they certainly do, however, think ill of them.) Therefore, as I said before, those who are despised are the men who 'help not themselves nor another', as the saying goes; they have in them no industriousness, no diligence, no concern.

(37) On the other hand men are regarded with admiration if they are thought to excel others in virtue, not only being free from all dishonour, but also resisting even those vices that others cannot easily resist. For pleasures themselves, those most alluring of mistresses, twist the hearts of most men away from virtue; and when the flames of pain are kindled most men are frightened beyond measure. Both life and death, both riches and poverty, powerfully perturb all men.

---

[1] *Fin.* v.66; *Tusc.* III.14; *Acad.* I.38. C. raises the issue in considering justice and good sense (the practical aspect of wisdom, I.153) because Carneades had attacked the idea that virtue, especially justice, and wisdom were compatible. C. had answered the point, particularly as regards states, in *De Re Publica* III.32ff.; as regards individuals, see below, III.40–96, especially 50–78, 89–92.

[2] The Stoics were charged with violating common usage as in the famous Stoic paradoxes and their idea that external advantages were not 'goods'. C. praises Panaetius for making concessions to ordinary language and notions in *De Finibus* IV.79.

But as for those who look down with a great and lofty spirit upon prosperity and adversity alike, especially when some grand and honourable matter is before them, which converts them wholly to itself and possesses them, who then will fail to admire the splendour and beauty of virtue? (38) Therefore, a spirit contemptuous in this way arouses great admiration; and justice most of all seems something admirable to the crowd; on account of that virtue alone are men called 'good'. And not unjustly: for no one can be just if he fears death, or pain, or exile, or need; or if he prefers their opposites to fairness. Men whom money does not move are also most greatly admired. If that quality is observed in someone, they regard him as having been tested by fire.[1]

To sum up then, the three things which I laid down as means to glory are all achieved by justice: goodwill, because it desires to benefit many; and for the same reason faithfulness; and admiration, because it scorns and ignores the very things towards which most men, inflamed by greed, are dragged.

(39) In my opinion, at least, every rational method or plan of life requires the assistance of other men, first of all so that one has others with whom one can share in friendly discussions. That is difficult if you do not present the appearance of a good man. The reputation for justice is necessary also even for a solitary man, or one who lives his life in the country; and all the more so because if they do not have it, having no defence at all to protect them they will have many injustices inflicted upon them.

(40) Justice is necessary also, so that they may carry out their business, for those who sell or buy, who hire or let, and who are involved in commercial transactions in general. Its effect is so great that not even those who win their bread from evil-doing and crime are able to live without any particle of justice. For if anyone steals or snatches something from one of his fellows in banditry, he leaves no place for himself even within the gang of bandits. And if the one called the pirate chief does not share the booty fairly, he will be killed or abandoned by his comrades. Indeed they say that there are even laws

---

[1] On the 'good' man, see p. 9, n. 1. The allusion to fire is to the testing of gold, for it was believed that only that metal was incombustible (Pliny *NH* XXXIII.59) and that its quality could be measured by observing the time it took to become incandescent.

among bandits which they obey and respect.[1] And so it was because of his fair distribution of booty that Bardulis, the Illyrian bandit, of whom we hear in Theopompus, had great influence, and Viriathus the Lusitanian much greater. Indeed our own generals and their armies surrendered to the latter. (It was Laelius, the one nicknamed 'the wise', who as praetor broke and crushed him, repressing his ferocity to such an extent that he left an easy war to his successors.)[2]

Justice has such great effect that it strengthens and increases the resources even of bandits. How great an effect, then, do we think it will have among laws and lawcourts and in a well ordered political community?

(41) It seems to me that it was not only among the Medes (as Herodotus tells us),[3] but also among our ancestors, that once upon a time men of good character were established as kings in order that justice might be enjoyed. For when the needy masses wẻre being oppressed by those who had greater wealth, they fled together to some one man who excelled in virtue. When he protected the weaker from injustice, fairness was established, and he held the highest and the lowest under an equality of justice. The establishment of laws and the institution of kings had the same cause. (42) For a system of justice that is fair is what has always been sought: otherwise it would not be justice. As long as they secured this from a single just and good man, with that they were content. When it ceased to be so, laws were invented, which always spoke to everyone with one and the same voice.[4]

This, therefore, is manifest: the men who are usually chosen to

[1] *Latro* (bandit) is used to cover a broad spectrum of people who threaten the social order by violence but are regarded neither as criminals to be dealt with by due process of law nor as legitimate enemies with whom formal war is waged. C. here, and in III.107, adduces pirates as the central case because of the scale of the nuisance and of the operations against it in his own lifetime: in this very year there had been a resurgence of the problem (*Att.* XVI.1.3).

[2] The Romans often described as bandits native bands within Roman provinces whom the governor had not succeeded in controlling (cf. C. writing to his brother in *QFr.* I.I.28). Like Bardulis and Viriathus, these bandits were sometimes guerrilla fighters opposing the rule of Rome. After Laelius' successes, Viriathus continued to cause Roman reverses until dealt with by treachery and assassination.

[3] Herodotus (1.96) describes how Deioces, who was famed for his just decisions, was made king by the Medes because they found that, when he ceased to give judgement, crime and anarchy increased.

[4] This schematic account of the rise and fall of the Roman monarchy adapts Roman history to a general account of political development such as Posidonius devised (Seneca, *Letter* 90.5). As Book II of C.'s *De Re Publica* shows, the Romans actually thought there were laws in operation under the kings, some of whom were great legislators.

rule are those who have a great reputation among the masses for justice. If in addition, indeed, they were thought also to be men of good sense, there was nothing that men would think they could not achieve under their leadership. Therefore justice must be cultivated and maintained by every method, both for its own sake (for otherwise it would not be justice) and for the sake of enhancing one's honour and glory. There is a rational method both of seeking money and of investing it, which ensures a continuous supply not merely of necessary, but even of liberal, expenditure; in a similar way, then, glory must be both sought and invested methodically.

(43) And yet, as Socrates declared splendidly,[1] the nearest path to glory, a short cut so to speak, is to behave in such a way that one is what one wishes to be thought. For men who think that they can secure for themselves unshakeable glory by pretence and empty show, by dissembling in speech and countenance, are wildly mistaken. True glory takes root and spreads its branches too; but everything false drops swiftly down like blossom; and pretence can never endure. There are witnesses in plenty to both those points, but for brevity's sake one family will suffice us. For Tiberius Gracchus, the son of Publius, will be praised as long as the memory of Roman deeds endures. His sons, however, while alive did not win the approval of good men; and now that they are dead they are numbered among those who were justly cut down. If anyone wishes, then, to win true glory, let him fulfil the duties of justice. And what they are, I have said in my first book.

(44) The greatest effect is achieved, then, by being what we wish to seem; however some advice should be given so that we might as easily as is possible be seen to be what we are. For if anyone from his early youth has cause to become famous and renowned, whether as the heir of his father (as I think has happened to you, my dear Cicero!) or through any other chance or fortune, the eyes of all are cast on him. They examine whatever he does, the very way in which he lives; he is, as it were, bathed in so brilliant a light that no single word or deed of his can be hidden. (45) Others, on the other hand, because of their humble and obscure background, spend their youth unknown by other men. As soon as they become young men, they ought to set their sights on great things and strive for them with

---

[1] Recounted by Xenophon in *Memoirs of Socrates* II.39.

unswerving devotion. They can do that with a steadier spirit because at that age they will not only not be envied, but will even meet with favour. Youth wins commendation primarily for any glory it may be able to gain in warfare. Many of our ancestors so distinguished themselves. For them wars were waged almost continuously. Your own youth, however, falls at the time of a war in which one of the sides possessed too much wickedness, the other too little luck. However, when Pompey put you in charge of a cavalry squadron in that war you won great praise, and that both from an outstanding man and from the army, by your horsemanship, your spear-throwing, and your endurance of every military hardship.[1] But the praise that was yours fell together with the republic. However, the subject of my discourse is not you, but this whole topic. And so let us proceed to what remains.

(46) Just as in other matters the efforts of the spirit are far more important than those of the body, here too the achievements of talent and reason win more gratitude than those of strength. One wins commendation primarily, then, for modesty, along with reverence for parents and goodwill to one's family and friends. Young men become known most easily, however, and in the best way, by attaching themselves to such famous and wise men as concern themselves with the good of the political community. By associating with such as these, they will inspire in the people the belief that they too will become like those whom they have chosen to imitate. (47) His visits to the house of Publius Mucius commended Publius Rutilius to public opinion as a person of integrity and of legal knowledge, while he was but a young man. But Lucius Crassus, when he was still a youth, did not borrow from elsewhere, but won for himself the greatest of praise for that noble and glorious prosecution of his. At an age when doing exercises normally wins praise, the young Crassus, like Demosthenes, as we are told, showed that he could already accomplish superbly in the forum things for which he could at the time have been praised for studying at home.[2]

---

[1] C. comes close to accepting here what he deplores at I.74 and II.46, that military glory counted for most at Rome. Young Cicero served at the age of 16–17 under Pompey in 49–8 in the civil war against Caesar.

[2] Lucius Licinius Crassus, C.'s Roman model as an orator, as Demosthenes was his Greek, was only twenty-one years old when he accused C. Papirius Carbo (cf. II.49) and drove him to suicide. C. pleaded his first public case in 80 BC at the age of twenty-six, preferring not to learn on the job (*Brutus* 311).

(48) There are two methods of speaking; under one falls conversation, under the other debate. There is no doubt that debate has the greater effect when glory is the object (for that is what we mean by eloquence). It is however difficult to say to what extent friendliness and an approachable manner of conversation will win over men's hearts. We have the letters which Philip wrote to Alexander, which Antipater wrote to Cassander, and which Antigonus wrote to his son Philip, the letters of three of the most sensible of men (for that is what we are told). In these they give the advice to woo the hearts of the crowds to goodwill with friendly talk, and to soothe their soldiers in conversation by gently beseeching them. But often when a speech is delivered to the masses in a debate, it arouses the whole crowd. Great indeed is the admiration aroused by an eloquent and wise speaker, whose hearers judge him wiser, and more understanding too, than the rest. And if in such a speech there is also a weightiness blended with modesty, then no achievement can be more admirable; and all the more so if these qualities are found in a young man.

(49) There are many types of case which call for eloquence, and in our republic many young men have won praise by speaking before the jurors, before the people, and before the senate. But the greatest admiration is inspired in lawsuits. The method required here is two-fold, as it consists of prosecution and of defence. Defence is indeed more likely to win praise, but frequently too a prosecution is approved. I mentioned Crassus just now. Marcus Antonius as a young man did the same. It was a prosecution also that brought to light the eloquence of Publius Sulpicius, when he summoned to court Gaius Norbanus, a seditious and worthless citizen.

(50) This should not, however, be done often. Further, it should only be done either on behalf of the community (as in the case of those I have mentioned) or for revenge (as in the case of the two Luculli) or to fulfil a patron's obligation (as I did for the Sicilians, and Julius in prosecuting Albucius for the Sardinians).[1] Again, the diligence showed by Lucius Fufius in prosecuting Manius Aquillius is recognized. It is a thing to be done once, then; certainly not

---

[1] Prosecution was the common way to make one's oratorical debut. Crassus was twenty-one (see p. 80, n. 2), Publius Sulpicius twenty; Marcus Antonius' first speech is unknown. C., who started with a defence, felt the need for excuses when prosecuting Verres at the age of thirty-six. Crassus' victim Carbo, like Sulpicius', was regarded by the Optimates as 'unsound'; the Luculli were avenging their father; C. and C. Julius Caesar Strabo were protecting the interests of the provinces they had governed.

frequently. If anyone has to prosecute more often, he should do so as a service to the nation: for avenging her enemies fairly often is not a thing to be condemned. But still due measure should be observed. For it seems a hard man indeed, or rather scarcely a man at all, who prosecutes a large number on charges that threaten their civic status. It both endangers a man and soils his reputation to allow himself to be viewed as a prosecutor. That happened to Marcus Brutus, who was born of outstanding stock and the son of one who was an expert before all in civil law.

(51) There is one piece of advice concerning duty which must be punctiliously observed, that is never to threaten the civic status of an innocent man by prosecution.[1] That could not fail to be a criminal deed. Is anything so inhuman as to take the eloquence that was given by nature for the protection and safekeeping of mankind and to turn it to the destruction or ruin of good men? But, on the other hand, though that must be avoided, still scruples should not prevent us from occasionally defending a guilty man, provided he is not wicked and impious. The masses want it; custom permits it; humanity tolerates it. In lawsuits, a judge[2] should always strive for the truth, but an advocate may sometimes defend what looks like the truth, even if it is less true. I should not dare to write that, especially when I am writing on philosophy, had it not been acceptable to Panaetius, a most respected Stoic. It is indeed defending that gives the richest yield of glory and gratitude, and the more so if it happens that the man you assist appears to be overwhelmed and oppressed because of the influence of some mighty individual. I myself have done that often; in particular I did so as a young man on behalf of Sextus Roscius of Ameria in the face of the influence of Lucius Sulla, who was then despot. That speech, as you know, is still in existence.[3]

(52) I have now explained such dutiful services of a young man as may be effective in securing glory. Next I must discuss beneficence

---

[1] C.'s expression here (literally: 'never to indict an innocent man on a capital charge') refers to the threat to a man's *caput*, his status as a citizen. In his day upper-class defendants were not retained in prison before or after sentence and usually withdrew into exile.

[2] The term applies not only to those who preside over trials, particularly civil ones, but, in criminal trials of C.'s time, to the members of the jury.

[3] Though later critical of its exuberant style, C. did publish *Pro Roscio Amerino*, his first speech in a public trial, delivered in 80 BC. He exaggerates his danger here, for though Sulla was consul, he had probably ceased to be dictator, and (despite Plutarch *Cicero* 3), C.'s trip abroad in 79–8 was not motivated by fear (*Brutus* 312–14).

and liberality. There are two methods here: one may show kindness to the needy either by personal services, or by giving money. The latter is easier, especially for a wealthy man; the former, however, is both more brilliantly illustrious, and more worthy of a brave and notable man. For both involve a liberal willingness to gratify others; but the one draws upon a money-chest, the other upon one's virtue. Again, gifts of money that come from personal wealth drain the very source of kindness: thus kindness is destroyed by kindness. For the more people that one has treated in that way, the less one is able so to treat many others. (53) If men are beneficent and liberal through services, that is through virtue and diligence, then, in the first place, the more men they benefit, the more helpers they will have in acting kindly. Secondly, the custom of being beneficent will make them the readier to deserve well of many and, so to speak, more practised in it.

Philip does splendidly to accuse his son Alexander in a letter, on the grounds that he has sought the goodwill of the Macedonians by gifts of money. 'What reason', he asked, 'led you – alas! – to entertain the thought that men you had corrupted with money would be faithful to you? Or are you trying to make the Macedonians hope that you will be not their king, but their servant and their provider?' 'Servant and provider' was well said, because it is degrading for a king; and it was better still to speak of gifts of money as a corrupting influence. For he who accepts them becomes a worse man, and the readier always to expect the same. (54) Philip wrote that to his son, but we may well think it good advice for everyone.

There is no doubt, therefore, that the kindliness that consists of personal effort and diligence is more honourable and extends more widely, and can benefit more people. But sometimes one should give money; that type of kindness should not be entirely rejected. To suitable men who are in need, one should often give a share of one's wealth; but one should do so with care and moderation. For many have squandered their patrimony by improvident gifts of money. But what is more foolish than to ensure that you are no longer able to do the very thing that you enjoy doing? Moreover, the giving of money brings robbery in its wake. For when men, because of their giving, begin to be in need themselves, they are forced to lay their hands on others' goods. Consequently, although they wish to be beneficent for the sake of acquiring goodwill, they do not gain as much support from those to whom they have given as hatred from those from whom they have taken.[1] (55) Therefore one's personal wealth is not to be locked in such a way that kindness cannot open it, nor so unsecured that it is open to everyone. Due limit should be observed, a limit determined with reference to one's capabilities. In sum, we should remember the phrase that has so often been employed by our countrymen that it has acquired the status of a proverb: 'bounty has no bottom'. For what limit can there be when both those who are used to it and those who are not alike desire the same thing?

In general there are two kinds of men who give amply, the one extravagant and the other liberal. The extravagant, with their banquets, their public distributions of meat, their gladiatorial performances, their spectacular provisions of games and of wild animals in combat, pour out their money on things for which they will be remembered briefly, if at all. (56) The liberal, however, out of their resources, ransom captives from bandits, or assume their friends' debts, or help them to finance their daughters' marriages, or give them assistance in acquiring or enlarging their property.[2]

I wonder therefore what could have been in Theophrastus' mind when he wrote in his book *On Riches* (which contains much that is splendid) something as absurd as the following: he is expansive in his praise of the personal provision of magnificent public events and he considers the harvest of riches to lie in having the resources for such expenditure. To me, however, it seems that the fruit of liberality, of which I have given a few examples, is much greater and much more certain. Aristotle speaks with far more weight and truth when he reprimands us for not being amazed at such squandering of money, the purpose of which is to soothe the masses.[3] If those who are under siege from an enemy are forced to buy water

---

[1] The example of Alexander who would become a king already blurs the issue, which is liberality from one's personal resources, and C. goes on to men like Caesar and Sulla who used their political position to increase their personal wealth which they then used to buy support. Later in 72–85 he discusses liberality with state money in an official capacity under liberality in services.

[2] C. distinguishes extravagance, i.e. spending on public entertainment to please the mob (56–60), from liberality, i.e. spending to help individuals (61–4). Note that ransoming from bandits, usually, in this period, pirates (p. 78, n. 1), appears as a routine occurrence, as also at II.63. Julius Caesar was captured by pirates as a youth.

[3] Theophrastus' book *On Riches* is lost. At II.60 another Peripatetic, Demetrius of Phalerum, is cited, and the whole discussion in 56–60, cf. 64, with its emphasis on the intermediate course, has a Peripatetic colour (see Introduction, pp. xvi–xvii).

at one *mina* a pint,[1] at first that seems unbelievable to us and everyone is surprised; but when they think more about it, they grant that necessity may excuse it. With regard to this enormous wastage and endless expense, however, we are not greatly surprised – and that though it serves no necessity and enhances no one's standing; indeed, though the very delight of the masses lasts but for a brief and paltry moment, and though that delight belongs only to the most frivolous, for whom the moment that their satiety dies, so does the very memory of their pleasure. (57) His conclusion is also a good one: those things are gratifying to boys and to weak women, to slaves and to those free men that are most like slaves;[2] but a serious man who weighs with steady judgement what is done cannot in any way approve of them.

And yet I do realize that even in the good old days it had become a tradition in our city to demand splendour from the best men in their aedileships.[3] Consequently Publius Crassus, 'Dives' (Rich) in both surname and substance, fulfilled his functions as aedile with extravagance. A little later, Lucius Crassus, together with that most moderate of all men, Quintus Mucius, discharged his aedileship with utmost magnificence; and then Gaius Claudius, the son of Appius, and many after him, the Luculli, Hortensius, Silanus. But in my consulship Publius Lentulus surpassed all his predecessors; Scaurus imitated him; and the events provided by my friend Pompey in his second consulship were extremely magnificent.[4] You can see what I myself would approve in all this.

(58) On the other hand, any suspicion of avarice must be avoided. There is the case of Mamercus, an extremely rich man, whose by-passing of the aedileship brought him rejection when he was a consular candidate. Therefore if something is demanded by the people, and

---

[1] A *mina*, to give an indication of its value at the height of the fifth century BC, was the amount Athenian jurors would receive from the state to cover bare subsistence for 200 days.

[2] Aristotle believed there were slaves by nature but did not think actual social status always coincided with natural distinctions (*Politics* 1.1254a14–1255b16). Thus there could be free men whose character showed them to be truly slaves.

[3] The aediles were in charge of the amenities of the city – street, markets, shrines – and fire-control. They also exercised minor jurisdiction and organized public games and festivals (*ludi*). There was a state allowance for these, but those in office could spend additional sums on them. In addition many gave entertainments, particularly gladiatorial games, at their own expense.

[4] Pompey as consul for the second time in 55 BC built the first permanent stone theatre in Rome (cf. II.60) and gave elaborate games. Note that these were not official games, as Pompey was not aedile at the time.

if good men, though they do not actually ask for it, do not however disapprove, it should be done – but only in proportion to one's resources (as I myself did); and similarly, when some greater and more useful thing may be achieved through gifts to the populace: the dinners which Orestes recently gave in the streets were nominally tithe-offerings, but won him great honour. Nor indeed was it counted a vice for Marcus Seius that when the price of corn was high he gave it to the people at only one *as* a measure. For he freed himself from a great and long-standing unpopularity, by a sacrifice that was neither dishonourable, as he was aedile, nor very great.[1] But the highest honour fell recently to my dear Milo, who bought gladiators for the sake of the republic (which depended on my safety) and suppressed all the insane ventures of Publius Clodius.[2]

(59) There is a case for lavish distribution, then, if it is either necessary or beneficial. However, in these very matters the rule of the intermediate course is best.[3] Lucius Philippus, the son of Quintus, a man of great talent and extremely notable, was accustomed to boast that without financing any public events he had achieved all the most highly regarded distinctions. The same was said by Cotta and Curio. I too may boast in a somewhat similar vein.[4] For compared with the distinction of the honourable offices which I achieved (elected to them unanimously and in the earliest possible year – something which happened to none of those I have just named) the expenditure during my aedileship was paltry indeed.[5]

(60) Again, money is better spent on walls, docks, harbours, aque-

---

[1] The *as* was the lowest denomination of the bronze coins in common use at Rome. The price Seius charged was low: when the sale of subsidized corn (see p. 92, n. 1) by the government, discontinued by Sulla in 81 BC, was resumed in 73, one year after this, the price was probably 6⅓ asses per measure. The shortages were caused by piracy and war. 'Since he was aedile' alludes to the suspicion that such distributions, when made by those without an official position, aroused.

[2] Milo, in using violence as tribune (not aedile) in 57 BC against his old enemy Clodius who had exiled C., is said to have acted for the good of the state, here identified with C.'s recall. By implication he disapproves of the enormous games Milo gave later in 55–4.

[3] See p. 35, n. 2.

[4] C.'s qualification is not intended to cover his failure to attain the censorship, as Cotta also failed to do so: 'the most highly regarded distinctions' are the praetorship and consulship. C. must mean that the other three gave *no* games, presumably because they were never aediles, whereas he had (cf. *Verr.* v.36).

[5] C. was elected praetor and consul by the Centuriate Assembly at the earliest age possible under the law of Sulla and by the unanimous vote of those centuries which had voted by the time he achieved a majority and was declared elected.

ducts, and everything else that concerns the needs of the nation; and these win greater gratitude from posterity, although what is present – what is in the hand, so to speak – is more pleasurable. On account of Pompey, I am embarrassed to criticize theatres, colonnades and new temples; but the most learned men do not approve of them, as Panaetius himself says (whom I am to a large extent following, though not expounding, in these books) and also Demetrius of Phalerum, who denounces Pericles, the foremost of the Greeks, because he threw away so much money on that splendid propylaea.[1] But I thoroughly discussed the whole topic in the books which I wrote *On the Republic.*[2]

To sum up, therefore, the whole system of lavish distribution is of its nature contrary to virtue; but due to circumstances, it may be necessary. Even then, it must be adapted to one's resources and moderated by the intermediate course.

(61) Now as for the other type of giving, that which proceeds from liberality, here we should not react in the same way towards different cases.[3] The case of a man overwhelmed by disaster is one thing, that of a man who seeks to improve his affairs though unaffected by misfortune, is another. (62) Kindness ought to incline itself more to those stricken by disaster, unless perhaps they deserve their disaster.

On the other hand, if others want assistance not in avoiding suffering, but in order to climb to a higher level, we ought to be not at all close-fisted, but to apply our judgement and care in selecting suitable men. Ennius wrote splendidly:

> Good deeds when badly placed I count as badly done.

(63) Furthermore, anything that is granted to a man who is good and grateful bears fruit both in him, and also in others. For liberality (when free from rashness) wins great gratitude, and most men praise it the more assiduously because the goodness of an excellent man

---

[1] The vestibule of the Parthenon on the Athenian Acropolis, built in the 440s BC, was criticized at the time, but because it was paid for with the tribute Athens collected from her allies for the ostensible purpose of mutual protection against Persian invasion.

[2] The passage, probably in the fifth book, is now lost.

[3] 1.42 laid down, from the point of view of honourableness, three principles for liberality; C. introduces the same three principles when discussing liberality from the point of view of benefit: giving should harm no one (II.64, II.68, II.73, II.78–9); should not exceed one's means (II.55, II.64); and should be in accordance with the standing of the receiver (II.61–3, II.69–71).

is the common refuge of all. Therefore we must make an effort to affect as many as possible by kind services of such a sort that the memory of them is handed down to children and children's children, so that they too may not be without gratitude. For everyone hates a man who is unmindful of kind services, and thinks that that injustice, because it discourages liberality, is inflicted also upon himself: the man who does such a thing is considered the common enemy of the poor.

A further kindness is that which benefits the nation also, for example, buying back captives from slavery and enriching the poor. We have plentiful evidence in that speech of Crassus' that such burdens were commonly assumed by our class.[1] Therefore I would value the habit of that type of kindness far above paying for public events. The former is the mark of a serious and great man, the latter of those who flatter the people, as it were, using pleasures to tickle the fickle fancies of the masses.

(64) It is fitting, moreover, both to be bountiful in giving and also to avoid harshness in making demands and in all transactions – selling, buying, hiring, letting, in issues concerning neighbours and boundaries – being fair, affable, often yielding much of what is rightfully one's own, certainly shunning litigation as far as possible, and perhaps even a little further than that. For it is not only liberal, but sometimes may even prove fruitful, occasionally to concede a little of one's right. One must take account of one's personal wealth (for it is criminal to allow that to slip away) but in such a way that there is no suspicion of meanness or avarice. For to be able to act with liberality, and yet not rob oneself of one's patrimony, is without doubt the greatest fruit that money can bear.

Again, hospitality was rightly praised by Theophrastus. For it is most seemly (or so it seems to me) for the homes of distinguished men to be open to distinguished guests. Furthermore, it reflects splendidly on the republic that foreigners do not in our city go short of that kind of liberality. For those who wish to possess great power honourably, it is also extremely beneficial to wield influence and command gratitude among foreign peoples through the guests one has

---

[1] The speech was delivered by L. Licinius Crassus in 106 BC in support of the bill of Servilius Caepio to end the equestrian monopoly of the juries, after many eminent senators had been convicted in 110 BC before the Mamilian tribunal. He argued that, because of their services to the state, senators deserved a fairer chance in the courts.

entertained. Theophrastus, indeed, wrote that in Athens Cimon was hospitable even to the Laciads, the members of his own ward; for he established the following practice, instructing his stewards accordingly, that everything should be offered to any Laciad who called at his country home.[1]

(65) Kind services which are effected by personal effort rather than by lavish distributions may be bestowed both on the nation as a whole and on individual citizens. For to attend to someone's interests in law, to help him by one's counsel, and generally to assist as many as possible with that sort of knowledge, tends strongly to increase one's own influence, and others' gratitude. Therefore, among the many splendid things about our ancestors was this, that they always held in highest honour the learning of our excellently constituted civil law, and its interpretation. Indeed, before the present unsettled time, our leading men themselves maintained the practice; but now, the resplendency of this knowledge, along with our honours and all our degrees of standing, has been eclipsed. And that is all the more unworthy because it has happened in the lifetime of a man who was equal in honour to all his predecessors, and in knowledge has easily surpassed them.[2] This type of service, then, is gratifying to many, and an appropriate way of binding men to you by kind services.

(66) Closely akin to this discipline, but an ability both weightier, and more gratifying and glamorous, is that of making speeches.[3] For what is superior to eloquence, whether the admiration of one's hearers, or the hope of those in need, or the gratitude of those whom one has defended, is in question? Therefore our ancestors gave to eloquence the foremost standing among civil professions. If a man is both a skilful speaker, and takes hard work lightly, and if he undertakes without reluctance or remuneration to defend a large number

---

[1] On Theophrastus, cf. II.56. The demes ('wards') were divisions of the ten Athenian tribes.

[2] S. Sulpicius Rufus, consul in 51 BC and one of C.'s friends and correspondents, is here praised anonymously because he was still alive. He not only gave legal advice and taught law but wrote a great deal, adding a new logical and systematic quality to legal discussion through his skill in dialectic (*Brutus* 152–3). In *Pro Murena* C. ridiculed his concern with the dry minutiae of law, but he made amends later. See Introduction, pp. xiii–xiv.

[3] Forensic oratory being the most important in politics, the Roman statesman needed to learn about the law. He did so by listening to great lawyers giving legal opinions, as C. did with Q. Mucius Scaevola (Augur).

of clients (as was the habit of our forefathers),[1] the opportunity for kind services and for patronage at law will be wide open for him.

(67) My very subject would advise me here also to deplore the interruption – not to say the destruction – of eloquence, did I not fear to seem to be complaining on my own account. But we can see how many orators have perished; we see that few who still live show promise, and fewer still ability – but how many are full of audacity!

It is true that not all, perhaps not even very many, can become experienced in law or skilled speakers. But it is still possible to assist many men by personal effort: by seeking kind services for them, recommending them to the jurors and the magistrates, by watching over another's interests, by soliciting for them those men that give advice or defend. Those who do this obtain the highest degree of gratitude, and their diligence spreads itself extremely widely.

(68) Now one does not need to be warned – for it is obvious – to take care that in trying to help some people one does not upset others. For often one may hurt either those whom one should not hurt, or those whom it is inexpedient to hurt. If one does so imprudently, one shows thoughtlessness; if knowingly, rashness. If you offend anyone unwittingly, you must to the best of your ability offer as excuses the reason why it was necessary to do what you did, and why you could not do anything else; and you must compensate for what seems to be an offence by other efforts and dutiful services.

(69) In assisting other men it is customary to regard either their conduct, or their fortune. Therefore it is easy for men to say, as they commonly do, that when bestowing kind services they respond to a man's conduct and not to his fortune. The words are honourable; but who is there in the end who does not, when giving service, prefer to the cause of an excellent but needy person the gratitude of a fortunate and powerful one? For our will, on the whole, inclines more to the man from whom a readier and swifter recompense seems likely to come. We should, however, attend more carefully to the nature of things. For the needy person, if he is also a good man, may indeed be unable to requite his gratitude, but he can certainly have it. As someone aptly said, 'The man who has a sum of money has not

---

[1] Though the Lex Cincia of 204 BC forbade lawyers to take fees or presents from their clients, there were many forms of indirect financial recompense. C. was once left a library in a will and once given a large loan in order to buy a house.

repaid it, and the man who has repaid it does not have it; but if someone has requited gratitude, he still has it, and if he has it, he has requited it.' But those who think that they are wealthy, honoured and blessed do not want even to be under obligation from a kind service. For they think that they have been benefactors themselves simply by accepting something, even if it is large; they suspect that something will be demanded or expected of them in return, and they consider that accepting patronage or being labelled as a client is tantamount to death.[1] (70) If, however, you do anything for a poor man, he thinks that you are observing not his fortune, but himself. He strives to appear grateful not only to the man who deserves his gratitude, but also to those others from whom he expects something (for he needs the help of many). Nor, if he happens to fulfil some service himself, does he boast of it exaggeratedly, but even depreciates it. Again, you must see that if you defend a wealthy and fortunate man, the gratitude that you will receive will be limited to him alone, or perhaps to his children. But if the man is poor but upright and modest, all lowly but decent men (of which there is a great mass among the people) see that there are defences prepared for them.

(71) Therefore I think it better to invest kind services among good men than among men of fortune. In general, every effort should be made so that we can satisfy every type; if, however, the matter leads to conflict, then we must surely summon Themistocles as our authority. Someone consulted him over whether he should give his daughter to a good but poor man, or to a less upright but wealthy one. 'I myself', he replied, 'prefer a man that lacks money to money that lacks a man.' And yet, conduct has been corrupted and depraved by admiration for riches. What does someone else's great wealth concern any one of us? It may perhaps help him who has it. It does not always even do that; but grant that it does. He may, it is true, be better provided; but how will he be more honourable? If he is also a good man, his riches should not hinder you from assisting

---

[1] Though the old formal and hereditary relationship of *clientela* (by which poorer men and those of lower social status were protected by the more powerful in return for certain services) may have been breaking down in the late Republic, the fact that this is Cicero's only reference to clientship also reflects his lack of interest in relations with social inferiors (see Introduction, pp. xxiii–xxiv). Even here he refers only to the marginal case of relationships formally equal, however *de facto* unequal, where the euphemism for *cliens* was *amicus* (friend). The persistence of the attitude here described is demonstrated by Seneca in *De Beneficiis* 2.23.

him, provided only that they do not help you to. Let every decision of ours depend not on how wealthy a man is, but on what he is like.

The final rule in providing kind services and personal assistance is to fight neither against fairness, nor on behalf of injustice. For justice is the foundation of lasting commendation and repute. Without it nothing can be worthy of praise.

(72) I have now spoken about the sort of kind services that regard individuals. Next, I must discuss those that concern everyone, and those that concern the nation. Of these, some are of such a kind as to concern all citizens, and others as to affect only individuals (these are also more productive of gratitude). Every possible effort should be made in both areas: one should consider the interests of individuals just as fully, but in such a way that the matter benefits – or at least does not harm – the republic. The corn dole of Gaius Gracchus cost a great deal of money; therefore he began to drain the treasury dry. More modest was that of Marcus Octavius; his could be borne by the republic, and yet could provide the needs of the poorer classes.[1] It was therefore healthy for both the citizens and the republic.

(73) The men who administer public affairs must first of all see that everyone holds on to what is his, and that private men are never deprived of their goods by public acts. Philippus acted perniciously in his tribunate in proposing an agrarian law (though when it was rejected, he accepted that readily, and showed himself here extremely restrained). But in promoting it he said many things as a *popularis* including the wicked claim that there were not two thousand men in the citizenship who possessed anything.[2] That speech deserved to lose him his civic rights, pointing as it did to an equalization of goods. What greater plague could there be than that? For political communities and citizenships were constituted especially so that men

[1] In 123 BC G. Gracchus introduced a law allowing every male freeborn citizen each month to claim five measures of corn (less than a family's full needs) at a subsidised price of 6⅓ asses per measure. This, together with his establishment of state granaries, was designed to lessen the hardship caused by the fluctuation of prices with supply. At an unknown date Octavius modified the arrangement by raising the price or reducing the number of recipients or both. (See also II.58 with n. 1.) In C.'s day the dole was free.

[2] On *popularis*, see p. 34, n. 2. Q. Marcius Philippus, later an arch conservative, made this speech, probably to gain popularity, in 104 BC. Most of Italy did not yet have citizenship, but the population of Rome itself may have been c. 500,000.

could hold on to what was theirs. It may be true that nature first guided men to gather in groups; but it was in the hope of safeguarding their possessions that they sought protection in cities.[1]

(74) Our ancestors, because the treasury was depleted and there was continual warfare, often used to impose a property tax. But we must make an effort to avoid this, and must provide long in advance so that it does not happen.[2] And, if the necessity for such a burden does befall any nation (I prefer to say that than to speak forebodingly of 'our nation'; for I am not discussing ours alone, but every one), then every effort must be made so that all understand that if they want to be safe, they must comply with that necessity. Furthermore, all those who control public affairs ought to plan for there to be a plentiful supply of necessities. We need not discuss how these tend to be or ought to be acquired, for that is obvious enough.[3] The topic had merely to be mentioned.

(75) The chief thing when undertaking any public business or public duty is that even the smallest suspicion of avarice should be expelled. Gaius Pontius the Samnite said, 'Would that fortune had reserved me until the day when Rome had begun to accept bribes! Would that I had been born then! In that case I should not have suffered their rule any longer.' And indeed he would have needed to wait many generations; for only now has that evil assailed our republic.[4] I am happy enough, therefore, that Pontius lived then, if he was indeed so mighty. A hundred and ten years have not yet passed since the carrying of Lucius Piso's bill to punish extortion; previously there had been no such law. But there have been so many laws since (and

---

[1] See 1.158 with n. 1.

[2] The property tax (*tributum*) levied on citizens was abolished in 167 BC after the conquest of Macedonia allowed Rome and Italy to live off Rome's subjects (II.76). As there was no income tax, and even indirect taxes were bitterly resented, it was vital for victorious commanders to feel obliged to spend their booty on public works and the rich generally to give largesse.

[3] A hint as to how this is to be done is given at 85. Essentially the money would have to come from outside as in the case of Aratus of Sicyon (81). The Gracchi's wish to use the legacy of King Attalus of Pergamum to finance their land programme might seem similar, but C. could not approve the programme nor the challenge to senatorial power posed by their use of popular legislation to secure the legacy.

[4] The incident is from the bitter Samnite Wars of the fourth and early third century BC. C. appears to date the beginning of the evil to 149 BC (see p. 94, n. 1) less than 150 years after the capture of Pontius in 291 BC. That approximates to one traditional date for Roman moral decline, i.e. after the destruction of Carthage in 146, though some put it earlier.

each one harsher than the one before), so many defendants, so many convicted.[1] The great Italian War was stirred up because of fear of the lawcourts; and when the laws and lawcourts[2] were overturned, there was widespread pillaging and plundering of the allies. Consequently, we are strong only through the failings of others, and not through our own virtue.[3]

(76) Panaetius praises Africanus because he was uncorrupted by greed.[4] Why should he not praise him? But there were other greater things about him; and praise for such incorruptibility belonged not only to the man, but also to his age. When Paullus won possession of all the treasure of the Macedonians – a great quantity indeed! – he brought into the treasury so much money that the booty of a single general put an end to all property taxes. But he took nothing to his own home except the everlasting remembrance of his name.[5] Africanus, emulating his father, was none the wealthier for his overthrow of Carthage. And what of his colleague as censor, Lucius Mummius? Was he a penny richer when he had razed to the ground that richest of cities?[6] He preferred to adorn not his house, but Italy; though by that very adornment of Italy, his own house, it seems to me, was ornamented the more.

(77) No vice, therefore, is more foul than avarice (to bring my discussion back to the point from where I digressed), particularly

[1] 110 years from 44 BC is a rough calculation for 149 BC, the date of the Lex Calpurnia *de repetundis,* the first of a series of laws against the extortion of money from Rome's subjects and (probably) citizens by Roman officials. Originally conviction led only to restoration of the money but later financial and other penalties were added. The latest of these laws, that passed by Julius Caesar in 59, had over 100 clauses.

[2] The immediate cause of the war of 90–88 BC, through which Rome's Italian allies secured Roman citizenship, was the failure of the attempt by the tribune Livius Drusus to legislate in their favour. Opposition to him was partly provoked by his bill to end equestrian immunity from prosecution under the extortion law. Hence C.'s implausible view that the Italian War was caused by fear of the courts.

[3] See p. 74, n. 1. Mistreatment of Rome's subjects has forfeited their goodwill and destroyed Rome's moral fibre and strength: hence Rome would lose her empire were it not for the weakness of her subjects, and possibly of other rival empires.

[4] See I.90 and Introduction, p. xx.

[5] On property taxes, see II.74 with n. 2. By tradition a portion of a general's booty went to his soldiers, and another to the state treasury. He was expected to spend a substantial part of the rest on public beneficence.

[6] Whereas Aemilius Paullus in 167 BC and Mummius after his destruction of Corinth in 146 enriched Rome and Italy with their spoils, Paullus' natural son Scipio, in the same year, not only refused to enrich himself (Polybius XVIII.35.9–12), but restored the statues Carthage had taken in previous wars to the cities of Sicily.

among leading men and those who control public affairs. For to use public affairs for one's profit is not only dishonourable, but criminal and wicked too. Pythian Apollo pronounced that Sparta would not perish unless through avarice; the oracle seems to have been a prophecy not only for the Spartans, but for all wealthy peoples.[1] There is nothing by which those in charge of public affairs can more easily endear themselves to the goodwill of the masses than by incorruptible abstemiousness.

(78) Those who wish to present themselves as *populares*,[2] and for that reason attempt agrarian legislation so that landholders are driven from their dwellings, or who think that debtors ought to be excused from the money that they owe, are undermining the very foundations of the political community: in the first place, concord, which cannot exist when money is taken from some and bestowed upon others; and secondly, fairness, which utterly vanishes if everyone may not keep that which is his. For, as I have said above,[3] it is the proper function of a citizenship and a city to ensure for everyone a free and unworried guardianship of his possessions.

(79) Moreover, even when they ruin the community in this way, they do not actually achieve what they think they will achieve, that is gratitude. For the man whose property has been stolen will be hostile; but the one to whom it has been given pretends that he did not want to receive it; and he hides his joy most of all when his debts are cancelled, so that it is not obvious that he was insolvent. The man who has been treated unjustly, however, remembers it indeed: he parades his anguish before him. Even if those who have been given things dishonestly are more numerous than those who have been unjustly deprived, they are not for that reason the more powerful. For these things are judged not by number, but by weight. Again, how can it be fair that when a piece of land has been owned for many years, or even generations, a man who has none should take possession of it, while he that had it should lose it?

(80) Now it was on account of injustice of this kind that the Spartans

---

[1] Sparta, because of her 'mixed constitution', was often seen as a parallel to Rome (e.g. Polybius VI.10; 48–9), a thought that C. has in mind in II.26 and 80, as here.

[2] See p. 34, n. 2 and p. 70, n. 1. C. implies that their interest in the people's welfare is only a pose to cover selfish ambition.

[3] At II.73. In discussing debts C. will have Caesar's measures in mind (see p. 98, n. 3). In speaking of agrarian programmes he may allude to Antony's measure in June 44 to complete the settlement of Caesar's veterans.

expelled the ephor Lysander and put to death the king Agis (something that had never happened before among them). From then on such great dissensions ensued that tyrants rose up, the *optimates*[1] were exiled, and a political community that had been splendidly organized began to crumble. Nor did it fall alone: for it overturned the rest of Greece too by the contamination of its evils; it began among the Spartans and spread widely.[2] And what should I say of our own Gracchi, the sons of that excellent man Tiberius Gracchus, the grandsons of Africanus? Was it not agrarian strife that destroyed them?

(81) Aratus of Sicyon, on the other hand, is justly praised. When his city had been held by tyrants for fifty years, he set out from Argos to Sicyon, entered the town secretly, and took possession of it. He overwhelmed the tyrant Nicocles, taking him unawares, he restored six hundred exiles who had been the wealthiest men in the city, and he liberated the political community by his coming. Then, however, he turned his attention to the great problem of their property and its occupancy: on the one hand, he considered it most unfair that those whom he had restored, whose property others were occupying, should be deprived; and on the other, he thought it by no means fair to displace those who had been in occupancy for fifty years, because after so long a stretch of time much of it was held as a result of inheritance, much had been bought, and much had been given as a dowry, all without injustice. Therefore he judged that he ought neither to deprive the one group nor to fail to compensate those whose property it had been.

(82) Consequently, when he had decided that what was needed to settle the affair was money, he told them that he wanted to journey to Alexandria, and ordered that the matter be left untouched until his return. He went swiftly to his friend Ptolemy, who was then reigning as second in line after the foundation of Alexandria. Explaining to him that he wanted to liberate his country, and telling him his reasons, that excellent man found it easy to obtain from the wealthy king the assistance of a large sum of money. He brought this back to Sicyon, and then took into counsel with him fifteen leading men.

---

[1] See p. 34, n. 2 and p. 95, n. 1.

[2] After the efforts of Agis IV ended in 241 BC, and Cleomenes III's attempts at similar measures ended in his defeat and banishment in 222 BC, Sparta was ruled by a succession of tyrants, including Nabis, who was defeated by the Romans in 195. C. here suggests that the Spartan reformers by causing dissension in a city famous for the stability of its constitution, eventually brought all of Greece under Roman rule.

With them, he looked into the cases both of those who were holding other people's land, and of those who had lost their own. After valuing the occupancies, he succeeded in persuading some that they would rather accept money and give up their occupancy, others to think it more advantageous to be allocated so much than to recover their property. In this way he brought it about that peace was established, and they all left without a quarrel.

(83) O great man, worthy to have been born in our republic! For that is the appropriate way to deal with citizens; and not, as we have twice seen, to plant the spear in the forum and to submit a citizen's goods to the cry of the auctioneer.[1] The Greek, as a wise and out-standing man, thought that he should consult the interests of all; and it showed the wisdom and extreme reasonableness that befits a good citizen that he did not dissever the interests of the citizens, but held everyone together under a single standard of fairness.

'Let them live free in another's house.'[2] But why? So that when I have bought it, have built it, and am now looking after it and spending money on it, you can, against my will, enjoy what is mine? What else is that but to snatch what is theirs from some, and to give to others what belongs to another? (84) Again, what is the point of wiping slates clean,[3] unless it is that you can take my money in order to buy a farm, which you will have, while I no longer have my money? For that reason provision must be made to avoid any debt that may harm the political community. There are many methods of guarding against this; but if it does occur do not let the rich lose that which is theirs while the debtors profit at others' expense. For there is nothing that holds together a political community more powerfully than good faith; and that cannot exist unless the paying of debts is enforced.[4]

---

[1] Aratus, like the Spartan reformers and the Gracchi (80), was concerned with genuine but conflicting claims to the same land. C. now adduces the proscriptions of Sulla and the confiscations of Caesar (cf. 1.43 with n. 2; 11.27–9 with p. 73, n. 1) in which property passed to those who had no original claim to it.

[2] As 84 fin. makes clear, C. is thinking of Caesar's measure of 48 BC providing for a one year rent remission.

[3] The phrase translates *tabulae novae*, the standard expression for cancelling debts by erasing all record of them and a rallying cry of reformers in Greece and Rome.

[4] 'Good faith' here translates *fides*, not the technical *bona fides* of 111.59–61. In financial contexts *fides* becomes the equivalent of our 'credit' (see Notes on Translation) and to lose one's *fides* was a stain on one's reputation. The Romans were regarded by the Greek historian Polybius (VI.58; XV.4.10), as harsh towards those who did not keep their word or maintain a contract and the sanctions of the Roman law of debt, designed to uphold *fides* (Gellius *Attic Nights* XX.1.41 ff.), were severe.

Efforts to prevent repayment were never more vigorous than they were in my consulship.[1] Every type and rank of men ventured such things, by means of arms and military camps. But I so resisted them that all such evil was removed from the republic. Indebtedness was never greater; but it was never better nor more easily discharged. For once the hope of defrauding had been taken away, the necessity to settle followed immediately.[2] And indeed the man who was now the victor, but had been among the vanquished, actually achieved when now it made no made difference to him, the things that he had contemplated when it would have affected him. For he had so great a desire to do wrong that the very doing of wrong delighted him, even if there were no cause for it.[3]

(85) This sort of lavish distribution, then, when one takes from some in order to give to others, is one from which those who are to protect the republic will refrain. Above all, they will make every effort to enable each man to keep that which is his, through the fairness of the law and of the lawcourts; and to stop the weak from being oppressed because of their lowly state and the rich from being prevented through envy from maintaining or recovering what is theirs; and besides this, by whatever means they can, whether in war or at home, to increase the republic in power, in land and in revenues. Such are the deeds of men who are great; such deeds were achieved in our forefathers' day.[4] Men who pursue these kinds of duties

---

[1] The conspiracy led by Catiline broke out after C. defeated a move for debt relief early in 63 BC. Debt was probably a severe problem at the time because the prolonged war with Mithridates had prevented the revenues of the province of Asia from reaching Rome. His booty began to make a difference in 62 BC.

[2] Catiline's followers, eventually defeated in battle, included rich but indebted aristocrats, veterans of Sulla farming poor land, and supporters of Marius dispossessed or having a precarious title to their land. C. concentrates on the first, who could have settled debts by selling property.

[3] Caesar is first charged with being in Catiline's conspiracy, but, though his debts early in his career were notorious, this was a flimsy charge which C. had ignored in 63; then with having cancelled debts as Dictator when, owing largely to his booty from Gaul, he was no longer insolvent. In fact the debt measures of 49 and 48 were both conciliatory and necessary in a situation where money was scarce. Caesar arranged for debts to be paid (minus interest already paid) by ceding property at pre-war prices. He may also have introduced in 46–5 a law providing for bankruptcy without disgrace or total impoverishment.

[4] See II.74 with n. 3. C.'s economic rationale for Roman imperialism even in the past is very hard to reconcile with his view of just wars (I.35–8) or with his view of the empire before Sulla as a 'protectorate of the world' (II.26–7).

will win, along with the utmost benefit to the republic, both great gratitude and great glory for themselves.

(86) On the question of advice about things beneficial, Antipater of Tyre, the Stoic who recently died in Athens, charged Panaetius with having omitted two things, the care of health and the care of money.[1] In my view, that excellent philosopher omitted them because they were easy; for they are certainly beneficial. But health is preserved by a knowledge of one's own body, and by observing what things usually benefit or harm it; by limiting the sustenance and the comforts of one's life in order to maintain one's physical health; by refraining from pleasures; and finally through the art of those to whose field of knowledge such things belong.

(87) Personal wealth, however, ought to be pursued by means that are free from dishonourableness, but to be preserved, and also to be increased, by carefulness and thrift. Xenophon the Socratic covered those matters most conveniently in his book entitled *Oeconomicus* (a book which I translated from Greek into Latin when I was just about the age at which you are now).[2] But the whole question of seeking profit and of investing money (I wish that I could say the same for using it!) is more conveniently discussed by those excellent men who sit at the central gate of Janus[3] than by any philosopher of any school. We must, however, learn about these things; for they are relevant to that which is beneficial, which is the topic of discussion of this book.

(88) It is, however, often necessary also to compare things that are beneficial. (This fourth topic was neglected by Panaetius.) For both bodily advantages are often compared with external ones, and external with bodily, and those of the body compared among themselves, and external with external. Bodily advantages are compared with external in this sort of way: you may prefer to have health than to be rich; external with bodily like this: you may prefer to be rich rather than to have the greatest possible bodily strength. Bodily advan-

---

[1] Clearly, Panaetius' work was still being read and discussed by Stoic philosophers. Antipater may have familiarized the younger Cato and other Roman readers with the work.

[2] Young Cicero was 21, so the translation must have been made *c.* 85 BC. The rest of this paragraph is found in the manuscripts at the end of 89. Editors agree that it ought to be here.

[3] Money-lenders who set up their tables under the central archway of the three on the east side of the Roman forum.

tages are compared among themselves when good health is put before pleasure, or strength before swiftness. Externals are compared, on the other hand, when glory is preferred to riches, or urban income to rural. **(89)** The words of the Elder Cato belong to this class of comparison. Someone asked him what was the most profitable activity for a family estate.[1] He replied, 'To graze herds well.' 'And what next?' 'To graze them adequately.' 'And what third?' 'To graze them, though poorly.' 'And what fourth?' 'To plough.' Then, when the questioner asked, 'What about money-lending?', Cato's reply was 'What about killing someone?'[2] From this and many other examples it ought to be understood that comparisons of benefits are often made, and it is correct for us to add the fourth type of question about duties.

(90) Let us then proceed to that which remains.

---

[1] The Elder Cato had composed a treatise on agriculture including pasturage. See p.59, nn. 1–2.

[2] For the odium attached to money-lending at interest, see I.150. In fact, though gentlemen lent and borrowed among themselves without interest, men like Atticus, Pompey and Brutus also lent money to Rome's subjects at rates well above the legal rate of 12% a year.

Book III

(1) Publius Scipio, the one first surnamed Africanus, was accustomed to say that he was never less at leisure than when he was at leisure, nor less alone than when he was alone. That, at any rate, Marcus my son, is what Cato, who was his approximate contemporary, wrote of him.[1] The words are magnificent, and worthy of a great and wise man; they testify that even in his leisure hours he reflected upon business, and that when he was by himself he used to talk with himself, so that he was never unoccupied, and sometimes did not even need another's conversation. Thus the two things that induce idleness in others used to make him more lively, that is to say leisure and solitude. I wish it were possible for me truly to say the same thing; however, though I may not be able to attain his intellectual excellence in imitating him, I can certainly come very close in my willingness. For I pursue leisure because I am barred from public life and from legal business by the force of accursed arms, and for the same reason I have left the city. Wandering around the countryside now, I am frequently alone.[2] (2) My leisure, however, cannot be compared with that of Africanus, nor my solitude with his. For he used to take leisure for himself occasionally, as a rest from his splendid

---

[1] See p. 41, n. 2. In 1–4 C. plays with the opposition in Latin of the terms *negotium* (business) and *otium* (leisure) here used in three senses: intervals of leisure (as with Scipio); total absence of public activity (enforced on C.); political stability (the 'repose for the city' of 3).

[2] C. was travelling from one of his country villas to another for security, first between 7 April and the end of August 44 because his open approval of Caesar's assassination had angered supporters of the Dictator, and again between mid-October and 9 December after he attacked Antony in the *First Philippic* on 2 September.

services to the republic, and from time to time he took himself into solitude, away from human crowds and gatherings, as if into a haven. But my leisure was determined by scarcity of business, not by my eagerness to rest; for when the senate has been suppressed and the lawcourts destroyed, what is there worthy of me that I can do in the senate house or in the forum?[1]

(3) Thus I, who once lived surrounded by crowds and under the gaze of the citizens, now hide myself as much as possible, fleeing the sight of wicked men, with whom every place overflows; I am often alone. However, we hear from learned men that we should not only choose the least among evils, but also extract from those very things whatever good may be in them. Therefore I make use of my leisure – though it is not the leisure that a man deserves who once secured repose for the city – and I do not allow my solitude to grow idle, although necessity rather than willingness brought it upon me.

(4) Africanus, however, in my judgement earned the greater praise. For there exist, entrusted to writing by him, no memorials of his talent, no achievement of his leisure, no product of his solitude. Consequently, we should understand that it was because his mind was active in investigating the objects of his reflection that he was never either at leisure or alone.[2] But I do not have enough strength to withdraw myself from loneliness by silent reflection; I have directed all my devotion and concern towards this type of literary work. As a result, I have written more in the short time since the overthrow of the republic than in the many years while it stood.[3]

(5) Now, my dear Cicero, while the whole of philosophy is fertile and fruitful, and no part of it uncultivated and abandoned, still none of its topics is more productive and richer than that of duties; we derive from them advice for living with constancy and honourably. That is why, even though I trust that you are continually hearing and absorbing all this from our dear Cratippus, who is the leading philosopher of living memory, I still consider it appropriate that your

---

[1] On such exaggerated expressions, see Introduction, pp. xiii–xiv. Antony surrounded the Senate with armed guards to prevent unrest, and the law courts were not functioning normally since Brutus and Cassius, two of the praetors, were away.

[2] Mock diffidence. At 1.156, C. clearly favours intellectual activity that is communicated to others over solitary study. Nor was country villa life usually solitary.

[3] For the flood of theoretical works produced since 46 BC, see Principal Dates, pp. xxxii–xxxiii, but see also p. 2, n. 2.

ears should be filled with such words, ringing with them from all sides, and should not, if it be possible, hear anything else. (6) Anyone who is thinking about embarking upon an honourable life ought to do so, but perhaps no one more than you. For you carry this burden: many expect you to emulate my diligence, most my honours, and some, perhaps, even my renown. Besides, you have incurred a weighty responsibility from Athens and from Cratippus; since you went to them as if going to purchase arts of good quality, it would be most dishonourable to return empty-handed, thus disgracing the authority of both city and master. Therefore, strive with as much spirit and struggle with as much effort as you can (if learning is an effort, and not a pleasure) in order that you may succeed, and not, instead, allow yourself to seem to have let yourself down, even though we have provided everything for you.

But that is enough of that; for I have often written to you many words of encouragement.[1] Now let me return to the remaining part of my proposed division. (7) Now Panaetius indisputably discussed the question of duties with extreme precision, and I have followed him in particular, though applying some amendments. He proposed three headings under which men are accustomed to deliberate upon and discuss the matter of duties: the first, when they doubt whether the course in question is honourable or dishonourable: the second, whether it is beneficial or harmful; and the third, if that which has the appearance of honourableness conflicts with that which seems beneficial, how one should decide between them. He gave an exposition of two of these topics in his first three books; but though he wrote that he was going to discuss the third in its turn, he did not, however, fulfil his promise.[2] (8) I am all the more surprised by this because his pupil Posidonius wrote that Panaetius lived for thirty years after he had produced those books. I am surprised also that Posidonius touched only briefly upon the topic in some of his notebooks, particularly when he writes that no topic in the whole of philosophy is so essential.[3]

(9) I do not at all agree with those who say that this topic was

---

[1] See Introduction, pp. xvi–xvii and Biographical Note on Tullius Cicero. Young Cicero, in writing to the beloved ex-slave Tiro speaks of his father's expressions of 'good will' towards him.

[2] Cf. I.9. C. covered the two topics of Panaetius' three books in Books I and II.

[3] See Introduction, pp. xix–xxi.

not overlooked by Panaetius, but deliberately omitted, and that in any case it ought not to have been written because what is beneficial could never conflict with what is honourable.[1] One may entertain a doubt on the latter question, whether the class that is third in Panaetius' division should have been added or should have been omitted altogether. On the former question, however, one cannot doubt that Panaetius undertook to include it, but omitted it. For if someone has completed two parts of a work divided into three, then necessarily the third remains to be done. Besides, in his third and final book he promises that he will go on to speak of this part in its turn. (10) Posidonius comes forward as a reliable witness to the same point; for he also wrote, in a letter, that Publius Rutilius Rufus, who was a pupil of Panaetius', was accustomed to say that just as no painter could be found who would complete the part of 'Venus of Cos' that Apelles had only begun, and then left (for the beauty of the face dispelled any hope of representing the rest of the body) so no one had attempted the part that Panaetius had overlooked, and not finished, because of the excellence of the part that he had finished.

(11) One can, therefore, have no doubt about Panaetius' decision. However, we can perhaps debate whether or not he was right to add this third class of questions about duty. For whether the honourable is the only good (as is Stoics' view) or whether what is honourable is the highest good (just as it seems to your Peripatetics) so that if everything on the other side were accumulated, it would hardly amount to the smallest weight[2] – in either case it cannot be doubted that what is beneficial can never compete with what is honourable. Consequently, we are told that Socrates used to curse those who first fancied that they could sever things that were by nature combined. The Stoics have so agreed with him that they hold that everything that is honourable is beneficial, and nothing beneficial that is not honourable.

(12) If, therefore, Panaetius were the kind of man to say that virtue should be cultivated on the grounds that it produces what is beneficial (as they do who measure the desirability of things by pleasure or

---

[1] For the view of the Stoics, and in particular Panaetius, on the relation between the honourable and the beneficial, see Summary, pp. xxxv–xxxvi.

[2] See Summary, pp. xxxvi–xxxvii.

absence of pain)[1] it would be possible for him to say that what is beneficial sometimes conflicts with honourableness. However, he is the kind of man who deems that the only good is that which is honourable – and moreover that life can be made no better by the presence of, nor any worse by the absence of, such things as conflict with it in so far as they appear to be beneficial. It seems, then, that he ought not to have introduced the sort of deliberation where that which may appear useful is compared with that which is honourable. (13) Indeed, when the Stoics say that the greatest good is to live agreeably with nature, this means, in my view, the following: always to concur with virtue; and as for other things that are in accordance with nature, to choose them if they do not conflict with virtue.[2] Since this is so, some think that it was not right to introduce this comparison, and that no advice at all should have been given about this category.

And what is more, the honourableness that is properly and truly so called is found in wise men only, and can never be severed from virtue. In those whose wisdom is not complete, this honourableness, complete as it is, cannot exist at all; however, semblances of the honourable can exist. (14) The duties that I discuss in these books are, then, those that the Stoics call 'middle'. They are shared, and widely accessible. Many achieve them by the goodness of their intellectual talent, and by their progress in learning. But the duty that the same men call 'right' is complete and unconditional and, as they say, 'fulfils all the numbers'; and it cannot belong to anyone except the wise man.[3] (15) However, when some action is performed where middle duties are in evidence, it is seen as being abundantly 'complete'. That is because ordinary people cannot really understand how it falls short of being complete. In so far as they do understand it, they think that nothing has been overlooked. The same thing tends to happen with poems, pictures and many other things, by which

---

[1] C. alludes to Aristippus and Epicurus for whom the end was pleasure, and to Hieronymus of Rhodes for whom it was lack of pain. (cf. III.116).

[2] This interpretation of following nature is not compatible with the original Stoic view that to live virtuously was to choose the things in accordance with nature. On that view, virtue and the things in accordance with nature could not be independently defined. However, developments in the Stoic view of virtue and of benefit made possible, for C. and presumably for Panaetius before him, the interpretation of 'following nature' given here (see Summary, p. xxxvi).

[3] Cf. I.8 with n. I.

inexperienced people are delighted, praising them when they ought not to be praised; the reason, as I believe, is that there is some worth in them that attracts the ignorant, but they are unable to judge what faults each may have. Therefore, when they are taught by experienced people, they readily abandon their view.

Such duties, then, which I am treating in these books, are said by them to be honourable in a second-rate way, so to speak; and they are not appropriate to wise men only, but shared with the whole human race. (16) Consequently, everyone who has the disposition for virtue is moved by them. Again, when the two Decii, or the two Scipiones, are mentioned as brave men, or when Fabricius or Aristides[1] is called just, we are not seeking an example of courage in the former, nor of justice in the latter, as if in a wise man; for none of them is wise in the way that we want to understand wise.[2] Not even Marcus Cato and Gaius Laelius were in fact wise, although they were called and considered wise; and nor were the famous seven.[3] Rather, because of their repeated practice of middle duties, they exhibited a kind of likeness to and appearance of wise men.

(17) It is therefore impious to compare that which is truly honourable with any conflicting benefit. Nor, on the other hand, must one ever compare profit with what we call honourable in the common sense, which men cultivate when they want to be thought good. For we ourselves must guard and preserve the honourableness that is accessible to our understanding, just as much as wise men must that other, which is appropriately and truly called honourable; for otherwise any progress that may have been made towards virtue cannot be maintained.[4]

But that is enough about those who have a reputation for goodness because of their observation of duties. (18) As for those who measure everything by profits and advantages and do not want these to be outweighed by honourableness, they are accustomed to compare in their deliberations what is honourable with what they think to be

---

[1] 'Or Aristides' is bracketed as an interpolation by some editors, since C. seems to be giving only Roman examples.

[2] Cf. 1.46, II.35.

[3] The seven wise men of Greece: Bias, Chilo, Cleobulus, Pittacus, Periander, Solon and Thales.

[4] Despite their rigour in not allowing degrees of virtue or vice nor any middle ground between them, the Stoics believed in moral progress. Performing middle duties could help one ultimately to acquire that virtuous disposition which would render them perfect.

beneficial.[1] Good men are not accustomed to do that. Therefore I am of the opinion that when Panaetius said that men were accustomed to hesitate about such a comparison, he meant only what he said: 'were accustomed to' and not also 'were right to'. For it is extremely dishonourable not only to value that which seems beneficial at more than that which is honourable, but even to compare the two with one another and hesitate between them.

What is it, then, that sometimes tends to raise a doubt and seems to need consideration? Such occasions arise, I believe, whenever there is doubt over the nature of the action that one is considering. **(19)** For often the occasion arises when something that is generally and customarily considered to be dishonourable is found not to be so. Let me suggest as an example something that can be more widely applied: what greater crime can there be than to kill not merely another man, but even a close friend? Surely then, anyone who kills a tyrant, although he is a close friend, has committed himself to crime? But it does not seem so to the Roman people, which deems that deed the fairest of all splendid deeds. Did the beneficial, therefore, overcome honourableness? No indeed; for honourableness followed upon what benefited.[2]

Therefore in order that we may pronounce judgement without error, if ever that which we call beneficial seems to conflict with that which we understand to be honourable, a rule of procedure must be established.[3] If we follow this when comparing courses, we shall never fall away from duty. **(20)** Moreover, this rule of procedure will be highly consistent with the reasoning and teaching of the Stoics. I am following their reasoning in these books for this reason: both the Old Academics and your Peripatetics (who were once the same as the Academics) prefer that which is honourable to that which seems beneficial; these things are discussed, however, more nobly by those for whom if anything is honourable, the same thing seems beneficial,

---

[1] These men appear again at III.26 and 37.

[2] Tyrannicide is C.'s favourite example of a duty in particular circumstances (cf. III.32 and p. 62, n. 1). The allusion is clearly to Caesar's murder, for many of those involved had been 'close friends'. C. exaggerates the unanimity of the Roman people.

[3] The term *formula* ('rule of procedure') is taken from Roman law. In civil cases the praetor (or other magistrate), after hearing the parties to a suit, set out the question of fact for the judge to establish and the legal decision that would follow depending on the facts. Similarly, the *formula* tells us what facts need to be determined before we can make a correct decision about how to act where apparent benefit is involved.

and nothing seems beneficial that is not honourable, than by those for whom there is something honourable but not beneficial, and something beneficial but not honourable.[1] In any case, our Academy grants us great freedom, so that we may be justified in defending whatever seems most persuasive.[2] But I return to my rule of procedure.

(21) Now then: for one man to take something from another and to increase his own advantage at the cost of another's disadvantage is more contrary to nature than death, than poverty, than pain and than anything else that may happen to his body or external possessions. In the first place, it destroys the common life and fellowship of men: for if we are so minded that any one man will use theft or violence against another for his own profit, then necessarily the thing that is most of all in accordance with nature will be shattered, that is the fellowship of the human race. (22) Suppose that each limb were disposed to think that it would be able to grow strong by taking over to itself its neighbour's strength; necessarily the whole body would weaken and die. In the same way, if each one of us were to snatch for himself the advantages other men have and take what he could for his own profit, then necessarily fellowship and community among men would be overthrown. It is permitted to us – nature does not oppose it – that each man should prefer to secure for himself rather than for another anything connected with the necessities of life. However, nature does not allow us to increase our means, our resources and our wealth by despoiling others.

(23) The same thing is established not only in nature, that is in the law of nations, but also in the laws of individual peoples, through which the political community of individual cities is maintained:[3] one is not allowed to harm another for the sake of one's own advantage. For the laws have as their object and desire that the bonds between citizens should be unharmed. If anyone tears them apart, they restrain

---

[1] See Summary, pp. xxxvi–xxxvii. The comparison of the Stoic and Peripatetic views is given more accurately at III.35 *fin.*, for whether the honourable is the only (Stoic) or the highest (Peripatetic) good, it will always be beneficial.

[2] Cf. p. 4, n. 2.

[3] The 'law of nations' is natural law (also divine law) which applies to all men and is the standard set for human laws by the providential reason that rules the world. In III.68–70 C. contrasts it with the civil law. (The distinction is different from that made by Roman lawyers in *Digest* I.I.3–4, where the 'law of nations' is not what is ordained by nature, but the actual common practice of men.)

him by death, by exile, by chains or by fine. Nature's reason itself, which is divine and human law, achieves this object to a far greater extent. Whoever is willing to obey it (everyone will obey it who wants to live in accordance with nature) will never act so as to seek what is another's, nor to appropriate for himself something that he has taken from someone else. (24) For loftiness and greatness of spirit, and, indeed, friendliness, justice and liberality, are far more in accordance with nature than pleasure, than life, than riches. Indeed to disdain these, when comparing them with the common benefit, and value them as nothing, is the mark of a great and lofty spirit. On the other hand, for anyone to take from someone else for the sake of his own advantage is more contrary to nature than death or pain or anything else of the type.

(25) The great Hercules undertook extreme toils and troubles in order to protect and assist all races of men. His reputation among mankind, recalling his kind services, has placed him in the council of the heavenly ones. It is more in accordance with nature to imitate him in this, if it can be done, than to live in solitude, even though you might be not only free from trouble, but also enjoying very great pleasures, endowed with plentiful resources and excelling too in beauty and strength. And so, the men with the best and most brilliant talent far prefer that life to this. Consequently, a man who is obedient to nature cannot harm another man.

(26) Again, if a man acts violently against someone else in order to secure some advantage himself, he either considers that he is doing nothing contrary to nature, or else he judges that death, poverty, pain, and the loss of children, relations or friends are more to be avoided than the doing of an injustice to someone. If he thinks that acting violently against other men involves doing nothing contrary to nature – then how can you argue with him? For he takes all the 'human' out of a human. If, on the other hand, he thinks that such action should be avoided, but that death, poverty and pain are far worse, his error is that he counts a failing of body or fortune as more serious than any failing of spirit.

Therefore all men should have this one object, that the benefit of each individual and the benefit of all together should be the same. If anyone arrogates it to himself, all human intercourse will be dissolved. (27) Furthermore, if nature prescribes that one man should want to consider the interests of another, whoever he may be, for the very reason that he is a man, it is necessary, according to the same nature, that what is beneficial to all is something common. If that is so, then we are all constrained by one and the same law of nature; and if that also is true, then we are certainly forbidden by the law of nature from acting violently against another person. The first claim is indeed true; therefore the last is true.

(28) Now surely it is absurd to say, as some do, that they would not deprive a parent or brother of anything for their own advantage, but that there is another rationale for the rest of the citizens. Such men decree that no justice and no fellowship exist among citizens for the sake of common benefit, an opinion that breaks up all fellowship in the city. There are others again who say that account should be taken of other citizens, but deny it in the case of foreigners; such men tear apart the common fellowship of the human race. When that is removed then kindness, liberality, goodness and justice are utterly destroyed. Those who destroy them must be judged irreverent even in respect of the immortal gods; for the fellowship among mankind that they overturn was established by the gods; and the tightest bond of that fellowship is that it be thought more contrary to nature for one man to deprive another for the sake of his own advantage than to endure every disadvantage,[1] whether it affects externals or the body or even the spirit itself – so long as it is free from injustice. For that single virtue is the mistress and queen of virtues.[2]

(29) But perhaps someone might object: would not a wise man, if he is dying of hunger, steal food from another man, if he could benefit no one? Not at all; for my life is not more beneficial to me than to be so disposed in spirit that I would not do violence to anyone for my own advantage. What if a good man were to be able to rob of his clothes Phalaris, a cruel and monstrous tyrant, to prevent himself from dying of cold? Might he not do it?

Such questions are very easy to decide.[3] (30) For if it is for your own benefit that you deprive even someone who is of no benefit whatsoever, you will have acted inhumanly and against the law of nature. If, however, you are the kind of person who, if you were to remain alive, could bring great benefit to the political community and to

---

[1] Cf. III.42 with n. I.

[2] The text is corrupt here: the manuscripts read 'so long as it is free from justice'; this is the simplest emendation, which gives an intelligible, if not strictly logical, sentence.

[3] C. now shows how to apply the 'rule of procedure' to decide cases.

human fellowship, and if *for that reason* you deprive someone else of something, that is not a matter for rebuke. In situations that are not of that kind, however, each man should endure disadvantage to himself rather than diminish the advantages that someone else enjoys. Illness, want or anything else of that sort are not, then, more contrary to nature than to take or to covet that which belongs to another. The neglect of the common benefit is, on the other hand, contrary to nature; for it is unjust. (31) Therefore the law of nature itself, which preserves and maintains that which is beneficial to men, will undoubtedly decree that the necessities of life should be transferred from an inactive and useless person to someone who is wise, good and brave, who, if he were to die, would greatly detract from the common benefit; he must, however, do this in such a way that he does not, out of self-esteem or self-love, find a pretext for injustice. In this way he will always discharge his duty by having consideration for what is beneficial to mankind and to human fellowship, which I so frequently mention.

(32) Now it is very easy to make a judgement in the case of Phalaris. For there can be no fellowship between us and tyrants – on the contrary there is a complete estrangement – and it is not contrary to nature to rob a man, if you are able, to whom it is honourable to kill. Indeed, the whole pestilential and irreverent class ought to be expelled from the community of mankind. For just as some limbs are amputated, if they begin to lose their blood and their life, as it were, and are harming the other parts of the body, similarly if the wildness and monstrousness of a beast appears in human form, it must be removed from the common humanity, so to speak, of the body. Of this sort are all those questions in which the issue is duty in particular circumstances.[1]

(33) I believe therefore that Panaetius would have pursued questions of this kind had not some mischance or other preoccupation spoiled his plan.[2] There is in the preceding books plenty of advice concerning these very problems, which may enable one to see what should be avoided because it is dishonourable, and what need not

---

[1] C. now explains what he said at III.19, that it is not dishonourable to kill in the case of a tyrant. Note, as in III.22, the metaphor of the body applied to society.

[2] The element of repetition in what follows results from C.'s first sketching in 20–32 what Panaetius might have said (perhaps with some help from Posidonius, see p. 62, n. 1) in a Stoic vein and then going on to his own development of the subject which is supposed to be compatible with Peripatetic views as well.

be avoided because it is not at all dishonourable.¹ But now we are placing the capstone, as it were, on work that is unfinished and yet almost complete. Therefore, just as geometers do not usually teach everything, but demand that certain things are granted them so that they may more easily explain what they want, in the same way, I demand that you, my dear Cicero, grant me, if you are able, that nothing except the honourable ought to be sought on its own account. If, because of Cratippus, you may not do that, you will at least concede that the honourable is the thing that is most greatly to be sought on its own account. Either of these is enough for me; sometimes the one and sometimes the other seems more persuasive; and no other possibility seems persuasive.

(34) In the first place, Panaetius must be defended on this count: it was not things actually beneficial that he said could sometimes conflict with honourable ones (for that was impious for him) but rather things that seemed beneficial. For he often witnesses that nothing is beneficial that is not also honourable, and nothing honourable that is not also beneficial; indeed, he claims that no greater plague has assailed human life than the fancy of those who have separated the two. Therefore he introduced the conflict that appears to, but does not in fact, exist, not in order that we should sometimes prefer beneficial things to honourable, but rather so that we may adjudicate these things without error if the circumstances should arise. The part that he left, therefore, I shall complete without any auxiliaries, but, as the saying goes, fighting my own battle. For there is no treatment of this question since Panaetius, at any rate such that meets with my approval, in the writings that have come into my hands.²

(35) When one encounters something that has the appearance of being beneficial, one is necessarily affected. But it may be that when you apply your mind to it, you see something dishonourable attached to the thing that has presented the appearance of benefit; if so, it is not so much that benefit should be abandoned, but rather that you must realize this: where dishonourableness exists there can be nothing beneficial. For if nothing is so contrary to nature as dis-

¹ The formulation here of the *regula* or 'rule' (as it is called in III.81), i.e. whatever is honourable is beneficial and whatever is *dishonourable* is not beneficial, is compatible with Stoic and Peripatetic principles. At the end of 33, C. prefers, and in 34 he ascribes to Panaetius, the Stoic form that allows for nothing beneficial between the honourable and the dishonourable, a formulation that recurs later, e.g. 78 *fin.*, 85 *fin.*, 110.
² Cf. III.89–92 and see Introduction, pp. xix–xxi.

honourableness (nature desires what is right and appropriate and constant, and rejects their opposites) and if nothing is so much according to nature as the beneficial, then certainly benefit and dishonourableness cannot coexist in the same thing. Similarly, if we are born for honourableness and that should be sought alone (as Zeno held) or at least should be thought entirely to outweigh everything else (as was Aristotle's view) it is necessary that what is honourable is either the only good or the highest; and what is good is certainly beneficial, and so whatever is honourable is beneficial.

(36) This, then, is the error made by men who are not upright: as soon as they seize upon something that seems beneficial, immediately they separate it from the honourable. This is the origin of daggers, poisons, and forged wills, of thefts and embezzlements of public funds and the pillaging and plundering of allies and of citizens; from this arises greed for excessive wealth, for unacceptable power, and finally, even in free cities, for monarchy. One cannot conceive of anything more foul and disgusting than such greed. In their mistaken judgements they see the profits in things, but they do not see the penalty; I do not mean the penalty of the laws – for they often ride roughshod over that – but that of dishonourableness itself, which is bitter indeed. (37) Therefore let us drive from our midst (for they are all wicked and irreverent) questioners of this sort, who deliberate over whether to pursue that which they see to be honourable or whether knowingly to contaminate themselves with wickedness. For there is wickedness in the hesitation itself, even if they do not go so far as the deed. One should not begin to deliberate questions, if the very deliberation of them is dishonourable.

Moreover, whenever we deliberate we must banish any hope or idea of hiding or concealing our actions. For if we have progressed but a little in philosophy, we ought to be sufficiently persuaded that nothing should be done greedily, unjustly, licentiously or without restraint, even if we could conceal it from all gods and men. (38) For this reason the well known story of Gyges was introduced by Plato:[1] one day, as a result of heavy rains, the earth gaped open, and Gyges went down into the chasm. There he noticed, so the story goes, a bronze horse with a door in its flank. He opened it, and inside he saw the body of a dead man of unusual size, with a golden

---

[1] *Republic* II.359 (for Gyges, see Biographical Notes).

ring on his finger. Gyges stole this and put it on himself; and then – he was one of the king's shepherds – he returned to the company of the shepherds. There he discovered that when he turned the stone in the ring towards his palm, no one could see him, while he himself could see everything. When he turned the ring back to its normal position, he became visible again. And so, using the opportunity given by the ring, he committed adultery with the queen, and with her complicity he murdered his king and master, and removed those whom he thought stood in his way; nor could anyone see him at his crimes. In this way, by courtesy of the ring, he rose swiftly to be king of Lydia.

If a wise man, then, were to have the same ring, he would think himself no more free to do no wrong than if he did not have it. For a good man pursues aims that are not secret, but honourable. (39) On this topic some philosophers[1] who are not at all bad men, but not clear-thinking enough, say that Plato has produced a fictional and fabricated tale, as if indeed he were justifying it either as actually having happened or even as possible. But the force of the ring, and of the example, is as follows: if no one were going to know, if no one were going even to suspect, when you did something for the sake of riches, power, despotism or lust, if it would be always unknown by gods and by men alike – then would you do it? They deny that that could have been possible, although it could indeed happen.[2] But I am in fact asking what they would do if the thing that they deny is possible were possible. They persevere in a boorish manner, they deny that it is possible and insist upon that, failing to see the force of this word [viz. 'if']. For when we ask what they would do if they could conceal it, we are not asking whether they could in fact conceal it. Rather, we are turning the screw, so to speak, so that if they reply that, given the proposed impunity, they would do the expedient thing,

---

[1] The Epicureans advocated virtue only as a means to pleasure and the avoidance of pain (118); just conduct was necessary because the fear of being discovered would always outweigh any pleasure derived from injustice. Epicurus' pupil Colotes attacked Plato for using myths in philosophical argument; C. here shows impatience with a similar Epicurean reluctance to consider a hypothetical case.

[2] Holden, among other editors, emends 'although it could indeed happen' to 'Of course it could not happen' (reading *nequaquam* for *quamquam*), to avoid attributing to C. an explicit rejection of divine providence. But C.'s own attitude is not so unequivocal. Moreover, as an Academic, he may simply be assuming an Epicurean premise (the rejection of providence) in refuting an Epicurean proposition.

they admit that they are iniquitous; if they deny it, they concede that everything dishonourable should on its own account be avoided.

But now let me return to my subject. (40) Many cases arise in which an appearance of benefit may trouble the spirit, that is, when one might deliberate not whether to abandon honourableness because the benefit is great (for that is certainly wicked); but rather whether it may be possible to do that which seems beneficial in a way that is not dishonourable. Brutus deposed his colleague Collatinus from his command; it could seem that he acted unjustly, for Collatinus had been Brutus' ally and assistant in his counsels when he expelled the kings. The leading men, however, had adopted the policy of removing Superbus' relations, the name of the Tarquins, and the memory of the monarchy. The thing that was beneficial, namely to consider the interests of the country, was for that reason honourable, and thus ought to have been agreeable even to Collatinus himself. Therefore benefit took its strength from honourableness, without which it could not even have been beneficial.[1]

(41) It was not so, however, in the case of the king who founded the city. For the appearance of benefit drove his spirit; and when it seemed more beneficial to him to rule alone than with someone else, he killed his brother. He abandoned both familial obligation and humanity in order to secure something that seemed beneficial, but was not; and to present the appearance of being honourable, he put forward the pretext of the wall, which was neither persuasive nor indeed serviceable. He did wrong, then – and I speak with all the respect due to him as Quirinus or as Romulus.[2] (42) However, we are not to neglect benefits to ourselves and surrender them to others when we ourselves need them. Rather, each should attend to what benefits him himself, so far as may be done without injustice to another. Among Chrysippus' many neat remarks was the following:

> When a man runs in the stadium he ought to struggle
> and strive with all his might to be victorious, but he
> ought not to trip his fellow-competitor or to push him
> over.

---

[1] C. here goes beyond giving first priority to one's obligation to one's country (1.57) and makes serving its interests honourable by definition. But note they must be the *true* interests of the country (cf. 1.159; III.90) and the country itself cannot honourably pursue its interests in contravention of justice (III.46–9, 86–8 and p. 134, n. 2).

[2] C. condemns him as a man (Romulus) or a god (Quirinus).

Similarly in life: it is not unfair for anyone to seek whatever may be useful to him, but it is not just to steal from another.[1]

(43) Another area where duties are greatly confused is friendships. Here it is contrary to duty either not to grant what you rightly may or to grant what is unfair. There is, however, some brief and easy advice available for all this sort of case: such things as appear beneficial – honours, riches, pleasures and things of that kind – should never be preferred to friendship. However, the good man will never, for the sake of a friend, act contrary to the republic, to a sworn oath, or to good faith. He will not do so even if he is a judge over his friends: for he lays aside the role of a friend when he assumes that of a judge. He will grant to friendship no more than that he would prefer his friend's case to be true, and that he would accommodate him over the time for pleading the suit, insofar as the laws allow. (44) Indeed, when he has to pronounce the verdict under oath, he should remember that he is calling as his witness a god, which is to say, as I judge it, his own mind; for that is the most divine thing that the god himself gives to man.[2] It is, therefore, a splendid custom that we have received from our forefathers, if only we would maintain it, of making requests of the judge 'provided that he can do the thing without breaking faith'.[3] A request of this form is appropriate to the type of concessions that, as I said just now, might honourably be made by a judge to a friend. For the kind of friendships in which everything that friends wish must be done should not be thought friendships at all, but rather conspiracies.

(45) I am speaking of course about the common[4] sort of friendships, for no such thing would happen among wise and perfect men. There is a story that reveals the spirit of the friendship between the Pythagoreans Damon and Phintias. When the tyrant Dionysius decreed that one of them should die on a certain day and the one whom he had condemned to death begged a few days in order to entrust his family to the care of others, the other stood as bail for his safe return; if his friend had not come back, he himself would

[1] Chrysippus is said to support the 'rule of procedure' (19–21), and we see the limits of our obligation to our fellow men (I.52 with n. 2 and III.28).
[2] C. interprets the oath of conventional religion in accordance with the Stoic view that divine Reason, immanent in the universe, is present in human beings as reason.
[3] The traditional form of words with which the parties to a civil action, in making requests to the judge, respect his oath to uphold the laws.
[4] The Latin word here *communis* is that translated as 'shared' in III.14–15.

have had to die. When the friend returned on the appointed day, the tyrant marvelled at his faithfulness and begged that they enrol him as a third partner in their friendship. (46) In friendships, then, when that which seems beneficial is compared with that which is honourable, let the appearance of benefit lie low, and let honourableness prevail. On the other hand, when something that is not honourable is demanded within a friendship, let pious faithfulness be preferred to friendship. In that way the selection of duty for which we are searching will be achieved.

In public affairs wrong is very often done because of the appearance of benefit. An example is our own destruction of Corinth.[1] The Athenians were even harsher; for they decreed that the Aeginetans, who had a powerful fleet, should have their thumbs cut off. It seemed to be beneficial, for Aegina was a threat to Piraeus because it was so near.[2] But nothing cruel is in fact beneficial; for cruelty is extremely hostile to the nature of man, which we ought to follow. (47) They also act badly who prevent foreigners from enjoying their city and banish them; Pennus did this in our fathers' time, and Papius recently. It is right not to allow one who is not a citizen to act as a citizen: those wisest of consuls Crassus and Scaevola carried that law. However, to prevent foreigners from enjoying the city is surely inhuman.[3]

Those cases are splendid in which the appearance of public benefit has been despised out of regard for honourableness. Our republic is full of such examples; on frequent other occasions, and especially during the second Punic war when the news of the disaster of Cannae was received. Then Rome contained men of greater spirit than ever in times of success: no evidence of fear, no mention of peace.[4] The force of the honourable is so great that it eclipses the appearance of benefit. (48) The Athenians, since they could not, however they tried, withstand the Persian onslaught, decided to abandon the city, leaving their wives and children at Troezen, and to put to sea and defend with their fleet the freedom of the Greeks. When a certain

---

[1] Cf. 1.35 and n. 1.

[2] Aegina, 'the eyesore of the Piraeus', is a large island off the coast of Attica opposite the port of Athens. The Aeginetans were expelled from the island in 431 BC, but this story does not appear in the older more reliable sources.

[3] For these measures of 126, 65 and 95 BC, see Biographical Notes under their authors.

[4] The Senate congratulated the surviving consul of 216 BC, C. Terentius Varro, for not despairing of the Republic.

Cyrsilus tried to persuade them to remain in the city and receive Xerxes, they stoned him to death.[1] Yet he appeared to be pursuing a benefit; but there was none, as it was in conflict with the honourable.

(49) After the victory in the war with the Persians, Themistocles announced in the assembly that he had a plan which would preserve the nation, but it was necessary that it should not be common knowledge. He asked that the people should give him someone with whom he could share it. Aristides was chosen. Themistocles told him that the Spartan fleet, which had been drawn ashore at Gytheum, could secretly be set on fire; if that were done, the Spartans' power would inevitably be crushed. When Aristides heard this, he went into the assembly amid great expectation. He said that the counsel offered by Themistocles was extremely beneficial, but not at all honourable. The Athenians considered that something that was not honourable was not even beneficial, and on Aristides' authority they rejected the plan completely, although they had not even heard it. They were better than us; for we let pirates go scot-free, while our allies pay tribute.[2] Let this, then, remain fixed: if something is dishonourable, it is never beneficial, not even when you acquire something that you think beneficial. For the very act of thinking something dishonourable to be beneficial is a disastrous one.

(50) Cases often do arise, however, as I have said already,[3] where benefit seems to conflict with honourableness. Then one must examine whether it clearly conflicts, or whether it could be combined with what is honourable. The following are questions of this type. For example, suppose that a good man had brought a large quantity of corn from Alexandria to Rhodes at a time when corn was extremely expensive among the Rhodians because of shortage and famine. If he also knew that several more merchants had set sail from Alexandria, and had seen their boats *en route* laden with corn and heading for Rhodes, would he tell the Rhodians? Or would he keep silent and sell his own produce at as high a price as possible? We are imagining

---

[1] Themistocles' strategy of evacuation led to the Greek victory at Salamis in 480 BC. An inscription from Troezen purports to record the actual arrangements made.

[2] Cf. Plutarch *Themistocles* 20. The Athenians refused to harm their ally in the Persian War in order to secure their own ascendancy; the Romans imposed taxes on their allies unjustly (explained in 87) while allowing Pompey to settle defeated pirates in Cilicia free of taxes.

[3] At III.40.

that he is a wise and good man;[1] our question is about the deliberations and considerations of a man who would not conceal the facts from the Rhodians if he judged it dishonourable, but is uncertain as to whether it is dishonourable.

(51) In cases of this type, Diogenes of Babylon, a great and respected Stoic, tended to have one view, his pupil Antipater, an extremely intelligent man, another. Antipater thought that everything should be disclosed, so that there was nothing at all that the seller knew and the buyer did not know. To Diogenes it seemed that the seller ought to mention such faults as the civil law requires, and to do everything else without trickery; but since he is selling, he ought to want to sell at the best price: 'I have transported this here, I have offered it for sale, and I sell it for no more than others do, perhaps even for less, when the supply is more plentiful. Who is treated unjustly?'

(52) On the other side, Antipater's argument is put forward: 'What are you saying? You ought to be considering the interests of men and serving human fellowship; you were born under a law, and you have principles of nature which you ought to obey and to follow, to the effect that your benefit is the common benefit, and conversely, the common benefit is yours. Will you conceal from men the advantages and resources that are available to them?'

Diogenes will perhaps reply: 'To conceal is one thing, to keep silent another. I am not at the present moment concealing from you the nature of the gods, or the end of good things,[2] if I am not telling you of it; yet to learn that would benefit you far more than to learn the cheap price of wheat. But it is not necessary for me to tell you everything that is beneficial for you to hear.'

(53) 'But no!' he will answer, 'It is necessary, if indeed you remember that men are bound together in fellowship by nature.'

'I remember,' the other will argue, 'But is that fellowship of a kind that nothing belongs to any one person? If that is so, then nothing can be sold at all, but must be given.'[3]

You will see that in the whole of this debate the following is never

---

[1] Cf. III.17 where the sage and the good man are contrasted; for the 'vir bonus' of common morality and of Roman law, see p. 9, n. 1.

[2] That is, the nature of the greatest good. See p. 3, n. 4.

[3] For the distinction between common property and private, see I.21, I.51, II.73 ff., III.42. The problem is how far commercial transactions protecting one's own interests are in practice compatible with not profiting at another's expense (see p. 124, n. 1).

said: 'Although this is dishonourable, however, I will do it, for it is expedient', but rather, 'It is expedient in such a way that it is not dishonourable.' On the other side again: 'It should not be done for the very reason that it is dishonourable.'

(54) Suppose that a good man is selling his house because of certain faults that he knows and that others do not know, say, that it is unsanitary but thought to be salubrious, or that it is not generally known that vermin can be found in all the bedrooms, or that it is structurally unsound and crumbling, but no one except the owner knows this. My question is this: if the seller does not tell the buyers these things, but sells the house at a higher price than that at which he thought he would sell it, will he not have acted unjustly or dishonestly?'

'He will indeed,' Antipater claims. (55) 'Give me an instance of "failing to show the path to someone who is lost" (something which is prohibited in Athens on pain of a public curse)[1] if it is not this: allowing a buyer to rush into a deal and succumb through his error to being thoroughly deceived. Indeed it is more than failing to show the path; rather it is knowingly to lead someone into error.'

And Diogenes again: 'If someone has not even encouraged you to buy, surely he hasn't forced you? He advertised something that he didn't want, and you bought something you did want. If those who advertise a villa as "good and well built" are not thought to have deceived you, even though it is neither good nor methodically built, then it's much less the case for those who haven't praised their house. Where it is up to the buyer to judge, how can there be deceit on the part of the seller? Indeed, if one need not accept responsibility for everything that was actually stated, do you really think that one need do so for something that was not stated?[2] What is more foolish than for a seller to recount the faults of the very thing he is selling? What could be more absurd than for the auctioneer to say, "I am selling an unsanitary house"?'

(56) In certain doubtful cases, therefore, honourableness is thus defended on one side, while on the other they argue the case for

---

[1] The prohibition also covered not giving the necessities of life such as fire and water: see 1.51 where these are given as examples of things that can be given to mankind in general *without loss to oneself*. The parallel ascribed to Antipater is therefore questionable.

[2] Diogenes is made to allude to a provision of Roman law (*Digest* XVIII.1.43) whereby the seller is not bound by professions he makes in advertising for sale as long as the qualities claimed are such as the buyer can judge for himself (cf. III.68).

benefit, but in such a way that it turns out not only to be honourable to do whatever seems beneficial, but even dishonourable not to do it. That is the kind of incompatibility that seems to arise between the beneficial and the honourable. And such cases must be adjudicated; for we did not set them out in order to ask questions, but in order to explicate them.

(57) Well then: it seems that the corn dealer ought not to have concealed anything from the Rhodians, nor the seller of the house from its buyers. For it is not concealment to be silent about anything, but when you want those in whose interest it would be to know something that you know to remain ignorant of it, so that you may profit.[1] Who cannot see what this kind of concealment is like, and what sort of man practises it? Certainly not one who is open, straightforward, well bred, just or good; but rather a twister, mysterious, cunning, tricky, ill-intentioned, crafty, roguish and sly. Surely it is not beneficial to subject oneself to all these allegations of viciousness and many others?

(58) Furthermore, if those who kept quiet are to be denounced, what are we to think of those who actually told lies as well? Gaius Canius, a Roman *eques*,[2] who was not without wit and fairly well read, went off to Syracuse for leisure, as he often put it himself, and not for business. There he used to say repeatedly that he wanted to buy some grounds where he could invite his friends and enjoy himself without people interrupting him. This became widely known; and a certain Pythius, who ran a banking house in Syracuse, said that he had some grounds which were not for sale, but which Canius might, if he wished, use as his own. At the same time he invited him to dine in these grounds on the following day. When Canius accepted, Pythius, who, as a banker, could command the gratitude of men of every order, called some fishermen together to him and asked them if on the next day they would fish in front of his grounds, explaining what he wanted them to do.

---

[1] C. here, using suitably convoluted language in his role as judge, applies the rule of procedure (III.21) to resolve the dispute: Antipater and Diogenes both fail to make a crucial distinction between cases in which silence is maintained *deliberately in order to profit at another's expense* and others. In C.'s view, the former, and only the former, involve concealment. C. agrees with Antipater on how to act, but not entirely on the reasons.

[2] The Latin word signifies the social order just below that of senator. The criterion was a census qualification of 400,000 HS plus free birth.

Canius arrived in time for the meal, and Pythius had had a sumptuous spread prepared. Before their eyes was a huge number of boats, and each man in turn brought in what he had caught. The fish were laid at Pythius' feet. (59) Then Canius said, 'What is this, Pythius? So many fish? So many boats?' He replied, 'It's not surprising, for this is where all the fish in Syracuse are; water is also drawn from here. They cannot do without this estate.'

Canius was inflamed with greed and urged Pythius to sell the place. At first he responded reluctantly. But what more need I say? Canius succeeded. He was rich and he was greedy for it, and he paid as much as Pythius wanted, including in his purchase all the fittings. Pythius entered it in his account book[1] and completed the business. On the following day Canius invited his friends, and arrived early himself. There was not a rowlock in sight. He asked his nearest neighbour whether the fishermen were on holiday, as he could not see any. 'Not as far as I know,' he replied, 'But there aren't usually any fishermen here. That's why I was wondering what happened yesterday.'

(60) Canius was furious. But what could he do? For my colleague and friend Gaius Aquillius had not yet introduced his rules of procedure concerning 'malicious fraud'.[2] On this question, when he was asked what 'malicious fraud' was, he used to reply, 'When one thing is pretended and another is done.' That is finely put, as one might expect from a man experienced in giving definitions. Both Pythius, therefore, and everyone else who does one thing and pretends another is treacherous, dishonest and ill-intentioned. No action of that sort can be beneficial, imbued as it is with so many vices. (61) If the definition of Aquillius is true, then both pretence and dissembling must be removed from our whole lives: the good man, then, will neither pretend nor dissemble, whether in order to sell or to buy at a better price.

Moreover, such 'malicious fraud' had already been liable to punish-

[1] By doing so, Pythius technically changed the contract from being one 'in good faith' (which a contract made by oral consent was) to being one 'of strict justice'. In the latter type of contracts the principle of *caveat emptor* held good, and Pythius now had no obligation to reveal the disadvantages of his property (see Notes on Translation p. xlvi under *Fides* and Crook, *Law and Life of Rome*, pp. 213–17).

[2] *Mala fides*, literally 'bad faith', the opposite of *bona fides*, 'good faith'. Aquillius devised *formulae* (p. 14, n. 1 and p. 107, n. 3) for bringing claims for restitution where fraud had been practiced in commercial transactions.

ment by the laws; for example in the matter of guardianships in the Twelve Tables, or that of defrauding minors, under the Plaetorian Law, and, without a specific law, in the lawcourts whenever the stipulation 'in good faith' is added.[1] From other court cases, moreover, the following phrases particularly stand out: in a judgement over a wife's property, 'better if fairer'; in the restoration of a trust, 'to act well, as among good men'.[2] Well then! Can the phrase 'better if fairer' countenance any share in deceit? And if one says, 'To act well, as among good men', can anything be done deceitfully or with ill intention? Malicious fraud consists in pretence, as Aquillius said. Therefore all untruthfulness must be removed from our dealings. The seller will not employ an artificial bidder, nor the buyer someone to bid low against him. If one of the two has come to declare a price, he should not do so more than once.

(62) Indeed, Quintus Scaevola, the son of Publius, once asked the man from whom he was buying a farm to name a definite price, and when he did so, Scaevola said he thought it worth more than that; he added 100,000 sesterces to the price. No one denies that a good man would do that; but they do deny that a wise man would, just as if someone had sold it at a lower price than he might have. Such things are ruinous; for their view is that the good and the wise are different.[3] Ennius said as a result, 'The wise man would be wise in vain if he could not profit himself.' That would indeed be true if Ennius and I were in agreement as to what it might be to profit.

(63) I see that Hecaton of Rhodes, Panaetius' pupil, said in the books about duty that he wrote for Quintus Tubero, that a wise man would, without acting contrary to customs, laws, and established practices, take account of his personal wealth. For we do not wish to

[1] The Twelve Tables were a codification of law dating originally from the fifth century BC and still studied in C.'s day. The Lex Plaetoria of 192 BC made fraud practiced on minors a criminal offence. The forms of trial not resting on statute are those under the formulary procedure (see p. 107, n. 3). The *formulae* could include the provision that the transaction was 'in good faith' (see III.70).
[2] C. goes on to other cases handled by the formulary procedure which involved the general notion, without the phrase 'malicious fraud'. Claims for return of dowry when a marriage was dissolved were handled before arbitrators who could award a sum different from that claimed. Cases of trust (*fiducia*) concerned property alienated on condition of its being eventually restored.
[3] They contrast the 'good man' (see p. 9, n. 1) with the 'wise man', not in the philosophical sense, but in the sense of 'worldly wise'. See p. 76, n. 1.

be rich for our own sake alone, but for our children, our friends, and most of all for the political community. The capacities and resources of individuals are the riches of the city. He would not be at all able to agree with Scaevola's action as I related it just now; for Hecaton declares that he would refrain from doing for the sake of his own gain only what is not permitted.[1] He should be accorded no great praise or gratitude.

(64) Anyway, if malicious fraud covers both pretending and dissembling, there are very few matters to which such malicious fraud is not relevant. Alternatively, if the good man is the one who assists whoever he can and harms no one, it is certain that such a good man is not easy to find. To sum up: it is never beneficial to do wrong, because it is always dishonourable; moreover, because it is always honourable to be a good man, it is always beneficial.

(65) It is indeed laid down in the part of our civil law concerning properties that when they are sold, whatever faults are known to the seller should be stated. In the Twelve Tables it was enough that one should accept responsibility for those faults that were verbally specified;[2] if the seller had denied these, he should face a double penalty. The jurisconsults, however, have even established a penalty for keeping quiet.[3] For they decided that if the seller knew about any fault in a property, unless he had expressly declared it, he ought to be responsible for it. (66) In one case of this type, the augurs were going to take an augury on the citadel, and they ordered Tiberius Claudius Centumalus, who had a house on the Caelian Hill, to demolish that part of it that was high enough to obstruct the auspices.[4] Claudius advertised the block for sale and Publius Calpurnius Lanarius bought it. The augurs made the same demand of him, and Calpurnius pulled down the required bit. When he discovered that Claudius had advertised the house after he had been ordered by the augurs to demolish some of it, he compelled him to go before the arbitrator as to 'what compensation he ought to have made in accordance with the demands of good faith'.

---

[1] Hecaton takes the same view as Diogenes (50–5). C., in accordance with his 'rule of procedure' (21), prefers the example of Scaevola who refused to enrich himself at the expense of another.

[2] By the buyer.

[3] I.e. through actions based on good faith under the formulary procedure.

[4] The augurs watched the flight of birds for omens from the citadel on the Capitoline Hill. The house on the Caelian Hill to the east of them might obstruct their view.

The verdict was given by Marcus Cato, the father of our Cato (for as other men take their name from their fathers this man, who fathered so bright a star, takes his from the son). He, then, as judge, pronounced that since the seller had known the facts when he sold and had not reported them, he ought to be responsible for the loss incurred by the buyer. (67) Thus he established that it was a part of good faith that the buyer should learn of any fault that the seller knew. If his judgement was correct, then neither the corn dealer nor the seller of the insanitary house were right to keep quiet.

The civil law cannot completely embrace reticences of this kind; in so far as it can, however, it carefully contains them. Marcus Marius Gratidianus, a relation of mine, sold to Gaius Sergius Orata a house that he had bought from the same man only a few years before. It was under a liability,[1] but Marius did not state that in the contract of sale. The matter was brought to court. Orata was defended by Crassus, and Gratidianus by Antonius. Crassus insisted on the law: 'The seller did not state the faults that he knew; therefore he ought to take responsibility.' Antonius urged fairness: 'Since the fault was not unknown to Sergius (for he had sold the house in the first place) there was no need to state it. He was not deceived, since he knew the legal position of the property that he had bought.' What is my point then? That you should realize that crafty men did not please our ancestors.[2]

(68) However, the laws and the philosophers remove craftiness in different ways: the laws, so far as they can, lay their hands upon it, philosophers, their reason and intelligence. Reason, then, demands that nothing is done insidiously, deceptively or with pretence. It is not insidious to set a trap even if you are not intending to startle the game or to hunt it? For wild beasts often fall into traps even when no one is chasing them. Is it not the same if you advertise your house, put up a notice just like a trap, sell it because of its faults, and let some foolish person run into it?

(69) I see that because custom is so corrupted such behaviour is neither thought dishonourable nor forbidden by statute and civil

[1] I.e. someone other than the owner had some right over the property. See Biographical Notes under Sergius Orata.
[2] See Introduction, pp. xxvi–xxvii. This last case in which equity was really on the side of the defendant, whose silence, not intended to deceive, was legally exploited by the plaintiff, leads into C.'s argument that civil law is an imperfect instrument for enforcing morality.

law.[1] It is, however, forbidden by the law of nature. For there is a fellowship that is extremely widespread, shared by all with all (even if this has often been said, it ought to be said still more often); a closer one exists among those of the same nation, and one more intimate still among those of the same city.[2] For this reason our ancestors wanted the law of nations and the civil law to be different: everything in the civil law need not be in the law of nations, but everything in the law of nations ought also to be a part of civil law. We, however, do not have the firm and lifelike figure of true law and genuine justice: we make use of shadows and sketches. I wish we would follow even those! For they are drawn from the best examples of nature and truth.[3]

(70) How valuable are the words, 'That I may not be caught or deceived because of you and my faith in you.' How golden are these, 'One must act well, as among good men, and without fraudulence'.[4] (But who the good are and what is acting well is a large question.) Indeed, Quintus Scaevola, the Pontifex Maximus, said that there was very great force in all judgements where the words 'out of good faith' were added. He thought that the expression 'good faith' had very wide application, that it was relevant to guardianships, to business fellowships, to trusts, to commissions, to purchases, to sales, and to hiring or letting. The fellowship of life consisted of these things; and it was the mark of a great judge to be able to decide in such cases, particularly when judgements are generally conflicting as to how far one man ought to accept his responsibility to another.[5]

(71) Therefore all craftiness should be removed, and also the ill will that wants to be seen as good sense, but is in fact different and very far removed from it. For good sense is located in the choice of things good and bad, while ill will – if everything dishonourable is bad – prefers bad things to good. Not only in property does the civil law, which is derived from nature, punish ill will and deceit,

---

[1] See p. 120, n. 2. 'Civil law' here is the praetor's formulary law (p. 123, n. 1).
[2] Cf. 1.50–8.
[3] The law of individual states is bound to be more detailed than the law of nations (= natural law, p. 108, n. 3), but should enforce its basic tenets.
[4] Clauses of contracts which rely on equity for their fulfilment.
[5] Cases arising on such contracts of good faith left a great deal to the discretion of the judge. Also, the two-sidedness of relationships of good faith meant that the possibility of counteraction by the defendant always existed.

but also in the sale of slaves deception on the seller's part is entirely excluded. For according to the aedile's edict if a man ought to know about a slave's health, his escapes or his thieving, he is responsible for them.[1] (The case of heirs is different.)[2] (72) Accordingly, we realize that since nature is the source of law, what is in accordance with nature is that no one should act so as to exploit another's ignorance. One can find nothing more destructive in life than ill will posing as intelligent behaviour;[3] this gives rise to countless instances where the beneficial seems to conflict with the honourable. For so few will be found who can refrain from injustice when granted both impunity and absolute secrecy!

(73) Let us, then, put this to the test, if you are agreeable, and even for those examples where the mass of men perhaps think that no wrong is done. For we should not discuss here assassins, poisoners, forgers of wills, thieves and embezzlers, who ought to be suppressed not by words and philosophical argument, but by chains and imprisonment. Here let us rather consider what is done by those who are thought of as good men.

Certain men brought from Greece to Rome a forgery of the will of Lucius Minucius Basilus, a rich man. In order more easily to achieve their aim, they wrote in as joint heirs with themselves Marcus Crassus and Quintus Hortensius, who were the most influential men of their day. Although these men suspected that the will was forged, since they were not a party to the guilty deed they did not reject the paltry gains from another's crime. What follows? Is it enough that they do not appear to have committed an offence? To me, it does not appear so, although I loved one of them when he was alive, and as for the other, now that he is dead, I do not dislike him.[4] (74) Basilus had wanted his sister's son Marcus Satrius to take his name and had named him as his heir. (I mean the Satrius who is patron of the Picene and Sabine territories – their very name brands

---

[1] The aediles regulated the markets and, using the formulary procedure, judged actions for voiding the sale of cattle and slaves sold under false pretences. The slave's 'thieving' is that from a third party for which the master could be sued.

[2] Heirs were not liable for the faults of slaves whom they had just inherited and whose faults they therefore could not be expected to know.

[3] See III.62 with n. 3.

[4] Hortensius who died *c.* 50 BC and Crassus who died in 54, respectively. See Biographical Notes.

the times with shame!)[1] It was not at all fair, then, that the leading citizens should take his property and that nothing except the name should come to Satrius. For if someone who does not resist and repel injustice when he can, acts unjustly (as I explained in my first book)[2] what are we to think of someone who not only did not avert an injustice, but even assisted it? In my view not even genuine inheritances are honourable if they are secured through ill-intentioned flattery and the pretence of dutiful service rather than the reality.

From time to time in such matters it happens that one thing seems beneficial and another honourable. That is a mistake: for the rule of what is beneficial and of what is honourable is one and the same. (75) If someone has not grasped that, no type of deceit or crime will be beyond him. For if he thinks, 'That is certainly honourable, but this is expedient', he will be daring to pull apart things that are united by nature; that error is the source of deceit, of misdeeds, and of all criminal activity. Therefore if a good man has the power to insinuate himself into a rich man's will by clicking his fingers, he should not make use of it, even if he has thoroughly ascertained that not a single person would even suspect. But grant such a power to Marcus Crassus, that the snap of a finger should have him written down as an heir although he was not heir in truth, and, believe me, he would dance in the forum.[3] The just, though, and the man whom we consider good,[4] will take nothing from anyone to transfer it to himself. If anyone is surprised at that, he should admit that he does not know what a good man is.

(76) If someone, however, were wanting to unfold the concept rolled up in his own mind, he would teach himself at once that a good man is one who assists whomever he can, and harms no one unless provoked by injustice. Well then? Would a man not be doing harm if he arranged, as if with some magic potion, to displace true heirs and to usurp their position? Someone will say, 'But shouldn't he do what is beneficial and expedient, then?' No! Let him understand that nothing is either expedient or beneficial that is unjust. Anyone who has not learnt this will not be able to be a good man. (77) When

---

[1] See Biographical Notes under Satrius.

[2] I.23, I.28–9.

[3] Crassus would go beyond intriguing to be named as heir: he would be willing to have himself inserted in a will *falsely* (as in 73) and then dance in the forum (cf. I.145) as a condition of entering on the inheritance (III.93).

[4] See I.20 with n. 1 for the 'just man' as the 'good man'.

I was a boy I used to hear from my father how Gaius Fimbria, the former consul, was judge in the case of Marcus Lutatius Pinthia, a Roman *eques*[1] and an honourable man. He had made a deposit, pledged as a forfeit 'if he did not prove himself a good man'.[2] Fimbria told him that he would never judge such a matter lest he should either deprive an honest man of his reputation by judging against him, or should appear to have decreed that someone was a good man, when such a thing depended upon countless duties and praiseworthy deeds. To a good man like this, recognized by Fimbria as well as by Socrates, nothing at all can seem beneficial that is not honourable.

Such a man will dare not even to think, let alone do, anything that he would not dare to proclaim. Is it not dishonourable that philosophers have doubts where even peasants do not doubt? For among peasants a proverb arose that is now trite with age: whenever they praise the faithfulness and goodness of anyone they say that 'he is worthy for you to play odds and evens with in the dark'. That can only mean this: nothing is expedient that is not seemly, even if you might acquire it without anyone convicting you. (78) You can see that this proverb grants no mercy to Gyges,[3] nor to the man I imagined just now who could sweep up everyone's inheritances by snapping his fingers. For just as something dishonourable can never become honourable even if it is hidden, similarly what is not honourable can never be done in such a way that it turns out beneficial; for nature opposes and resists this.

(79) But when the rewards are very great is there not a case for wrongdoing? Gaius Marius was far from the hope of a consulship, remaining in obscurity still in the seventh year after his praetorship, and he was looking as if he would never even stand as a consul. He was sent to Rome by his general Quintus Metellus, a fine man and citizen, whose legate he was.[4] Then, in front of the people of Rome, he charged Metellus with prolonging the war, saying that

---

[1] See p. 121, n. 2.

[2] Laying a wager, which the winner would recover and the loser forfeit to the state, was used in the older form of civil law at Rome and could also be used to settle extra-judicial disputes, as here to vindicate one's reputation.

[3] See III.38–9.

[4] The minimum interval between these magistracies, achieved by C., was two years. Only C. represents Marius as deceitful in securing the command against Jugurtha: Sallust and Plutarch say that Metellus insulted him when he revealed his consular ambitions.

if they would make him consul he would in a short time reduce Jugurtha, alive or dead, into the power of the Roman people. And so he was indeed made consul; but he departed from faithfulness and justice by arousing hostility with a false accusation against an excellent and most respected citizen, even though he was his legate and had been sent by him.

(80) Even my kinsman Gratidianus once failed to discharge the duty of a good man. He was praetor, and the tribunes of the people had summoned the college of praetors[1] to settle by a common decision a standard of currency (for the currency was so fluctuating then that no one could know how much he had). They drew up in common an edict, including the questions of punishment and judgements, and decided that they should all ascend the rostra together in the afternoon. The rest departed in different directions; but Marius, on leaving the tribunes' benches, made directly for the rostra; then, by himself, he published the edict that had been composed in common. If you ask, the affair did indeed bring him great honours: statues in every street, incense and candles in front of them.[2] Need I say more? No one was ever dearer to the masses.

(81) Such are the questions that sometimes confuse one's deliberations, when the point in which fairness is violated seems not so very great, while the result of it seems extremely important. Thus Marius' usurping of the popular gratitude due to his colleagues and to the tribunes of the people seemed to be not so dishonourable, while to become consul because of it, which had been his aim, seemed extremely beneficial. But there is one rule for all cases; and I desire you to be thoroughly acquainted with it: either the thing that seems beneficial must not be dishonourable, or if it is dishonourable, it must not seem beneficial.[3] Well then? Can we judge the one Marius or the other a good man? Unravel and sift your understanding in order to see the form and concept of a good man that is there. Does it become the good man to lie or slander for his own profit, or to usurp or to deceive? Unquestionably, no.

(82) Is there any matter so valuable or any advantage so desirable

---

[1] At this date (85 BC) there were six praetors. The ten tribunes summoned them to the low benches on which they themselves sat (the higher magistrates occupied chairs). The rostra was the speaking platform in the forum.

[2] Worship of living men was not a Roman custom: these are to be construed as extravagant honours.

[3] See p. 112, n. 1.

that you would abandon the name and splendour of a good man for it? What can the said benefit bring that is worth as much as what it takes away, if it removes the name of a good man and deprives one of keeping faith and of justice? What difference does it make whether someone changes from a man into a beast or remains in human form while possessing the savagery of a beast? As for those who neglect everything upright and honourable provided that they can win power, are they not acting just like the man who wanted to have for a father-in-law one whose audacity would make him powerful himself?[1] It seemed beneficial to him to secure great power by means of someone else's unpopularity. He did not see how unjust that was towards his country, and how dishonourable. The father-in-law himself always had upon his lips those Greek verses about the Phoenician women; I will express them as I can, awkwardly perhaps, but still so that the point is intelligible:[2]

> If justice must be violated for sovereignty's sake, it must
> be violated: you may indulge your scruples elsewhere.

He[3] deserved to die for having exempted the one thing that is most criminal of all.

(83) Why then do we collect petty examples – fraudulent inheritances, trading and sales? Here you have a man who longed to be king of the Roman people and master of every nation; and he achieved it![4] If anyone says that such a greed is honourable, he is out of his mind: for he is approving the death of laws and liberty, and counting their oppression – a foul and hateful thing – as something glorious. But if anyone admits that it is not honourable to reign in a city that has been free and ought to be so, but says that it is beneficial to the man who can do it – what reproach, or rather what abuse, can

---

[1] Pompey, who married Caesar's daughter Julia in 59 BC when Caesar, as consul, used force to pass bills ratifying Pompey's arrangements in the East and settling his veterans, but also laid the basis for his own power.

[2] C. translates into Latin verses 524–5 spoken by Eteocles in Euripides' play *The Phoenician Women*. Though editors punctuate Euripides' and C.'s texts to read 'If justice must be violated it must be violated for sovereignty's sake', this punctuation makes better sense of both versions.

[3] The manuscripts give 'Eteocles or rather Euripides' as the subject of this sentence, but the reference is probably to Caesar.

[4] Caesar never actually accepted the title *rex*, a term of opprobrium for the Romans since the expulsion of the last Tarquin, but it was applied to him by his enemies in the sense of 'tyrant'.

I use to try to tear him from so great an error? Immortal gods! Can the most disgusting, the foulest of parricides, that of one's fatherland, be beneficial to anyone? Can it be so, even if the man who took it upon himself is named 'father' by the citizens he has oppressed?[1] Benefit must therefore be measured by honourableness, and in such a way that in name the two seem discordant, in substance to sound as a single note.

(84) In the opinion of the ordinary man, I can think of nothing that could be a greater benefit than to be king. Conversely, when I begin to bring my reasoning back to the truth, I find nothing less beneficial for the man who has achieved it unjustly. Can worry, anxiety, fears by day and night, and a life full of treachery and dangers, be beneficial to anyone?

> Many are unfair and unfaithful to a throne, and few
> have goodwill,

as Accius said. And which throne did he mean? One that was held by right, handed down from Tantalus and Pelops.[2] Then how much more true do you think it is of the king who oppressed the Roman people themselves with the Roman people's army, and forced a city that was not just free, but even the ruler of the nations, to be his slave? (85) What stains of guilt, what wounds, do you think he had in his heart? Can a man's life be beneficial to him, when he lives it on these terms: that anyone who takes it from him will be held in the greatest gratitude and glory? If such things, though they seem to be extremely beneficial, are not in fact so, because they are full of disgrace and dishonourableness, we ought to be well persuaded that nothing is beneficial that is not honourable.

(86) Such a judgement has indeed often been made; and in particular by Gaius Fabricius, as consul for the second time, and our senate, in the war against Pyrrhus. King Pyrrhus had declared war upon the Roman people unprovoked; the contest was for empire, and with a noble and powerful king. A deserter came from him into Fabricius' camp and promised that if Fabricius would offer a reward, he would

---

[1] Caesar was called 'Father of his Country' after his final victory in the civil war in 45 BC. The title had been conferred on C. in 63, not without opposition.

[2] The play of Accius must be one about the house of Atreus, descendants of Tantalus and his son Pelops (see Biographical Notes).

return to Pyrrhus' camp as secretly as he had left it, and would kill him by poison. Fabricius arranged for the man to be returned to Pyrrhus, and his action was praised by the senate. And yet, if we are looking for the appearance of benefit and to ordinary opinion, one single deserter would have put paid to that great war and to a serious foe of our empire. It would, though, have been a great disgrace and an outrage to overwhelm by crime rather than by virtue a man with whom we were competing for praise.[1] (87) Then which was more beneficial to Fabricius, who was for this city what Aristides was for Athens,[2] or to our senate, who never separated benefit from standing: to fight the enemy with arms or with poison? If empire is to be sought for the sake of glory, then away with the crime! For there can be no glory in it. If, on the other hand, one is seeking power, by any means whatever, it cannot be beneficial when combined with disrepute.

The well known proposal of Lucius Philippus, the son of Quintus, was therefore not beneficial. Lucius Sulla had, in return for a sum of money, freed certain cities from taxation, in accordance with a senatorial decree; Philippus proposed that they should become liable to tribute once more, but that we should not return the money that they gave in return for their liberty. The senate agreed to this. Shame upon the empire! The faith of pirates is better than that of the senate.[3] 'But revenues were increased, therefore it was beneficial.' How long will men dare to say that something is useful if it is not beneficial? (88) Indeed, can hatred or disrepute be beneficial to an empire, which ought to be supported by glory and by the goodwill of the allies?

I too have often disagreed with my friend Cato; for he seemed to me to guard the treasury and the revenues too rigidly, denying everything to the tax-collectors and much to the allies, when we ought to have been kind towards the latter and to have been dealing with the former as we are accustomed to with our tenants. That was all the more true because such solidarity of the orders was connected

---

[1] The incident took place in 278 BC. Cf. 1.38 on Pyrrhus.
[2] Both were nicknamed 'The Just' (III.16). Cf. III.49.
[3] In the 70s BC when Rome's many wars had led to financial crisis, the states freed by Sulla from tribute, in return for payments made during the First Mithridatic War, had taxes reimposed. Pirates release their captives after ransom is paid, cf. also II.40.

with the safety of the republic.[1] Curio also was in the wrong when he used to say that the cause of the Transpadani was fair, but always added, 'Let benefit prevail!' He should have taught that it was not fair because it was not beneficial to the republic rather than admit its fairness while denying that it was beneficial.[2]

(89) The sixth of Hecaton's books on duties is full of questions of this kind: would a man who is good fail to feed his slave household when corn is extremely dear? He argues on either side, but in the end he measures duty by what is beneficial, as he thinks, rather than by humanity. He asks whether, if some cargo must be thrown overboard at sea, one should sacrifice an expensive horse rather than a cheap little slave. Personal wealth draw us one way, humanity the other.[3]

'If a foolish man in a shipwreck seizes a plank, will the wise man wrest it from him if he can?'

'He denies that, because it would be an injustice.'[4]

'Well then. Will the master of the ship snatch what is his?'

'Not at all, no more than he would be willing to throw a passenger from the ship on to the sea, because the ship is his. For until they arrive at the place for which the ship is chartered it belongs not to its master, but to the passengers.'

(90) 'Well, suppose there is one plank and two sailors, both of them wise men. Would each of them grab it for himself, or would one give in to the other?'

'One should give in to the other, that is, to the one whose life most matters for his own or the republic's sake.'

'And what if such considerations are equal for both?'

---

[1] For the two incidents, see Biographical Notes under M. Porcius Cato (the Younger). The tax-collectors were the most organized part of the equestrian order (see p. 21, n. 2) whose support of the senatorial order C. regarded as vital. The comparison with tenants is that Roman landlords often remitted rents in years of bad harvest.

[2] For the episode, see Biographical Notes under C. Scribonius Curio. Curio may have argued that whoever got credit for granting the Transpadani citizenship would acquire too much political power, which was against the interests of the Republic. Though C.'s suggestion would have improved Curio's argument, it would not have justified Rome's adoption of the policy (p. 115, n. 1).

[3] As the first two cases clearly involve Hecaton's rule (III.63), law and custom must have allowed the master to sacrifice his slave household rather than exhaust his wealth and fail to provide for his own family. See p. 18, n. 3.

[4] Cf. III.29–30.

'There will be no contest, but one will give in to the other as if losing by lot, or by playing odds and evens.'

'All right, then. Suppose that a father despoil a temple, or dig a tunnel to the treasury, will his son denounce him to the magistrates?'

'That would be impious. He should rather defend his father if he is charged.'

'Does one's country not, then, take precedence in all duties?'

'Yes, indeed. But it actually assists one's country to have citizens who revere their parents.'[1]

'And if a father should try to impose a tyranny, or to betray his country, will the son keep silent?'

'He will beseech his father not to do it, and if he has no success, he will rebuke him and threaten him. In the last resort, if the affair would lead to the ruin of his homeland, he will put its safety before that of his father.'[2]

(91) He also asks this:[3] if a wise man has foolishly accepted counterfeit coins for good ones, when he discovers it, would he pay with them any debt he my have, instead of with good coins? Diogenes says yes; Antipater says no, and I agree rather with him.[4] If a man is knowingly selling a wine that will not keep, ought he to say? Diogenes thinks it unnecessary, Antipater considers that a good man would do so. Such matters are for the Stoics like disputed points of law.

Should one declare the faults of a slave whom one is selling? Not of course the faults one is required by civil law to state, or else to have the slave returned, but these: that he is untruthful, or a gambler, or steals, or drinks? It seems to one of them that you should declare them, and to the other not.[5] (92) If anyone is selling gold, but thinks

---

[1] Cf. 1.159 with n. 1.

[2] On C.'s view, the father would put himself outside the circle of human obligations by becoming a tyrant (III.32).

[3] In the cases in 91–2, as in those debated by Diogenes and Antipater in III.51–2, one partner in a commercial transaction practises reticence which is not against the law.

[4] At this date it was illegal under the *Lex Cornelia de falsis* to counterfeit silver coins, to connive at the offence, or to buy and sell them (*Dig.* XLVIII.10.9), and it was legal to reject such a coin (Paul. *Sent.* v.25.1). Hence C. explains that the wise man acquired the counterfeit coins unknowingly and hence legally. Paying his debts with it would presumably have exploited some legal loophole.

[5] There is no contradiction with III.71 (see p. 127, n. 1), as the seller had to disclose acts of theft for which the master was liable, not a habit of stealing from the master (*Digest* XXI.1.52).

that he is selling brass, will the good man inform him that it is gold, or buy it for one denarius when it is worth a thousand? It is by now clear both what my view is,[1] and what the dispute is between the philosophers whom I have named.

Should agreements and promises always be kept, which have been made (as the praetors usually put it) 'without force or malicious fraud'.[2] Suppose that one man has given another a cure for the dropsy and has stipulated that if he is made healthy by the cure he should never use it again. If a few years later the same man falls ill with the same disease, and does not succeed in obtaining permission to use the cure again from the man to whom he gave the promise, what should he do? Since the man who does not permit it is inhuman, and no injustice is being done to him, the sick man should consider his own life and safety.

(93) Well then, suppose that someone is making a wise man his heir, and asks him, when he leaves him 100,000,000 sesterces in the will, to dance openly by daylight in the forum before he receives the inheritance;[3] suppose that he has promised that he will – for otherwise the man would not name him as his heir. Should he do what he has promised or not? I would prefer that he had not made the promise; that, I think, would have befitted his seriousness. Since, however, he has promised, if he thinks it dishonourable to dance in the forum, he will act more honourably by falsifying his promise and taking nothing from the inheritance, than if he accepts it; unless perhaps he contributes the money to the republic to meet some important contingency. For in that case, dancing in the interests of one's country would not be dishonourable.

(94) Furthermore, promises need not be kept if they are not beneficial to the very people to whom you made the promise. Sol told his son Phaethon (to return to mythology) that he would do whatever his son wished. What he did wish was to be taken up in his father's chariot; and he was taken up in it. But before he came to rest he was burnt up by a bolt of lightning. How much better would it have been if in this case his father's promise had not been kept. And what of the promise that Theseus required Neptune to fulfil? Neptune

---

[1] As in III.57, C. would abide by the rule of procedure (III.21): one cannot profit at another's expense.

[2] Cf. I.32, I.40, III.107, III.110–13.

[3] Cf. I.145 and III.75 with n. 3.

had given him three wishes, and he wished for the death of his son Hippolytus, since his father had suspicions concerning him and his step-mother. When Theseus obtained what he had asked for, he was stricken with great grief.[1]

(95) And again: because Agamemnon had vowed to Diana the most beautiful creature born that year in his kingdom, he sacrificed Iphigenia; for in that year nothing more beautiful than she was born. He should rather have broken his promise than commit so foul a deed. Sometimes, therefore, promises ought not to be kept and deposits not always returned. If someone has deposited his sword with you when he was of sound mind, and asks for it back when insane, it would be wrong to return it, and your duty not to return it.[2] Again, if a man who has deposited money with you were to make war on your country, would you return the deposit? I believe not; for you would be acting contrary to the republic, which ought to be the dearest thing to you.[3] (96) In this way, many things that seem to be honourable by nature become honourable no longer through circumstance: to keep promises, to stand by agreements, and to return deposits become no longer honourable, if what is beneficial changes.

I think that I have said enough about things which, though contrary to justice seem, by posing as good sense, to be beneficial. In my first book, however, I derived duties from the four sources of honourableness; let us now therefore deal with the same four, wanting as we do to show how things that seem beneficial but are not are hostile to virtue. I have debated good sense, which ill will wants to mimic, and similarly justice, which is always beneficial.[4] There remain two parts of honourableness, of which one is to be seen in the greatness and excellence of an outstanding spirit, and the other in being moulded and moderated by temperance and restraint.

(97) Ulysses' plan seemed beneficial to him, at least as some tragic poets have related it (for there is no such suspicion of Ulysses in Homer, that finest of authors). However, the tragedians pretend that he wanted to evade military service by pretending to be

---

[1] Cf. 1.32.
[2] The example in Plato's *Republic* I.
[3] Cf. 1.57–8; 1.160; III.89.
[4] C. only now reveals that from 40 on he has been discussing the first two virtues, wisdom and justice, and not, as he implies, in sequence but together (see p. 76, n. 1). Throughout the book, justice is given priority, see Introduction, pp. xxiii ff.

mad.[1] His plan was not honourable, but beneficial, or so someone might say: to rule and to live at leisure in Ithaca with his parents, his wife, his son. Do you think you can compare with such tranquillity any dignity that daily toil and danger might bestow? But in my view his tranquillity should have been despised and rejected; for I do not count anything that is not honourable as beneficial. (98) What do you think that Ulysses would have heard said of him if he had persisted in his pretence? For even when he had done very great deeds in war, he could still hear the following from Ajax:

> He was the first to swear the oath, as you all know;
> but he alone broke its faith. He began to pretend to
> be mad, so that he need not join us. Had Palamedes'
> penetrating good sense not grasped his ill-intentioned
> daring, he would have evaded the justice of his sacred
> vow for ever.[2]

(99) Indeed it was better for him to struggle not only with the enemy, but also with the waves, as in fact he did, than to desert a Greece united in its aim of warring with barbarians.[3]

Let us now leave myth and foreigners' tales, and return to events of our own history. Marcus Atilius Regulus, as consul for the second time, was captured by ambush in Africa, when the Spartan Xanthippus was leading the Carthaginian troops (the general, though, was Hamilcar the father of Hannibal).[4] He was sent to the senate, having sworn that he would return to Carthage unless certain noble captives were returned to the Carthaginians. When he reached Rome, he could see the thing that was apparently beneficial, but, as events reveal, he judged it specious. It was this: to remain in his own country, to be at home with his wife and children, to maintain his rank and standing as an ex-consul,[5] counting the disaster that had befallen him in war as common to the fortune of warfare. Who can deny that such things are beneficial? Whom do you think? Greatness of spirit and courage deny it. (100) Surely you are not seeking authorities

---

[1] The Greek tragedians Sophocles and Euripides and the Latin ones Pacuvius and Accius told this story.

[2] From Pacuvius' *Judgment of Arms*.

[3] In Homer's *Odyssey* v.365 ff. Ulysses struggles with the waves as he swims to the land of the Phaeacians.

[4] C. confuses Hannibal's father with an older Hamilcar who commanded at the battle of 255 BC in which Regulus was captured.

[5] In the Senate ex-consuls were called on for their opinions before the other ex-magistrates.

still more reliable? For it is characteristic of these virtues to fear nothing, to disdain everything human, and to think nothing that can happen to a man unendurable.

What, therefore, did he do? Entering the senate, he revealed his instructions; then he refused to vote himself, saying that as long as he was held under oath by the enemy, he was not a senator. And furthermore – 'Foolish man,' someone will say, 'To oppose his own benefit!' – he even claimed that it was not beneficial to restore the captives: for they were young men and good leaders while he was worn out by old age. His authority prevailed, and the captives were kept there. He himself returned to Carthage, held back by love neither for his country nor for his family and friends. Moreover, he knew well that he was going to a very cruel enemy and most sophisticated torture. For all that, he thought that his oath should be kept.[1] And so, even while he was dying through enforced wakefulness he was better off than if he had remained at home, a consular but elderly, captive, and foresworn.

(101) 'But he acted foolishly! For he not only failed to recommend that the captives be returned, but even spoke against it.' But why is that foolish? Even if it was to the advantage of the republic? In any case, can anything that is harmful to the republic be beneficial to any citizen? When men separate benefit from honourableness they subvert the foundations of nature. We all seek what is beneficial; we are pulled towards it; we can do nothing else. Who is there who would avoid things beneficial? Or rather, who would not pursue them most assiduously? But it is because we can never find beneficial things except in what is praiseworthy, seemly and honourable, and because we deem these things highest and first, that we consider the word 'benefit' not so much splendid, as necessary.

(102) Someone will say, 'But what, then, is there to a sworn oath? Surely we do not fear the wrath of Jove? For all philosophers, not only the ones who say that a god is free of business himself and imposes none on others, but also those who wish the god to be active and labouring all the time, share the view that he is never angry and never does harm.[2] In any case, how could a wrathful Jove have

---

[1] Though C. is supposed to be discussing courage or greatness of spirit (96), he now begins to concentrate on the oath (cf. 102–10) which brings justice into consideration (also in III–15). He returns to the courage of Regulus at 110 and at the end of 115.

[2] Cf. II.12 and see Summary, pp. xxxv–xxxvi.

harmed Regulus more than he harmed himself? Therefore, religious respect that subverts something so beneficial has no force.'

'Or was he avoiding acting dishonourably? First of all, "The least of evils". Surely that dishonourableness did not include as much evil as the torture he endured. And again, there are the words of Accius:

> Have you broken faith? I gave none; and nor do I, to
> any faithless man.[1]

That was, it is true, said by an irreligious king, but the words are very fine.'[2]

(103) Furthermore, they add this: we say that some things seem beneficial that are not; similarly they say that some things seem honourable that are not. Thus it seems honourable to have returned to torture in order to keep a sworn oath; it was not, however, honourable because something exacted by the enemy through force ought not to have been authoritative.[3] They argue in addition that anything that is extremely beneficial becomes honourable even if it did not seem so beforehand. Those, roughly, are the arguments raised against Regulus. Let us, then, look at the first ones.

(104) 'He ought not to have feared that a wrathful Jove would harm him, because it is his wont neither to be angry nor to do harm.' Such reasoning has no more force against Regulus than it does against any sworn oath. One ought to understand not what fear there is in such an oath, but what force: for a sworn oath is a religious affirmation; and if you have promised something by affirmation with the god as witness you must hold to it. What is relevant here is not the anger of the gods, which does not exist, but justice and faith. For what about Ennius' splendid words, 'O winged and nurturing Faith, and oath sworn in Jupiter's name'? Therefore anyone who violates a sworn oath violates Faith, whom our ancestors wanted to dwell on the Capitol, as 'neighbour to Jove, the greatest and best', as the speech of Cato puts it.[4]

(105) 'But not even a wrathful Jove would have harmed Regulus

---

[1] Atreus to Thyestes in the *Atreus* of Accius.
[2] Regulus had been captured by ambush (99), and the Carthaginians were generally regarded as a treacherous people (cf. 1.38).
[3] See 1.32 *fin.*
[4] The cult of Fides had a shrine built in 249 BC on the Capitoline next to the temple of Jupiter. The speech of the Elder Cato is lost.

more than he did himself.' That would certainly be true if nothing were evil except to suffer pain. However, philosophers of the greatest authority assert not only that that is not the greatest evil, but that it is not an evil at all.[1] Do not, I pray, find fault with Regulus, who is no humble witness in such matters, but, I suspect, one to be taken very seriously indeed. For whom could we request more reliable than a leader of the Roman republic who voluntarily accepted torture in order to discharge his duty?

As for the saying, 'the least of evils'; that is, act dishonourably rather than disastrously, is there any greater evil than dishonourableness? If something offensive is found in a bodily disfigurement, then how much deformity and foulness ought to be apparent in a spirit made dishonourable! (106) Therefore those who discuss these matters with more verve dare to say that the only evil is what is dishonourable; and even those who do so more laxly do not doubt that that is the greatest evil.

And as for the words, 'I gave none; and nor do I to any faithless man', the poet was right to use them because when he was handling Atreus he had to serve the needs of his role. But if they adopt for themselves the view that faith given to a faithless person is nullified, they should take care that they are not seeking a hiding place for perjury.

(107) Moreover, there are laws of warfare,[2] and it often happens that faith given to an enemy must be kept. For if an oath has been sworn in such a way that the mind grasps that this ought to be done, it should be kept; if not, then there is no perjury if the thing is not done. For example, if an agreement is made with pirates in return for your life, and you do not pay the price, there is no deceit, not even if you swore to do so and did not. For a pirate is not counted as an enemy proper, but is the common foe of all.[3] There ought to be no faith with him, nor the sharing of any sworn oaths. (108) For it is not perjury to swear something false; but if you swear something 'in accordance with your mind's opinion' to use the words

---

[1] The Stoics, contrasted at the beginning of 106 with the Peripatetics. See Summary, pp. xxxv–xxxvii.

[2] Cf. 1.35–8.

[3] Cf. p. 78, n. 1. Later when civil war and invasion made brigandage prevalent, lawyers felt it necessary to say that no action for division of property could be brought by plunderers (*praedones*) because there can be no valid contract or agreement with them (*Digest* x.3.7.4).

with which we customarily express it,[1] to fail to do that is perjury. For as Euripides neatly said:

'I swore with my tongue; I have kept my mind unsworn.'[2]

But Regulus was right not to overturn by perjury stipulations and agreements made with an enemy in war. For the enemy with whom the war was being waged was just and legitimate. The whole of our fetial code is about such an enemy and we have many other laws that are shared. If that were not so, the senate would never have delivered notable men in chains to the enemy.[3] (109) Yet Titus Veturius and Spurius Postumius, in their second consulship, after fighting unsuccessfully at Caudium, when our legions were sent under the yoke, had made peace with the Samnites. As a result, they were handed over to them: for they had done it without the order of senate and people. Tiberius Numicius and Quintus Maelius, who were then tribunes of the people, were also handed over at the same time, by way of rejecting the peace with the Samnites; for the peace had been made with their authority. Furthermore, the man who was the author and advocate of their being handed over was Postumius, who was being handed over himself.[4]

The same thing happened many years later, when Gaius Mancinus, who had made a treaty with the Numantini without senatorial authority, proposed a bill to the effect that he be handed over to them. Lucius Furius and Sextus Atilius carried it in accordance with a senatorial decree. This was passed, and he was handed over to the

---

[1] *Ex animi tui sententia* was a formula used in solemn oaths. C.'s point is not that one can break promises that one did not really mean at the time, but rather that oaths in certain categories need not be kept, e.g. those given to men outside society. It would, however, be perjury to break a solemn promise freely made to an appropriate person, such as a legitimate enemy; then the mind would 'grasp that this ought to be done' (107).

[2] *Hippolytus* 612.

[3] See 1.36 with n. 1 on the fetial code. In 109 C. gives examples from 321 (Caudine Forks) and 136 (Mancinus), and a counter-example from 139 BC. By listing them out of chronological order he gives the impression that Roman moral standards have declined (see Introduction, p. xxvii).

[4] According to Livy IX.5 ff., the peace was a *sponsio*, a pledge to negotiate a peace on their return, guaranteed by the lives and property of the Roman officers who were party to it. It was repudiated by Rome as invalid because it had been made without the authorization of the Roman people. The men were surrendered to release Rome from any moral obligation.

enemy.[1] Mancinus acted more honourably than Quintus Pompeius, who in a similar case made a plea against the law, which was not passed. In this case, what seemed to be beneficial carried more weight than honourableness; in the previous ones, the false appearance of benefit was overcome by the authority of honourableness.

(110) 'But an oath exacted through force ought not to have been authoritative.' As if force could be used against a brave man![2]

'Why then did he go to the senate, when he was intending specifically to dissuade them in the matter of the captives?'[3] Here you are criticizing what in fact is the greatest thing about it. For he did not rely on his own judgement, but he took up the case so that judgement might belong to the senate. If he had not been its author, the captives would immediately have been handed back to Carthage; and thus Regulus would have remained in safety in his country. But it was because he thought that that was not beneficial to his country that he believed it honourable for himself to make such a proposal, and to suffer. As to their claim that what is extremely beneficial becomes honourable – it does not *become* so; rather it is so. For nothing is beneficial that is not honourable; but it is not honourable because beneficial, but beneficial because honourable.

Out of the many amazing examples there are, therefore, one could not easily produce one more praiseworthy or outstanding than this one. (111) Of all the praise due to Regulus, however, this one thing is worthy of marvel, that he proposed retaining the captives. It seems amazing to us now that he returned, but in those days he could not have done otherwise. Praise for that belongs not to the man, but to his times; for our ancestors desired that no bond should bind faith more tightly than a sworn oath. The laws of the Twelve Tables show that, as do the sacred laws and those treaties by which our faith is pledged even with an enemy: and again, the investigations and punishments of the censors, who used to render judgements nowhere with greater care than in the case of sworn oaths.

(112) When Lucius Manlius, son of Aulus, was dictator, Marcus

---

[1] The Mancinus case, unlike the first case, involved a formal treaty, but the precedent was held to apply so as not to break the agreement without compensation to the enemy.

[2] Cf. 103. In 1.32 C. admitted that justice does not require fulfilment of oaths taken under compulsion. Here he defends Regulus' behaviour not as *just* but as *brave* (cf. p. 139, n. 1): since the wise man does not regard pain as an evil, he cannot be forced to behave badly.

[3] C. returns to the first objection (101).

Pomponius, a tribune of the people, indicted him on the grounds that he had added a few days to his tenure of the dictatorship. He also charged him with having sent his son Titus, who was later called Torquatus, away from other men, ordering him to live in the country. When the young man, his son, heard that someone was giving his father trouble, he hurried to Rome; at daybreak, so the story goes, he arrived at Pomponius' house. This was announced to Pomponius, who, thinking that the angry man was about to bring him some more information against his father, rose from his bed, sent away any witnesses, and bid the young man to come in. He entered; and at once he drew his sword swearing that he would kill the man immediately if he did not swear an oath that he would have his father discharged. Pomponius was driven by his fear to swear it; he reported the matter to the people, telling them why it was necessary for him to withdraw the case, and he had Manlius discharged. That is how great the power of a sworn oath was in those days. He was, by the way, the same Titus Manlius who was challenged by a Gaul at the Anio and killed him, then by taking his torque acquired his surname. In his third consulship the Latins were routed and put to flight at the Veseris. He was a great man, among the best; very indulgent towards his father, and at the same time harshly severe towards his son.[1]

(113) On the other hand, just as Regulus must be praised for keeping his oath, similarly the ten men whom Hannibal sent to the senate after the battle of Cannae must be condemned, if in fact they did not return. For they were under oath to return to the camp, which the Carthaginians had seized, if they did not succeed in arranging for the captives to be ransomed. Not everyone has the same account of this; for Polybius, a fine author and among the best, records that of the ten eminently noble men who were sent on that occasion, nine did return from the senate after failing to secure their request.[2] One of the ten, he goes on, who had returned to the camp a little after he had left it, as if he had forgotten something, remained at Rome. His explanation was that by his return to the camp he had

[1] He put his son to death for disobeying his orders at Veseris in 340 BC. Though this was legally within the power of a Roman father, C. regards his action as harsh. Note the disapproval of his father's action even in the 4th century BC.

[2] In 216 BC after the Roman defeat of Cannae. At 1.40 (see n. 2), C. says nothing of alternative versions and tells the story differently from Polybius (VI.58 ff.) and Acilius: all stayed in Rome and were dishonoured by the censors (as in Livy XXII.61.9), but only one practised the sophistry.

freed himself from his sworn oath. He was not right, for deceit does not undo perjury, but rather it binds it tight. This was a foolish craftiness, crookedly imitating good sense. Therefore the senate decreed that the crafty old rogue should be bound and taken to Hannibal.

(114) But this was the greatest thing: Hannibal was holding 8,000 men, who had neither been taken in battle by him, nor fled through fear of death, but who had been left in the camp by the consuls Paullus and Varro. The senate decided that they should not be bought back, although this could have been done for a small price; thus it would be implanted in our soldiers that they must either conquer or die. The same writer records that when Hannibal heard this his spirit was broken, because the senate and Roman people had shown such a lofty spirit in time of adversity. In this way things that seem beneficial are defeated in a comparison with what is honourable. (115) On the other hand, Caius Acilius, who wrote a history in Greek, says that several men had returned to the camp, employing the same deceit in order to be freed from their oath; he reports that they were branded by the censors with all kinds of disgrace.

Let that be the end of this topic. For it is clear that things that are done with timid, lowly, dejected and broken spirit (as Regulus' action would have been if he had either proposed doing with the captives what seemed to be in his own interest rather than that of the republic, or else been willing to remain at home) are not beneficial, because they are disgraceful, shameful, dishonourable.

(116) There remains the fourth section, which consists of seemliness, moderation, modesty, self-control and restraint. Can anything, then, be beneficial that is counter to such a chorus of virtues as this? The Cyrenaics and the philosophers named Annicerii,[1] who follow Aristippus, placed all good in pleasure and considered that virtue should be praised only on the grounds that it was productive of pleasure. They are outdated now; but Epicurus flourishes, and he is the author and promoter of more or less the same proposal. We must fight against these 'with horse and foot' as the saying goes, if it is our proposal that honourableness be guarded and preserved. (117) For if, as Metrodorus has written, not only what is beneficial, but the happy life in its entirety, consists in strength of constitution along with an examined hope of its continuance, then such benefit

---

[1] See Biographical Notes under Amniceris and Plan, p. xxxiv.

(which in their view is, of course, the highest) will conflict with honourableness.

First of all, where will good sense find a place? In seeking high and low for pleasant experiences? What wretched servitude for virtue to wait upon pleasure! What will be the office of good sense? To select those pleasures intelligently? Grant that nothing could be more enjoyable than that; but what could be thought of that is more dishonourable? Again, if someone says that pain is the greatest evil, what place does courage, which is the disdaining of pain and toil, have with him? For Epicurus may speak bravely about pain in many places, as indeed he does; but we should not look at what he might say, but at what accords with the words of a man who has defined goods by pleasure, and evils by pain. Similarly, if I listen to him, he says many things in many places about self-control and restraint; but 'the water sticks', as the saying goes. For how can a man praise restraint when he places the highest good in pleasure? For restraint is hostile to the passions; but the passions are pleasure's adherents.

(118) However, they still twist and turn over these three classes of virtue in whatever way they can, and not without craftiness:[1] they bring in good sense as a knowledge that provides pleasures and repels pains; they also explain courage in a way, by leaving us a reasoned method of ignoring death and enduring pain.[2] They even introduce restraint, not very easily, it is true, but however they can; for they say that the limit of the greatness of pleasure is the removal of pain. Justice totters, or rather falls flat, along with all the virtues that are found in sociability and in the fellowship of the human race.[3] For there can be neither goodness nor liberality nor courteousness, no more than friendship,[4] if these are not sought for their own sakes, but are directed towards pleasure or benefit.

Let me condense all that, then, in a few words. (119) I have taught

---

[1] Though C. introduces his attack on the hedonists under the fourth virtue because he regards the pursuit of pleasure as incompatible with modesty and restraint, he thinks they undermine all four virtues.

[2] Epicurus claimed that he had kept the balance of pleasure over pain even in his last agony.

[3] C. holds that the Epicureans can accommodate, however implausibly, three of the virtues, but not justice, the most important (but cf. p. 114, n. 1). In particular, abstention from public life conflicted with one of C.'s basic requirements of justice (e.g. 1.28).

[4] A shrewed hit, as the Epicureans attached great value to the pleasure derived from friendships.

that there is nothing of benefit that is contrary to honourableness; similarly I say that all pleasure is contrary to honourableness. I judge that Calliphon and Dinomachus ought to be criticized all the more because they thought that they would dissolve the controversy by coupling pleasure with honourableness, as if man with beast. But honourableness does not accept the union; she spurns it, rejects it. Indeed the end of good things, which ought to be single, cannot be mixed and blended out of dissimilar things. But I have spoken about this elsewhere at length (for it is an important matter).[1] Now to return to the subject.

(120) We have sufficiently debated above the way in which one must adjudicate the matter whenever what seems to be beneficial conflicts with what is honourable. But if pleasure, too, is said to have the appearance of the beneficial, there can be no union of it with honourableness. To grant something to pleasure, it may perhaps provide a little spice; but it will certainly provide nothing really beneficial.

(121) Here you have a present, Marcus my son, from your father; something great, in my view, but it will be as you receive it. These three books should be accepted as fellow guests, as it were, among your lecture notes from Cratippus.[2] If, however, I had come to Athens in person (as indeed I should have done had not my country called me back in a loud voice in the middle of my journey)[3] you would sometimes be hearing me also. In the same way, then, since now my voice reaches you in these volumes, may you give them as much time as you can; you can, of course, give them as much time as you wish. When I understand that you are enjoying this type of learning, then I shall discuss it with you, from afar as long as you are away, but very soon, as I hope, face to face. Farewell, then, my dear Cicero, and be assured that you are very dear indeed to me, and will be far dearer if you take delight in such guidance and advice.

[1] *De Finibus* II contains a general critique of Epicurean ethics; V.21–2 deals with combining pleasure and virtue in the definition of the end of life.
[2] Cf. I.1–2. Young Cicero refers to his lecture notes in writing to Tiro (*Fam.* XVI.21.8).
[3] See Introduction, pp. xiv, xviii.

Biographical Notes

(These notes include only persons mentioned in the text of *De Officiis*. For the Greek philosophers, consult also the Plan and the Summary of the Doctrines of the Hellenistic Schools)

ACCIUS (170–*c*.90 BC). Roman writer, particularly acclaimed for his tragedies of which fragments of 46 have come down to us. He handled his Greek models, notably Euripides, freely and also wrote on Roman subjects. In youth C. had met him.

ACILIUS, GAIUS (mid second century BC). A Roman senator and historian who acted as interpreter when the famous Athenian embassy composed of philosophers addressed the Senate in 155 BC. He wrote a history in Greek from early Italian times down to at least 184 BC, which was then translated into Latin.

AEACUS, in mythology, grandfather of Achilles, who became a judge in the underworld.

AELIUS TUBERO, QUINTUS. Nephew of P. Cornelius Scipio Aemilianus and a pupil of the Stoic philosopher Panaetius, he was a senator and an accomplished lawyer. According to C., his Stoic austerity affected his oratory adversely (*Brutus* 117).

AEMILIUS LEPIDUS LIVIANUS, MAMERCUS. He was consul in 77 BC after having been defeated for the office, possibly in 78, because of his failure to hold the aedileship earlier in his career, an office that offered opportunities for pleasing the populace.

AEMILIUS PAULLUS, LUCIUS (1). As consul in 219 BC he won a brilliant victory in the Second Illyrian War, but as consul in 216 he was in command during the terrible Roman defeat at Cannae against Hannibal and was killed in battle.

AEMILIUS PAULLUS, LUCIUS (2), the natural father of P. Cornelius Scipio Aemilianus. In his third tenure of the consulship in 168 BC, he ended the Third Macedonian War by a victory at Pydna and took as his own booty only the library of King Perseus. His triumph was saddened by the death of his two younger sons, the two eldest having been adopted by a Fabius and a Cornelius Scipio.

AEMILIUS SCAURUS, MARCUS (1), a statesman of the late second and early first century BC whom C. admired. He came from an impoverished aristocratic family but rose to be consul in 115 BC and censor in 109 BC. Known for his conservative politics, he appears in Sallust as a dishonest intriguer.

AEMILIUS SCAURUS, MARCUS (2), son of the above. He gave particularly magnificent games as aedile in 58 BC, was praetor in 56, and then in 54 was successfully defended by C. in a trial for alleged extortion during his governorship of Sardinia. In 52 he was convicted of electoral malpractice in his campaign for the consulship.

AESOPUS, a famous actor, more sedate than his contemporary Roscius and hence unfit for the part of Ajax who went mad. He gave C. elocution lessons.

AFRICANUS: see CORNELIUS SCIPIO AFRICANUS

AGAMEMNON, king of Mycenae or Argos who, in Homer's *Iliad,* leads the Greek expedition against Troy. The tradition that he sacrificed Iphigenia is not in Homer. This occurred because a seer blamed the becalming of the fleet on the offence given to Artemis (the Roman Diana) by Agamemnon while hunting. Iphigenia's mother, Clytemnestra, in revenge killed her husband on his victorious return from Troy.

AGESILAUS (440–360 BC). As Spartan king from 399, he enjoyed military success against the Persians and the Boeotians until he was decisively defeated by Epaminondas at the Battle of Leuctra. His virtues were celebrated by his friend Xenophon in his *Agesilaus.*

AGIS IV became king of Sparta in 244 BC. He sought to increase manpower and reduce inequalities of wealth by restoring the 'constitution of Lycurgus'. This involved the cancellation of mortgages. He was deposed and executed by command of the ephors in 241.

AJAX, a hero of great strength and courage, who in Homer's *Iliad* is matched with Odysseus (Ulysses) in a wrestling match as a contest of strength against cunning. In Sophocles' play of the name, he goes mad and kills himself when the armour of the dead Achilles is given to Odysseus rather than to him.

ALBUCIUS, TITUS, praetor *c.*105 BC. After governing Sardinia *c.*104, he was convicted of extortion and went into exile in Athens, where he pursued his passion for Greek culture and for Epicurean philosophy.

ALEXANDER THE GREAT (356–332 BC). His father Philip II, whom he succeeded as king of Macedonia, had secured him Aristotle as his tutor. A magnificent general, he founded a great overseas empire by conquering the Persian Empire, including Egypt, and annexing areas of northwest India. His violent and vengeful nature led him into crimes that tarnished his glorious reputation.

ALEXANDER of PHERAE, ruler of Pherae in Thessaly (369–358 BC). He married his niece Thebe, daughter of his predecessor Jason. She killed him, assisted by her three brothers.

ANNICERIS, a philosopher of the Cyrenaic school founded by Aristippus. He died in 283 BC. He modified the doctrine but still held that pleasure was the goal of life.

ANNIUS MILO, TITUS, one of Cicero's political allies who opposed his enemy Clodius and supported Cicero's return from exile in 57 BC. Milo's career illustrates the use of organized violence in the politics of the Late Republic. His feud with Clodius ended in the latter's death at the hands of Milo's gangs in 52. Though Cicero defended him at his trial, the hostility of Pompey ensured his conviction. In 48 he returned to Rome from Massilia to press for radical economic reforms but was captured and executed at Cosa.

ANTIGONUS (*c.*382–301 BC), one of the generals of Alexander the Great and father of Demetrius Poliorcetes. After Alexander's death he tried to reunite Alexander's kingdom but was defeated and killed in the Battle of the Ipsus against rival generals including Cassander.

ANTIPATER (397–319 BC), close military and political associate of Philip II of Macedon and his son Alexander. He remained in charge of Macedonia after Alexander's death. His two books of letters to his son Cassander are lost.

ANTIPATER of TARSUS, successor of Diogenes of Babylon as head of the Stoic school at Athens in the mid-second century, and teacher of Panaetius who succeeded him. He defended himself in writing against the criticisms of Carneades, the sceptical leader of the Academy.

ANTIPATER of TYRE, a Stoic philosopher with whom the younger Cato studied moral and political philosophy in youth: not to be confused with the older Antipater above.

ANTONIUS, MARCUS, consul of 99 BC and the grandfather of Mark Antony (Marcus Antonius). In C.'s view, he was one of the leading orators of his age, the other being L. Licinius Crassus who appears with him as a speaker in *De Oratore*. He defended C. Norbanus in 95 BC and was killed after Marius' return to Rome in 87 BC.

APELLES, renowned Greek painter of the fourth century BC. He died in Cos while making an improved copy of his painting of Aphrodite (Venus).

AQUILLIUS, MANIUS. After serving under Marius in the war against the Cimbri, he was his colleague as consul in 101 BC. Though successful in crushing a slave revolt in Italy in that year, he was later prosecuted for peculation but was supported by C. Marius and M. Antonius and acquitted. He served on a mission to Asia which provoked Nicomedes of Bithynia to attack Mithridates, who captured and killed Aquillius in 88.

AQUILLIUS GALLUS, GAIUS, senator and jurist and, like C., a pupil of Q. Mucius Scaevola the Pontifex. After being praetor in 66 BC, the same year as C., he devoted himself to the law. He created the *formulae de dolo malo* which enabled either party to plead the bad faith of the other in a lawsuit (cf. *De Natura Deorum* III.74) and also improved procedures for discharging debts.

ARATUS (271–213 BC). After his father's murder in 264, he went to Argos from which he returned to liberate his native Sicyon from the rule of Nicocles, the last of a series of tyrants. He avoided further civil dissension by securing money from Ptolemy Philadelphus of Egypt. He attached Sicyon to the Achaean Confederacy of which he became the leader.

ARISTIDES, Athenian statesman of the fifth century, often called 'The Just' because of his reputation for honesty. He was a general at the Battle of Marathon in 490 BC and held the post of archon in 489. Worsted in his political conflict with Themistocles, he was ostracized in 482, but, after being recalled on the eve of Xerxes' invasion, he co-operated with Themistocles in winning the Battle of Salamis in 480 and later in rebuilding the walls of Athens. The architect of the Delian League, he fixed the tribute for the member states. He died a poor man.

ARISTIPPUS, traditionally the founder of the Cyrenaic school in the late fifth century BC and a companion of Socrates. He taught that sensual pleasure was the proper goal of life.

ARISTOTLE (384–22 BC). Born in Stagira in Chalcidice, he was a student in the Academy at Athens until Plato's death. He founded the Lyceum, the Peripatetic School. His learning was encyclopaedic: he developed the disciplines of ethics, politics and history, of rhetoric and poetics, of psychology, natural philosophy and metaphysics, and founded the systematic study of meteorology, logic and zoology. His popular dialogues, now lost, were still available in C.'s day. The 'esoteric works' that we know, however, may have been little studied until a thorough edition of them was prepared by Andronicus, assisted by C.'s friend Tyrannio, perhaps after C.'s death.

ATILIUS REGULUS, MARCUS. As consul in 267 BC, he captured Brundisium. Consul again in 256, he fought successfully against Carthage but was defeated and taken prisoner in 255. Five years later, after some noble Carthaginians had been captured, he was sent to Rome to negotiate for their return, under oath to come back if he failed to persuade the Roman Senate. The story of his self-sacrifice is also celebrated by Horace in *Odes* III.5.

ATILIUS SERRANUS, SEXTUS. Consul in 136 BC, he and his colleague, with the support of the Senate, put through the assembly the bill authorizing the surrender of C. Hostilius Mancinus to the Numantines in Spain as expiation for the Senate's repudiation of the treaty made with them by Mancinus.

ATREUS, father of Agamemnon. According to Greek mythology, he laid his family under a curse by killing the children of his brother Thyestes and serving them at a banquet to which Thyestes had been lured by deception or, in the version in III.102, by oath.

AUFIDIUS ORESTES AURELIANUS, CNAEUS. Aedile by 79 BC, he became praetor in 77 but apparently never reached the consulship despite the popularity he secured as aedile.

AURELIUS COTTA, GAIUS, one of three brothers active in Roman politics. His oratory is praised by C. in several of his rhetorical works. An associate of L. Licinius Crassus in youth, he was exiled and then restored by Sulla. As consul in 75 BC he supported a concession to the popular demand for the restoration of their powers to the tribunes of the plebs. He speaks for the sceptical Academic position in C.'s *De Natura Deorum*.

BARDULIS, a leader of the Illyrians who founded a kingdom north of Macedonia in the fourth century BC. He died fighting Philip II of Macedonia in 358.

BRUTUS: see JUNIUS BRUTUS.

CAECILIUS METELLUS MACEDONICUS, QUINTUS. In 146 BC he celebrated a triumph over the King of Macedonia. In 143, as consul, he fought successfully against the Numantines and in 131 he was censor. He opposed the attempt by Tiberius Gracchus to secure by popular legislation the legacy of King Attalus of Pergamum for his land programme.

CAECILIUS METELLUS NUMIDICUS, QUINTUS. As consul in 109 BC, he had some success against Jugurtha in Africa but was then superseded in his command by C. Marius who was appointed by popular legislation. In contrast to III.79, the other sources say that Metellus insulted Marius when he asked to be allowed to return to Rome to stand for the consulship. In 100 Metellus was the only senator who refused to take the oath to observe the agrarian law of Saturninus. He was sent into exile but was recalled a year or two later. C. saw him as a model for his own exile and return.

CAESAR, GAIUS LUCI FILIUS = JULIUS CAESAR STRABO VOPISCUS, GAIUS.

CALLICRATIDES, the commander of the Spartan fleet when the Athenians in 406 BC gained a great victory at Arginusae off the coast of Asia Minor, two years before their final defeat in the Peloponnesian War.

CALLIPHON, Greek philosopher of uncertain date who tried to reconcile Epicurean and Stoic views of the goal of life by saying that virtue is first pursued as a means to pleasure but afterwards becomes an end in itself.

CALPURNIUS LANARIUS, PUBLIUS. Probably the same as an officer serving in Spain in 81 BC under C. Annius.

CALPURNIUS PISO, LUCIUS. He passed the first extortion law as tribune of the plebs in 149 BC and went on to become consul in 135 and censor in 120. His historical work *Annales* recounted Roman history from the origins of the city to his own time, and dated the decline of Roman morality from 154 BC.

CALYPSO, a nymph in Homer's *Odyssey* who detained the hero for seven years on the island of Ogygia.

CANIUS, GAIUS, a Roman *eques* known only from III.58–9, an episode clearly dated by III.60 to before 66 BC.

CASSANDER (358–297 BC), son of Antipater. He served under Alexander the Great in Asia and, after his father's death, resisted the plan of Antigonus to reunite Alexander's kingdom, fighting to keep his own hold on Macedonia and Greece.

CATO: see PORCIUS CATO

CATULUS/I: see LUTATIUS CATULUS

CHRYSIPPUS (250–207 BC), the third head of the Stoa, after Zeno and Cleanthes. He was regarded as the second founder of the Stoic school because in his voluminous writings he set out the doctrines fully in their logical order.

CICERO (the son): see TULLIUS CICERO

CIMON, Athenian statesman of the first half of the fifth century BC. The son of Miltiades, general at the Battle of Marathon in 490, Cimon came to prominence after the final victory over Persia in 480/79. His naval victories increased the Athenian empire and secured a period of peace with Persia. His admiration for Sparta, constitutional conservatism and aristocratic style of largesse set him in opposition to his democratic political rivals.

CIRCE, a nymph in Homer's *Odyssey* who detained the hero on her island for a year.

CLAUDIUS CENTUMALUS, TIBERIUS, known only from III.66, an episode dateable to before 91 BC when the Porcius Cato mentioned there died.

CLAUDIUS MARCELLUS, MARCUS. Consul five times, he slew the king of the Insubres, a Gallic tribe, with his own hand in 223 BC, thus becoming the third and last general to win the *spolia opima* ('rich spoils'). Later he captured Syracuse in Sicily in 212 during the Second Punic War against Carthage.

CLAUDIUS PULCHER, GAIUS. As aedile in 99 BC, he exhibited elephants for the first time in the Circus Maximus. He became consul in 92.

CLEOMBROTUS, the Spartan commander at the Battle of Leuctra when the Thebans under Epaminondas inflicted a disastrous defeat on the Spartans. His rashness stemmed from his desire to counter the suspicion that he was sympathetic towards the enemy.

CLODIUS PULCHER, PUBLIUS. Really one of the patrician Claudii, he used the popular spelling of his name and later transferred to plebeian status in order to become tribune of the plebs in 58 BC. As tribune he forced C., who had given evidence against him during his trial for sacrilege in 61, into exile. Among other democratic measures, he passed a bill against those who had put Roman citizens to death without trial, as C. had done with the Catilinarian conspirators. After the conference at Luca in 56, he supported the coalition of Pompey, Caesar and Crassus. In 52, when he was a candidate for the praetorship, he was killed by Milo's gangs.

COCLES: see HORATIUS

COLLATINUS: see TARQUINIUS COLLATINUS

CONON, a late fifth-century Athenian admiral. After Athens was defeated by Sparta in 405, he tried to win Persian help for Athens and succeeded in defeating Sparta in 394.

CORNELIUS LENTULUS SPINTHER, PUBLIUS. As aedile in 63 BC, the year of C.'s consulship, he had the stage lavishly decorated for performances. As consul in 57, he was active in supporting C.'s recall from exile.

CORNELIUS SCIPIO, CNAEUS. Though the younger brother of Publius Cornelius Scipio (1), he was consul earlier in 222 BC. He was killed in Spain during the Second Punic War after defeating Hannibal's brother Hasdrubal and capturing Saguntum in 212.

CORNELIUS SCIPIO, PUBLIUS (1). As consul in 218 BC, he fought and died with his brother Cnaeus (above). He was the father of Scipio Africanus who finally defeated Hannibal.

CORNELIUS SCIPIO, PUBLIUS (2), elder son of Africanus (below). An outstanding orator, he wrote a history in Greek, but ill health prevented him from taking up a public career. He adopted the elder son of L. Aemilius Paullus.

CORNELIUS SCIPIO AFRICANUS, PUBLIUS (236–184/3 BC), usually referred to by C. as the 'first' or 'elder' Africanus. Entrusted when very young by the people with the command in Spain during the Second Punic War, he was brilliantly successful. As consul in 205 BC, he invaded Africa, despite senatorial opposition, and in 202 defeated Hannibal at the Battle of Zama for which he acquired the cognomen Africanus. In 194 he was consul again, accompanied his brother Lucius who was in command in the East and was then implicated in his prosecution for misconduct in office.

CORNELIUS SCIPIO AFRICANUS AEMILIANUS, PUBLIUS. As his name indicates, he was born a son of L. Aemilius Paullus and was adopted by P. Cornelius Scipio (2). In 147 BC, during the Third Punic War, he was elected consul, despite having held none of the lower offices. He conquered and destroyed Carthage in 146. Consul again in 134, he was sent to deal with the difficult war in Spain where he destroyed the city of Numantia in 133. On his return to Rome the next year, he made clear his disapproval of Tiberius Gracchus' methods, and in 129 he championed the cause of the Italians due to lose holdings of public land under the Gracchan legislation. When he was found dead, there were rumours of murder. On the basis of his friendship with the Greek historian Polybius in youth and with the philosopher Panaetius in the 130s, C. created a picture of him as a statesman who combined Roman patriotism, morality and good sense with Greek culture, and made him the principal speaker in *De Re Publica*.

CORNELIUS SCIPIO NASICA, PUBLIUS, son of Scipio Nasica Serapio (below).

Consul in III BC, he died in that year. C. praised him for his wit (*Brutus* 128), and Posidonius for his virtue.

CORNELIUS SCIPIO NASICA SERAPIO, PUBLIUS, grandson of Scipio Africanus (the elder) and cousin of the Gracchi brothers, he was *pontifex maximus* (head of the state religion) and consul in 138 BC. When Tiberius Gracchus tried to be re-elected as tribune in 133 and was accused of aiming at tyranny, he took the law into his own hands, and led a band of senators against Tiberius, who was killed in the skirmish. Regarded as a villain by the people, he was sent by the Senate to Asia as an ambassador and died at Pergamum.

CORNELIUS SULLA, LUCIUS (*c.*138–78 BC), the Dictator. After being consul in 88 and marching on Rome with his army in order to retain his command against Mithridates King of Pontus, Sulla concluded the peace of Dardanus with the king and invaded Italy in 84. He defeated his political enemy Marius and became Dictator in 82. He first carried out a proscription of his enemies, confiscating their property and denying them the protection of the law, and in 81 he enacted a legislative programme designed to give an enlarged Senate political control. C. deplored his methods but respected his legislation.

CORNELIUS SULLA, PUBLIUS, a relative of the Dictator (above) who profited in the proscriptions and helped to found a veteran colony at Pompeii. Elected consul in 65 BC, he was permanently disqualified for office after being convicted of using bribery to be elected. In 62 he was successfully defended by C. when put on trial as a confederate of the conspirator Catiline. Later he joined Caesar's side in the civil war against Pompey.

CRASSUS: see LICINIUS CRASSUS

CRATIPPUS (MARCUS TULLIUS CRATIPPUS), eminent Peripatetic philosopher born at Pergamum. Inscriptions there show that he took the name and tribe of C. after being granted Roman citizenship, at C.'s request, by Caesar (cf. Plutarch, *Cicero* 24). Originally a pupil of Antiochus of Ascalon, he deserted the Academy and was teaching as a Peripatetic in Mitylene on Lesbos by July of 51 BC when he went to meet C. on his way to his province of Cilicia. He was of the social class that mixed easily with Roman aristocrats, like Pompey and Brutus. C. persuaded the Areopagus to invite him to teach in Athens, where he taught and socialized with C.'s son, dining with him (*Fam.* XVI.21.3) and offering to travel with him (*Fam.* XII.16.2).

CURIO: see SCRIBONIUS CURIO

CYRSILUS, an Athenian who was stoned to death in 480 BC by his fellow citizens when he proposed surrendering to the Persian King Xerxes instead of evacuating Attica and resisting. The story, not in Herodotus (our main historical source for the events of 481–479 BC), is told by the orator Demosthenes (*On the Crown* 204).

CYRUS, founder of the Persian Empire which he ruled from 559–529 BC. He was for the Greeks a model ruler despite his subjection of the Greeks on the coast of Asia Minor. Xenophon gave an idealized picture of him in the *Education of Cyrus*, a work which was well known at Rome.

DAMON, a Pythagorean from Syracuse. His friendship for Phintias was demonstrated, and in one version deliberately tested, when he stood bail for his friend who had been sentenced to death by Dionysius II, tyrant of Syracuse.

DECIUS MUS, PUBLIUS. Father and son of the same name sacrificed themselves for Rome, the father in a battle against the Latins in 340 BC, the son in a battle against the Samnites, Umbrians and their allies in 295 (Livy VIII.9; X.28).

DEMETRIUS of PHALERUM, an Athenian Peripatetic philosopher and statesman. Appointed by Cassander, then ruler of Macedonia, as absolute ruler of Athens for ten years (317–307 BC), he passed just legislation under the influence of Theophrastus but was ousted when Demetrius Poliorcetes took Athens. C. praises him as a rare example of the philosopher–ruler (*Leg.* III.14). He was for a time in charge of the library at Alexandria.

DEMETRIUS POLIORCETES (336–283 BC) succeeded his father Antigonus as King of Macedonia in 294 and followed his policy of reconquering Alexander's kingdom but was deserted by the Macedonians for the invaders Lysimachus and Pyrrhus.

DEMOSTHENES (384–322 BC), Athenian orator particularly admired by C. (see ISOCRATES).

DANA, an Italian goddess identified with the Greek Artemis, the huntress.

DICAEARCHUS, a fourth-century Peripatetic philosopher from Sicily, a pupil of Aristotle and contemporary of Theophrastus. Only fragments of his works survive.

DINOMACHUS, Greek philosopher of uncertain date who tried to reconcile Epicurean and Stoic views of the goal of life. He is regularly coupled with Calliphon in the ancient sources.

DIOGENES of BABYLON (*c.*240–152 BC) was a pupil of Chrysippus and teacher of Antipater of Tarsus who succeeded him as head of the Stoa in Athens.

Along with Carneades the Academic and Critolaus the Peripatetic, he was sent as ambassador to Rome in 155 BC to plead for the remission of a fine imposed on Athens for sacking Oropus.

DION (*c.*408–354 BC), the uncle of Dionysius II who was the ruler of Syracuse. He was impressed by the teaching of Plato who visited there in 389 and tried to train his nephew as a philosopher–ruler but was forced into exile. He then seized Syracuse in 357 when Dionysius was away and ruled himself in an autocratic style which led to his assassination in 354 by his fellow Academic Callippus.

DIONYSIUS I, ruler of Syracuse (406–367 BC). He extended the control of Syracuse over Sicily and southern Italy and brought prosperity to the city. His reputation suffers from Plato's failure to exercise influence over him and his son (below).

DIONYSIUS II, son of Dionysius I and ruler of Syracuse (367–344 BC), who rejected the teaching of Plato and the influence of his uncle Dion. After Dion temporarily seized control of Syracuse, Dionysius returned in 347 but was then defeated by Timoleon in 344. He lived in exile at Corinth for many years.

DRUSUS: see LIVIUS DRUSUS.

ENNIUS, the first Latin poet to write an epic, the *Annals* in twelve books, in the hexameter metre taken over from the Greeks. He also wrote plays, from which come most of C.'s quotations, as the metre reveals.

EPAMINONDAS. An important figure in the restoration of his native Thebes to a position of importance in Greece during the 370s BC. At the Battle of Leuctra in 371 he decisively defeated the invading Spartan army and went on to liberate Arcadia and Messenia from Spartan control.

EPICURUS (341–271 BC). An Athenian citizen born in Samos, he founded in 307 a philosophical school called the Garden from its premises in Athens. In ethics he taught that the goal of life was pleasure, though his interpretation of living pleasantly was quite austere. He adopted and modified the atomic theory of Democritus.

ERILLUS: see HERILLUS

EURIPIDES (*c.*485– *c.*406 BC), Athenian playwright. Of his eighty plays, most of them tragedies, we have nineteen. C. quotes here from *The Phoenician Women* and the *Hippolytus*.

FABIUS LABEO, QUINTUS, consul in 183 BC. In the *Brutus* 81 C. describes a man of this name, probably his son, who was an expert in law, literature and antiquities.

FABIUS MAXIMÚS VERRUCOSUS, QUINTUS. He acquired the nickname Cunctator (Delayer) because of the tactics he developed to fight Hannibal during the Second Punic War. As dictator in 217 BC and later, during his third to fifth consulships, he conducted a war of attrition enabling Rome to recover from her disastrous defeats at the Battle of Lake Trasimene in 217 and the Battle of Cannae in 216.

FABRICIUS LUSCINUS, GAIUS. As consul in 282 and 278 BC, he was a successful military commander in the war with King Pyrrhus and acquired a lasting reputation for incorruptibility from the incident reported in I.40 and III.86–7.

FLAVIUS FIMBRIA, GAIUS (called 'ex-consul' by C. to distinguish him from his notorious contemporary of the same name who killed and supplanted his commander in 86 BC). The first consul of his family, he served as Marius' colleague in 104 BC, then governed a province and was later prosecuted and acquitted on a charge of extortion. He was dead by 91. C. praises his good sense and reliability as an orator and a senator in the *Brutus* 129.

FUFIUS, LUCIUS, mentioned several times as a mediocre orator by C. He was unsuccessful in prosecuting Manius Aquillius.

FURIUS PHILUS, LUCIUS. As consul in 136 BC with Sextus Atilius Serranus, he and his colleague put through the assembly the bill authorizing the surrender of Hostilius Mancinus to the Numantines. He carried out the surrender and, as one of the speakers in C.'s *De Re Publica*, relates the episode (III.28).

GRACCHUS/I: see SEMPRONIUS GRACCHUS

GYGES king of Lydia (*c.*685–657 BC). He secured the throne and founded the Mermnad dynasty by murdering King Candaules with the co-operation of the king's wife. C. uses the version in Plato's *Republic* according to which he was a shepherd who achieved this by the help of a magic ring that made him invisible. Herodotus ascribes the opportunity to his service in the king's bodyguard.

HAMILCAR (BARCAS), father of Hannibal. He was an important Carthaginian general fighting Rome for control of Sicily from 247–229/8 BC during the First Punic War and then, after the Carthaginian defeat in 241, for control of Spain. In the latter campaign he was accompanied by his son.

HANNIBAL (247–*c.*182 BC), the great Carthaginian general. He inherited from his father (above) an imperialistic policy towards Spain and a hatred of Rome. His capture of Rome's ally, the city of Saguntum, precipitated the Second Punic War (218–201) in which he invaded Italy from the north. Having failed to detach most of Rome's allies from their allegiance, he finally withdrew his army and was defeated in north Africa by Scipio Africanus at the Battle of Zama in 202.

HECATON, Stoic philosopher from Rhodes. A pupil of Panaetius, he is credited with works on ethics, including the one mentioned at III.63 and 89, but only fragments (many of them problematic) survive.

HERCULES, Roman name for the Greek mythical hero Heracles, known for his twelve labours and other feats of strength and endurance. C. alludes at I.118 to one tradition that he was one of the many illegitimate sons of Jupiter, the king of the gods.

HERILLUS of Carthage. A pupil of the Stoic Zeno, he founded a separate Stoic sect which died out by 200 BC. On his unorthodox views, see p. 4, n. 1.

HERODOTUS, the first Greek historian. Born in Halicarnassus, he composed in the second half of the fifth century BC a history of the relations between Greeks and Persians down to the Persian defeats at Plataea and Mycale in 479 BC.

HESIOD, Greek poet who lived in Boeotia probably in the second half of the eighth century BC. His most notable poems are the *Theogony* on the relationships between the gods and the *Works and Days* on the farmer's life.

HIPPOLYTUS, in Greek mythology, the son of Theseus by the Amazon Hippolyta. Several ancient tragedies, notably a surviving one by Euripides tell the story of his stepmother Phaedra's tragic passion for him. When rejected by him, she made false accusations about him which enraged Theseus on his return home and moved him to use one of the three wishes previously granted him by Neptune, the god of the sea, to ask for his death. The god sent a sea monster to kill Hippolytus.

HOMER, the blind poet of the *Iliad* and the *Odyssey* according to Greek tradition. The date of Homer, his birthplace and the common authorship of both poems were disputed even in ancient times. It is clear that each poem in the form we have them contains material carefully selected from a larger store of traditional stories and unified by a consummate artist earlier than 700 BC.

HORATIUS COCLES. Roman tradition held that he defended the bridge over the Tiber single-handed against the army of Lars Porsena, the Etruscan invader (Livy II.10).

HORTENSIUS HORTALUS, QUINTUS (114–50 BC). Consul in 69 BC, he was the greatest orator of his generation until surpassed by C. He had a florid ornate style and a magnificent memory. C., whose good relations with his older rival are credited to a common friendship with Atticus by Nepos (*Atticus* 5), pays a particularly handsome tribute to him in the *Brutus*.

HOSTILIUS MANCINUS, GAIUS. As consul in 137 BC, he was defeated by the Numantines in eastern Spain and negotiated a peace treaty through his quaestor Ti. Sempronius Gracchus. When the Senate repudiated the treaty at the suggestion of Cornelius Scipio Aemilianus, he supported the bill passed by the consuls of 136, L. Furius Philus and Sex. Atilius Serranus, to surrender him to the enemy in expiation. The Numantines returned him, and he was later readmitted to Roman citizenship and held office again.

IPHIGENIA: see under AGAMEMNON

ISOCRATES (436–338 BC), great Athenian orator of whose speeches twenty-one survive. He was the rival of the orator Demosthenes whose policy of hostility to Macedonia he opposed, in favour of a united Greek and Macedonian attack on Persia.

JASON of Pherae. As tyrant of Pherae in Thessaly from *c.*385–370 BC, he managed to create and rule a united Thessalian state, but his more ambitious designs were cut short by his assassination.

JOVE, or Jupiter, a Roman sky-god identified with the Greek Zeus, King of the gods, and associated with the protection of treaties and oaths.

JUGURTHA. Designated in the will of King Micipsa who died in 118 BC as one of three joint rulers of Numidia in Africa, he had one of them murdered and attacked the other. Popular opinion finally forced the Senate to take strong action and dispatch Q. Caecilius Metellus (later Numidicus). C. Marius then secured the command from the people in 107, but Jugurtha was not captured until 105. He was led in triumph and then executed at Rome.

JULIUS CAESAR, GAIUS (the Dictator). He was proud of his connection by marriage with C. Marius and pursued a *popularis* course in politics. In addition to securing the ordinary magistracies, he was elected *pontifex maximus* through a lavish use of bribery in 63 BC. In that year suspicions of his implication in the Catilinarian conspiracy were fed by his opposition to the imposition of the death penalty on the conspirators in the senatorial debate conducted by C. He passed radical legislation by force during his consulship of 59, after forming a coalition with Pompey and M. Licinius Crassus, commonly known as the 'first triumvirate'. He invaded Italy in 49 rather than give up his command in Gaul and face a possible politically motivated prosecution. In the intervals of fighting a civil war against Pompey and his supporters, he had himself chosen Dictator and passed a great deal of legislation. He was assassinated on 15 March 44.

JULIUS CAESAR STRABO VOPISCUS, GAIUS. A distinguished orator, he appears as the chief speaker on wit in C.'s *De Oratore*. Having prosecuted T. Albucius successfully in youth, he became aedile in 90 BC and then tried the next year to be elected consul illegally without having held the praetorship. He was killed after the return of Marius to Rome in 87. Through his mother Popilia, he was the half-brother of Q. Lutatius Catulus (1).

JUNIUS BRUTUS, LUCIUS, the traditional founder of the Roman Republic. He led the revolt against the Tarquin kings and was one of the first pair of consuls at Rome. When he discovered that his sons were plotting with the nephews of his consular colleague L. Tarquinius Collatinus, he killed his sons and caused his colleague to abdicate his office and leave Rome. He passed a law banishing all Tarquins.

JUNIUS BRUTUS, MARCUS. He was the son of a famous jurist and a member of the family of L. Junius Brutus (above). He was also related in an uncertain way to M. Junius Brutus who killed Caesar the Dictator. He was active in the early part of the first century BC. By choosing to appear regularly in the courts as a prosecutor, he acquired a bad reputation.

JUNIUS PENNUS, MARCUS. As tribune of the plebs in 126 BC, he carried a law, over the opposition of C. Sempronius Gracchus, to prevent non-citizens from settling in Roman towns and to expel those who had done so.

JUNIUS SILANUS, DECIMUS. He was aedile by 70 BC. Later, as consul-elect in 63, he spoke first in the session of the Senate convened by C. as consul to debate the fate of the Catilinarian conspirators. He proposed the death penalty but then changed his mind, influenced by the speech of C. Julius Caesar urging lifelong imprisonment.

LAELIUS, GAIUS (called 'The Wise'). A close friend of Cornelius Scipio Aemilianus, he served under him at the siege of Carthage in 146 BC. He then served in western Spain as praetor fighting Viriathus and in 140 became consul. In 132 he was on the senatorial commission to punish the followers of Ti. Sempronius Gracchus. C. made him the principal speaker in *Laelius de amicitia,* and a participant in *De Re Publica.* C. at one time saw himself as a Laelius to Pompey's Scipio (*Fam.* v.7).

LENTULUS: see CORNELIUS LENTULUS SPINTHER

LICINIUS CRASSUS, LUCIUS (140–91 BC). C., who had studied with teachers approved by him at his house, regarded Crassus as the greatest orator of the preceding generation and made him the principal speaker in *De Oratore*. C. also admired his moderate conservative politics. Crassus was the colleague of Q. Mucius Scaevola the Pontifex as aedile, praetor and finally consul in 95 BC, when they legislated against aliens who tried to pass as citizens. Their *Lex Licinia Mucia* enraged the Italians and was a cause of the Social War that followed four years later. In 92 as censor, he prohibited the teaching of rhetoric in Latin, and in 91 he died while supporting the programme of the tribune Livius Drusus who wished to make concessions to various disaffected groups including the Italians.

LICINIUS CRASSUS DIVES, MARCUS. A supporter of Sulla in the civil war with Marius in the 80s BC, he suppressed the slave revolt led by Spartacus in the late 70s, and then became consul with Pompey in 70. He was a member of the so-called 'first triumvirate' (see under JULIUS CAESAR), held the consulship again in 55 and was killed in 54 while holding a special command in Syria against the Parthians. In *De Finibus* III.75 C. plays on his family name Dives ('rich') in ascribing his desire for this command to greed (cf. III.73 and 75). At I.25 C. describes his greed as a means to political influence, a view supported by the historian Sallust who notes the effect of the loans and gifts he had made to many senators (*Catiline* 48.5). He believed C. had been behind the rumours of his involvement in the Catilinarian conspiracy, a charge C. did make in secret memoirs left unpublished at his death.

LICINIUS CRASSUS DIVES, PUBLIUS, father of the above. Since he was consul in 97 BC, he must have given his magnificent games as aedile *c.*103 (II.57). He killed himself after the victory of Marius and Cinna in 87.

LICINIUS LUCULLUS, LUCIUS. A prominent supporter of Sulla in youth, he gave splendid games as aedile in 79 BC, became consul in 74 and received a special command from the Senate against King Mithridates of Pontus. He had notable military successes, but a mutiny by his soldiers and opposition from Roman interests, provoked by his equitable tax settlement in Asia, led to his being replaced in his command by Pompey. He retired in 59 to a life of cultured luxury in his villas at Tusculum and Misenum. C. made him the spokesman for the views of Antiochus of Ascalon, who had accompanied him on his eastern campaigns, in the first edition of the *Academica*.

LICINIUS LUCULLUS, MARCUS, younger brother of the above. After adoption he bore the name Marcus Terentius Varro Lucullus. Also a supporter of Sulla, he was aedile in the same year, praetor in 76 and consul in 73. He triumphed in 71 for victories as proconsul in Macedonia.

LIVIUS DRUSUS, MARCUS. Son of the tribune of the plebs of 122 BC who used *popularis* methods against C. Sempronius Gracchus, he too defended the interests of the Senate as tribune in 91 BC, but in a more imaginative way. His programme aimed to satisfy the grievances of various groups, offering land distribution to the poor, a share in the criminal courts to the senators, possibly entry to the Senate for some *equites*, and citizenship to the Italians. He met opposition on all sides in Rome and was murdered. His legislation was rescinded.

LUCULLUS/I: see LICINIUS LUCULLUS

LUTATIUS CATULUS, QUINTUS (1): Of a noble but submerged family, he finally, after three electoral defeats, became consul in 102 BC and helped his colleague C. Marius to win the final battle against the Cimbri in 101. In 87 he opposed Marius and Cinna, was threatened with prosecution and committed suicide. He wrote prose and verse and was interested in philosophy and in the arts, as we learn from C., especially in *De Oratore*. He was an adherent of the sceptical Academy like C.; it is his view that his son was made to expound in the first edition of the *Academica*.

LUTATIUS CATULUS, QUINTUS (2), son of the above. He was a supporter of Sulla and his favoured candidate for the consulship of 78 BC. When his colleague M. Aemilius Lepidus became a revolutionary, Catulus, with help from Pompey, defeated him. Regarded as one of the leaders of the *optimates* in the Senate, he opposed alterations to Sulla's laws, the special commands conferred on Pompey in 67 and 66, and the attempts of his colleague in the censorship in 65 to give Roman citizenship to the Transpadani. He was defeated by Julius Caesar in the election for *pontifex maximus* in 63 and thereafter his influence declined until his death *c*.61. C. gave him the role of defending philosophy in the *Hortensius*, and originally made him one of the speakers in the *Academica*, but, meeting with criticism because of Catulus' well known lack of expertise in philosophy, he transferred the part to himself in the second edition.

LUTATIUS PINTHIA, MARCUS, a Roman *eques* who lived in the early first century BC. All that is known of him is the story at III.77 which belongs before the death of C. Flavius Fimbria in 91 BC, perhaps after his consulship in 104 BC.

LYCURGUS, legendary founder of Sparta's constitution and of her distinctive military and social institutions. Ancient traditions about the date and occasion of his reforms are various and confused.

LYSANDER (1), Spartan general and statesman. As admiral of the fleet in the last stages of the Peloponnesian War, he finally secured Persian aid and defeated the Athenians at Aegospotami in 405 BC. After his blockade of the Piraeus brought about the surrender of Athens in 404, he instituted the rule of The Thirty there. His ambition earned him distrust at Sparta. He died in 395 during the Corinthian War.

LYSANDER (2), the ephor. As one of the annually elected ephors, he introduced bills to implement the reforms of King Agis IV in the middle of the third century BC.

LYSIS, a fourth-century BC Pythagorean philosopher from Tarentum in southern Italy. When his sect was persecuted, he fled to Greece, where he taught Epaminondas in Thebes.

MAELIUS, QUINTUS. He was probably tribune-elect in 321 BC when he served on the consuls' staff at the time of the Roman defeat by the Samnites at the Caudine Forks. (Actual tribunes of the plebs were not allowed to leave Rome.)

MAMERCUS: see AEMILIUS LEPIDUS LIVIANUS

MANCIA, possibly identical with the Helvius Mancia adduced in *De Oratore* II.266 and 274 as a wielder and target of wit in the 90s BC. Years later, when taunted with his age and low origins (his father was an ex-slave), he called Pompey 'teen-age murderer'. The identification at I.109 is difficult, because he is made, with three well-born senators, an example of 'great power' combined with easy social manner; if it is correct, either he was a prominent senator despite his origins or the 'great power' must in his case have been his outrageous outspokenness.

MANCINUS: see HOSTILIUS MANCINUS

MANLIUS CAPITOLINUS IMPERIOSUS, LUCIUS, dictator in 363 BC. He was indicted for trial before the popular assembly by the tribune Marcus Pomponius in 362 BC (see also under Pomponius).

MANLIUS IMPERIOSUS TORQUATUS, TITUS, the son of the above, whose indictment included the charge of mistreating his son. He saved his father from prosecution and went on to acquire the name Torquatus by killing a Gaul in combat and taking his torque as booty. He was consul three times. In his last tenure of 340 BC his own son disobeyed his orders and engaged the enemy in single combat during the battle against the Latins at Veseris. For this Manlius put him to death.

MARCELLUS: see CLAUDIUS MARCELLUS

MARCIUS PHILIPPUS, LUCIUS. After behaving like a demagogue while tribune of the plebs in 104 BC, he went on to become a formidable conservative, opposing, as consul in 91, the moderate measures of Livius Drusus. He joined Sulla's side in the civil conflict with Marius and supported the appointment of Pompey to two commands in 78 against Lepidus and in 77 against Sertorius. C. heard him speak in the Senate in old age and admired him.

MARCUS (CICERO); see TULLIUS CICERO

MARIUS, CAIUS (*c.*157–86 BC). Born in C.'s home town of Arpinum, he was related by marriage to C.'s grandmother. He achieved the lower magistracies with difficulty, despite the support of the Metelli. While serving on the staff of Metellus Numidicus in Africa, he exploited discontent with senatorial policy there to secure election to the consulship of 107 BC, aged fifty, and then to the command against Jugurtha. When the Cimbri threatened to invade Italy from the north, Marius was elected consul for 104 and then four more times in succession. He defeated the Cimbri in 101, but his collaboration with radical politicians in his last consulship of 100 led to a period of eclipse, until in 88, he tried to wrest the eastern command from Sulla and found himself embroiled in civil war. In 86 he captured Rome with Cornelius Cinna and became consul again, but died before he could take up the eastern command.

MARIUS GRATIDIANUS, MARCUS, nephew by birth and by adoption of C. Marius. His natural father, Marcus Gratidius, was the brother-in-law of C.'s grandfather, with whom he clashed over the introduction of the secret ballot at Arpinum. Like his father, he was a *popularis* in politics, taking the side of Marius against Sulla in the 80s. As praetor in 85, he published an edict enforcing the official exchange rate of bronze to silver at a time of financial instability, thus acquiring all the popularity for a measure that was to have been a joint declaration (III.80). He became praetor again in 84 and was killed in the Sullan proscriptions of 82.

MAXIMUS: see FABIUS MAXIMUS VERRUCOSUS

METELLUS: see CAECILIUS METELLUS

METRODORUS of LAMPSACUS (331–227 BC), the most important disciple of Epicurus. Only fragments of his works survive. C. regarded his philosophy as even more sensual than that of Epicurus because of its emphasis on bodily pleasure.

MILO: see ANNIUS MILO

MINOS, legendary king of Crete who became a judge in the underworld.

MINUCIUS BASILUS, LUCIUS. He served under Sulla when he occupied Rome in 88 BC and later in the East against Mithridates. He had died in Greece by 70 when C. mentioned his will in his speeches in defence of Verres.

MUCIUS SCAEVOLA, PUBLIUS. An eminent jurist like his father and son, he was consul in 133 BC. Having advised the tribune Tiberius Gracchus on his agrarian bill, he refused to use violence against the tribune, though he later defended the action of P. Cornelius Scipio Nasica Serapio. *Pontifex maximus* from 130 to his death *c.*115, he was credited with compiling and publishing the yearly pontifical records called the *annales maximi.*

MUCIUS SCAEVOLA, QUINTUS (1), called 'The Augur'. Cousin and younger contemporary of the above, he was also a jurist. He was the son-in-law of Laelius and is credited with Stoic sympathies. Consul in 117, he opposed the radical tribune Saturninus in 100, but also defied Sulla after his march on Rome in 88. C. studied law with him when he was an old man.

MUCIUS SCAEVOLA, QUINTUS (2), called 'The Pontifex'. The son of P. Mucius Scaevola (above), he was also a jurist and published the first systematic treatise on civil law. He shared the aedileship, praetorship and consulship with L. Licinius Crassus. As governor of Asia sometime in the 90s BC, he introduced a reorganization which remained a model for subsequent governors, though it offended the tax collectors. He became *pontifex maximus* in 89 but was killed in 82 at the command of the consul C. Marius.

MUMMIUS ACHAICUS, LUCIUS. He sacked and destroyed Corinth in 146 BC and shipped its art treasures back to adorn Rome and other Italian cities. He received the name Achaicus for his victory over the Achaean Confederacy. He was later censor with Scipio Aemilianus.

NEPTUNE, the Italian god Neptunus, identified with the Greek sea-god Poseidon.

NICOCLES, tyrant of Sicyon. He was deposed by Aratus in 251 BC.

NORBANUS, GAIUS. As tribune of the plebs in 103 BC, he supported his radical colleague Saturninus. He was prosecuted in the *optimate* interest by P. Sulpicius in 95 and defended by M. Antonius under whom he had served as quaestor. He became consul in 83 during the civil war, was defeated by Sulla and fled to Rhodes where he committed suicide.

NUMICIUS, TIBERIUS. He was probably tribune-elect, not tribune, in 321 BC (see under Q. Maelius) when serving on the consuls' staff at the time of the Roman disaster at the Caudine Forks.

Biographical Notes

OCTAVIUS, CNAEUS. Probably the son of a praetor, he became consul in 165 BC. His brother was the great-grandfather of the later Emperor Augustus.

OCTAVIUS, MARCUS, probably a tribune of the plebs when he changed the legislation about subsidized corn (Cic. *Brutus* 222 and n. 1 on *Off.* II.72).

ORESTES: see AUFIDIUS ORESTES AURELIANUS

PALAMEDES, a proverbially clever hero, often associated with the cunning Ulysses. At III.97–8 C. alludes to his exposure of Ulysses for feigning madness in order to avoid joining the Greek expedition against Troy. Ulysses yoked an ass and ox to a plough and began to sow salt, but when Palamedes placed Ulysses' son Telemachus in front of the plough, Ulysses gave up his pretence. In revenge he forged a letter from the Trojan king to Palamedes arranging for him to betray the Greeks and hid money in Palamedes' tent. Palamedes was then put to death as a traitor by the army.

PANAETIUS (*c.*180–109 BC). Born at Rhodes, he became a pupil of Diogenes of Babylon in Athens and then of Antipater of Tarsus, whom he succeeded as head of the Stoa in 129 BC. He was a friend of Cornelius Scipio Aemilianus, whom he accompanied on an embassy to the eastern Mediterranean in 140/39. In physics he rejected the Stoic tenets of divination and periodic universal conflagration. His ethics were directed towards the man making moral progress, not the sage. For C.'s use of his work, see Introduction, pp. xix–xxi.

PAPIUS, GAIUS. As tribune of the plebs in 65 BC, he passed a law expelling from Rome foreigners from beyond Italy (as then defined) and set up tribunals to check illegal assumption of citizen rights. The law, probably aimed originally at settlers beyond the Po (Transpadani), whose claim to citizenship was being supported in that year by M. Licinius Crassus as censor, was later invoked against the poet Archias, whom C. successfully defended in 62.

PAULLUS: see AEMILIUS PAULLUS

PAUSANIAS. An older relative of the young Spartan king Pleistoanax, he commanded the combined Greek land forces successfully against the Persians at Plataea in 479 BC and then led the Greek counter-offensive in 478. His arrogant behaviour led to the rejection of Spartan leadership and the formation of the Delian League led by Athens. Recalled to Sparta on a charge of Medism, he took refuge in a temple and starved to death.

PELOPS. In Greek mythology, the son of Tantalus and the father of Atreus and Thyestes.

PENNUS: see JUNIUS PENNUS

PERICLES (*c*.495–429 BC), Athenian statesman. He became prominent in the 460s BC when the Athenian democracy was becoming more radical and her imperialism more ruthless. From 443 he was elected one of the ten generals every year until he died of the plague. He initiated a great building programme and took Athens into the Peloponnesian War by resisting the demands of Sparta and her allies in the 430s. He was a powerful orator in the 'Olympian' style of his statesmanship.

PHAETHON, in mythology, the son of Helios (Sol), who was allowed to drive his father's chariot one day but was killed by Zeus (Jupiter) when his inability to control the immortal horses threatened the world with conflagration.

PHALARIS, tyrant of Agrigentum in Sicily in the second quarter of the sixth century BC. He also established his rule in Himera before being stoned to death by his subjects. He was notorious for his cruelty, especially for roasting victims alive in a hollow brazen bull.

PHILIP, son of Antigonus and brother of Demetrius Poliorcetes.

PHILIP II, King of Macedonia (359–336 BC) and father of Alexander the Great. He unified Macedonia, improved the training tactics of the Macedonian army, and, by a combination of force and diplomacy, conquered Greece. He was assassinated when about to lead combined Greek and Macedonian forces against Persia.

PHILIPPUS: see MARCIUS PHILIPPUS

PHINTIAS: see under DAMON

PISO: see CALPURNIUS PISO

PLATO (429–347 BC). He was a pupil of Socrates and founder of the Academy in Athens. Probably the most influential philosopher in western history, he raised in his dialogues fundamental questions of ethical and political theory, of epistemology and of metaphysics. C.'s main philosophical mentors, Philo, Antiochus, Panaetius and Posidonius, were great admirers of Plato, whose *Republic* and *Laws* inspired C.'s works of the same name. C. frequently quoted Plato and translated some of his works.

PLAUTUS, Latin playwright of the later third century BC. Twenty-one of his comedies, loosely based on Greek originals, survive.

POLYBIUS (*c*.200–after 118 BC), Greek historian. He was sent to Rome from Arcadia as one of those suspected of sympathy with King Perseus of Macedonia, who had just been defeated at the Battle of Pydna by the Romans in

168 BC. He remained in Rome, became a friend of Scipio Aemilianus, and wrote his history of the growth of Roman power from the Second Punic War to his own time.

POMPEIUS, QUINTUS. He was the first member of his family to gain the consulship, in which office he suffered a reverse in the war against the Numantines in Spain in 140 BC. He negotiated a treaty which he then repudiated on the arrival of his successor. The Senate approved of his action, and he was acquitted on a charge of extortion. He went on to become censor in 131.

POMPEIUS, SEXTUS, the uncle of Pompey the Great. In *Brutus* 175, C. tells us that he devoted himself not only to geometry, but to law and Stoic philosophy as well, and was not an orator. The avoidance of public life by a man of his background illustrates C.'s second 'fault' at 1.19, though he avoids explicitly saying so.

POMPEIUS MAGNUS, CNAEUS (Pompey the Great) (106–48 BC). An exact contemporary of C., he was a military and political prodigy in youth, defeating Sulla's enemies in the 80s and Sertorius in Spain in the 70s. As consul in 70 with M. Licinius Crassus, he supported the restoration of the powers removed by Sulla, to the office of tribune of the plebs and allowed the juries of the standing courts, entrusted by Sulla to senators, to include *equites*. In 67 BC the popular assembly gave him the command against the pirates and rewarded him for his dazzling successes with the eastern command against Mithridates King of Pontus in 66. On his return to Rome in 62, he faced opposition in securing rewards for his veterans and confirmation of his eastern arrangements, and therefore supported Julius Caesar for the consulship of 59. These two with Crassus, P.'s consular colleague again in 55, dominated politics for the next decade as 'the first triumvirate'. After the death of Crassus in 54, Pompey remained near Rome, governing his province of Spain through subordinates, then became sole consul in 52, and finally sided with the senatorial diehards who refused to make concessions to Caesar. He was eventually defeated at Pharsalus and then murdered as he attempted to land in Egypt. C. defended his restoration of the tribunician powers in *De Legibus* II, hoped to detach him from Caesar in the 50s, and finally went east to join him in the civil war. To the end he admired him, though not uncritically.

POMPONIUS, MARCUS. As tribune in 362 BC, he indicted L. Manlius before the assembly for prolonging his dictatorship beyond the legitimate time and for mistreating his son. Other charges not mentioned by C. at III.112 concern religion and the levy.

PONTIUS, GAIUS, a leader of the Samnites. In 321 BC he defeated a Roman army at the Caudine Forks and made them pass under the yoke. Twenty-nine years later, he was captured, led in triumph and executed.

POPILIUS LAENAS, MARCUS. As consul in 172 BC, he conquered the Ligurians with great brutality.

PORCIUS CATO, MARCUS (1), the Elder (234–152 BC). The first in his family to hold the consulship (in 196 BC), he was sometimes called 'Cato the Censor' from the energy with which he pursued moral reform in that office in 184. At the end of his life he was particularly associated with an uncompromising hostility to Carthage. He was known for his vigorous defence of traditional Roman values and his lambasting style of oratory, but he was also a cultured man and an innovator in literature, composing a treatise *On Agriculture* and a history called *Origins*. His portrait is softened by C. in the *Cato Maior de senectute*.

PORCIUS CATO, MARCUS (2), the father of the Younger Cato and grandson of the above. He started on a public career, becoming tribune of the plebs in 99 BC, but died in 92 or 91 while seeking election to the praetorship.

PORCIUS CATO, MARCUS (3), the Younger, sometimes called 'Cato of Utica' (95–46 BC). Great-grandson of the Elder Cato, he added Stoic convictions to the latter's moral rigour and sense of Roman tradition, thus achieving an even more austere reputation. As quaestor in 64, he straightened out the treasury records; as tribune in 62, he extended the number of recipients of subsidized corn. In 61 C. disagreed with his insistence that the tax-collectors not be granted a revision of their contract when revenue proved less than they expected. An outspoken opponent of 'the first triumvirate', he was removed from Rome in 58 by a law of the tribune Clodius sending him to annex Cyprus. He brought back to Rome much money and treasure from the royal possessions, after the king of Cyprus committed suicide. When C. wanted Clodius' measures (which included his own exile and confiscation of his house) cancelled, on the grounds that his tribunate was illegal, Cato objected: C. apparently attributes this (III.88) to his concern for the revenue he had brought back. Cato became praetor in 54 but failed to be elected consul for 51. He joined Pompey in the civil war and, when defeated by Caesar at Utica in Africa, committed suicide.

PORCIUS CATO LICINIANUS, MARCUS, son of the Elder Cato. He did his military service (1.36) and held the lower magistracies, but died in 152 BC, after being elected as praetor for the next year.

POSIDONIUS (135–51 BC). Born at Apamea in Syria, he became a pupil of Panaetius. He travelled widely in the Mediterranean, gathering material for scientific and cultural research. He settled in Rhodes where he held a priesthood. The leading Stoic philosopher of his day and a polymath, he wrote on ethics, physics, logic, theology, psychology, astronomy, geography and history. He was on good terms with Pompey and with C., who first heard him in Rhodes as a young man and later tried unsuccessfully to elicit from him an account in Greek of C.'s consulship.

POSTUMIUS ALBINUS, SPURIUS. As consul for the second time in 321 BC, he and his colleague T. Veturius Calvinus, when defeated at the Caudine Forks, made peace by a *sponsio* (pledge) in which they and others pledged their lives and property as guarantors of the peace. On their return, the Senate took Postumius' advice, rejected peace, and surrendered him and the others pledged to the Samnites, who rejected them.

PRODICUS of CEOS, a sophist and contemporary of Socrates, the author of the famous myth about the choice of Hercules.

PTOLEMY PHILADELPHUS (308–246 BC) became king of Egypt in 283 in succession to his father Ptolemy Soter who had secured control of Egypt after the death of Alexander the Great. He created the Ptolemaic financial administration and cultural institutions.

PYRRHO of ELIS (*c.*365–*c.*270 BC), founder of the Pyrrhonists, who held that withholding judgement and having no beliefs led to the ethical goal of tranquillity. He left no writings. In C.'s day Aenesidemus of Cnossus initiated a revival of Pyrrhonism. His followers later became known as 'Sceptics', literally, 'inquirers'.

PYRRHUS (*c.*319–272 BC), King of Epirus. He reigned from 297 to his death, freed his kingdom from Macedonian influence, and expanded its territory at the expense of its neighbours. His invasions of Macedonia were less successful. Taking the pretext provided by a request for help from the Greek city of Tarentum in southern Italy, he won two victories against the Romans in 280–279, invaded Sicily, returned to Italy, and was finally narrowly defeated in 275 at Beneventum.

PYTHAGORAS. Born in Samos in the latter part of the sixth century BC, he fled from the tyranny of Polycrates to Croton in southern Italy where he founded a philosophical and religious order, of which the last traces disappeared in the late fourth century BC. He left no writings and soon became a legendary figure, who attracted great interest in Rome in C.'s day. The 'unity in plurality' idea (I.56) finds an echo in the later idea of a friend as an *alter ego*.

PYTHIUS, a banker from Syracuse, known only from III.58–9, an episode dated to before 66 BC by the praetorship of Aquillius mentioned in III.60.

QUIRINUS: see ROMULUS

REGULUS: see ATILIUS REGULUS

ROMULUS. He was the legendary founder of Rome with his brother Remus whom he killed for leaping over the walls he had built around the new settlement. After forty years as king, he is supposed to have vanished and become the god Quirinus.

ROSCIUS AMERINUS, SEXTIUS. He was the son of a prosperous citizen of Ameria with whose murder he was charged in 80 BC by two relatives. They, with the help of Sulla's minion Chrysogonus, had actually secured his father's death by having his name entered on the proscription lists. C. defended Roscius in his first public case, being careful, when attacking Chrysogonus, to separate him from Sulla, who, though no longer dictator, was consul at the time.

RUPILIUS, an actor known only from C.'s reference in I.114.

RUTILIUS RUFUS, PUBLIUS. He studied with Panaetius and observed Stoic teaching even in his austere style of oratory. Consul in 105 BC, he served under Q. Mucius Scaevola (2) when the latter was governor of Asia. He was unjustly condemned for extortion in 92 BC by a jury of *equites* dominated by the tax collectors, who had suffered from the reforms introduced by Rufus and Scaevola. While in exile at Smyrna, he wrote memoirs and history.

SATRIUS, MARCUS, called after his adoption by his uncle, L. Minucius Basilus (Satrianus). Mentioned in III.74 as an unwelcome patron of territory in Picenum and the Sabine country, he is also attacked by C. in the Second Philippic Oration as an associate of Antony: he must have been involved in distributing land to veterans in these areas. He is probably distinct from Caesar's assassin L. Minucius Basilus.

SCAURUS: see AEMILIUS SCAURUS

SCIPIO: see CORNELIUS SCIPIO

SCRIBONIUS CURIO, GAIUS. Having fought under Sulla in the East, he became consul in 76 BC and censor in 61. The incident recorded by C. at III.88 must belong before his death in 53, and after 89 when most of the Transpadani received Latin rights, whereas the rest of Italy, including those south of the Po River, received full Roman citizenship. As censor in 65, M. Licinius Crassus unsuccessfully supported their demand for Roman citizenship, which was ultimately granted by Julius Caesar in 49.

SEIUS, MARCUS, a Roman *eques* who, having lost that status as a result of a conviction, was elected aedile for 74 in spite of aristocratic competition. In that office he established his popularity by subsidizing wheat and oil in a time of scarcity caused by the prevalence of piracy and war.

SEMPRONIUS GRACCHUS, GAIUS. He and his brother Tiberius were the sons of Cornelia, the daughter of Scipio Africanus and mother-in-law of Scipio Aemilianus. For their distinguished father, see below. Gaius served under Scipio Aemilianus in Spain and was appointed in 133 BC to his brother's agrarian commission. As tribune of the plebs in 123 and 122, he not only renewed his brother's agrarian law but instituted more sweeping reforms. He was killed in a riot early in 121. Though his move to give citizen rights to the Italians failed and his colony Junonia was cancelled, much of his legislation survived, such as his law assuring citizens wheat at a stable and subsidized price.

SEMPRONIUS GRACCHUS, TIBERIUS (1), the consul of 177 BC. A famous general, he conquered the Celtiberians and founded the city of Gracchuris in Spain, later subjugating Sardinia. He was known for his conservative principles and personal austerity. He died in 154 when his surviving sons, Tiberius (2) and Gaius (above), were only boys.

SEMPRONIUS GRACCHUS, TIBERIUS (2), elder surviving son of (1) above. As tribune of the plebs in 133 BC, he sought to remedy the declining numbers of Roman citizens (and probably Italians), especially those with the property qualification for military service, by limiting holdings of land belonging to the Roman state and distributing the excess to the poor. The methods he used in forcing through this bill and in securing the legacy of King Attalus of Pergamum to help finance his land programme caused outrage then and later. He was killed in a riot while trying to be re-elected tribune. The view of C. that the Gracchi were rightly killed (II.43, cf. I.76) goes back to a speech of Scipio Aemilianus about Tiberius. C. is condemnatory of the brothers, except in some of his speeches to the people.

SERGIUS ORATA, GAIUS, a clever Roman business man of the first century BC. He was the first to use the Lucrine lake near Baiae on the Bay of Naples to breed oysters for commercial purposes. The case related in III.69, dated to 91 BC or shortly before by *De Oratore* I.178, may have concerned a house in this area, perhaps bought as an investment. If it is identical with a case against Considius, the liability may have been a ban on fishing rights in some part of the property on the Lucrine Lake where the Roman state had a right of taxation (Valerius Maximus IX.I.I). The participation of the two most famous orators of the day in such a case may partly be explained by their possession of property on that coast.

SILANUS: see JUNIUS SILANUS

SOCRATES (469–399 BC). A philosopher and citizen of Athens, who showed great courage both under the democracy and under the regime of the Thirty Tyrants. He was tried in 399 by a popular jury under the restored democracy and condemned for impiety and corruption of the youth. His speech in self-defence and his last days in prison were recounted by his pupil Plato, who also made Socrates the principal speaker in most of his other dialogues. As Socrates wrote nothing himself, it is difficult to be sure how much, if any, of the positive philosophical views in Plato derive from him, but his pretence of knowing nothing himself, his way of leading his interlocutors to question inherited ethical views, and his concentration on human conduct, described in Plato's early dialogues, were accepted by C. as true to his method (*Fin.* II.I ff.; *Rep.* I.I6). Plato's Academy, Aristotle's Peripatos, and the Stoa all claimed to descend from him.

SOL, the Roman sun-god.

SOLON, Athenian statesman and poet of the early sixth century BC. Having fought in Athens' war with Megara for the possession of Salamis, he became chief archon in 594/3 BC when he resolved a political and economic crisis by abolishing debt bondage, basing eligibility for office on property rather than birth, creating the *Boule* (a council that prepared business for the assembly) and establishing the *Heliaia* (the people sitting as a court of appeal). He then left Athens to travel for ten years. Many of his measures survived, and he was later regarded as the founder of the Athenian democracy.

SOPHOCLES (*c.*494–406 BC). He was an Athenian statesman as well as being one of the greatest Athenian playwrights. He served as imperial treasurer and was twice elected general, first in 440 when, along with Pericles, he helped to suppress the revolt of Samos.

SULLA: see CORNELIUS SULLA

SULPICIUS GALUS, GAIUS. He was praetor in 169 BC and consul in 166. When serving under L. Aemilius Paullus in 168 during the wars against Macedonia, he put his astronomical skill at the service of the state by predicting a lunar eclipse and thus preventing a panic among the soldiers on the eve of battle.

SULPICIUS, PUBLIUS, tribune of the plebs in 88 BC. He was related to C.'s close friend Atticus and appears in *De Oratore* as one of the young men associated with Livius Drusus, the tribune of 91. In 95 he made his oratorical debut prosecuting Norbanus. In 88 he tried, in the spirit of Livius Drusus, to have the newly enfranchised Italians distributed fairly throughout the Roman tribes and, when opposed, allied himself with Marius to whom he had Sulla's command against Mithridates transferred. When Sulla marched on Rome, he fled but was captured and killed. His legislation was abrogated.

TANTALUS. In Greek mythology, he was the father of Pelops and the son of Jupiter. Having eaten divine food, he was immortal and therefore had to suffer eternal punishment for his various transgressions against the gods.

One version gives this punishment as being 'tantalized' by food and drink that forever eluded him.

TARQUINIUS COLLATINUS, LUCIUS. He was the husband of Lucretia, whose rape by the last Tarquin king impelled him to join the conspiracy to end the Roman monarchy. He and Lucius Junius Brutus were the first pair of consuls of the new Republic, but (depending on the source) he either abdicated or was removed from office, either because he was thought to be sympathetic to a conspiracy to restore the Tarquins or because the Tarquin name attracted too much odium.

TARQUINIUS SUPERBUS (Tarquin the Proud), the last of the Roman Kings, who traditionally reigned from 534–510 BC and was expelled by Lucius Junius Brutus.

TERENCE (P. Terentius Afer), Latin playwright of the first half of the second century BC. Born in North Africa, he came to Rome as a slave and was freed by his senatorial master whose name he thus acquired. His six plays are all comedies freely based on Greek originals.

TERENTIUS VARRO, GAIUS. Consul in 216 BC, he was thanked by the Senate for not despairing of the Republic after Hannibal's victory at Cannae. In the later tradition, he alone was blamed for the defeat, as his consular colleague was killed on the battlefield.

THEBE, wife of Alexander of Pherae whom she conspired to kill.

THEMISTOCLES (*c.*528–462 BC), Athenian statesman credited with starting Athens on the path to naval supremacy before the invasion of Xerxes. As general in 480 BC, Themistocles commanded the Athenian fleet and persuaded the Spartan commanders to fight at Salamis and the Athenians to evacuate their homes and meet the Persians at sea. By the time his exploits were celebrated by Aeschylus in *The Persians* (472), he had been ostracized and then condemned in absence for alleged intrigues with Persia, to which he fled. King Artaxerxes made him governor of Magnesia where he died, probably of illness, though C. adheres to the tradition of suicide. C.'s letters show that he was much in C.'s thoughts in 49. C. compared his strategy of evacuation to Pompey's plan to leave Italy and fight Caesar in the East, and saw in the exile and suicide of the far-seeing Themistocles an indication of what might befall himself should his expectations of Caesar's fall prove wrong.

THEOPHRASTUS, pupil and successor of Aristotle as head of the Peripatetic School in Athens. Only a small fraction of his writings, which enjoyed great popularity, survive. His interests were scientific research and scholarship; in philosophy he largely followed Aristotle.

THEOPOMPUS, a Greek historian of the fourth century BC. Nothing but fragments survives of his work. He continued the history of Thucydides down to 394 BC and wrote the history of the reign of Philip II of Macedonia.

THESEUS, legendary king of Athens. He is credited with bringing the different villages of Attica into political union. He is the hero of many adventures, e.g. the killing of the Minotaur in Crete. He defeated the Amazons and won for himself Hippolyta who became the mother of his son Hippolytus.

TIMOTHEUS, Athenian statesman of the fourth century BC. He implemented an imperialistic policy for the Second Athenian League but was ultimately impeached and fined. A pupil of Isocrates, he is often praised by C. as an orator.

TUBERO: see AELIUS TUBERO

TULLIUS CICERO, MARCUS, C.'s only son. He was born in 65 BC when his sister Tullia was already 13 or 14 years old. He accompanied his father to Cilicia in 51 and assumed the *toga virilis* (the adult toga) in 49 BC. He went with his father to join Pompey in the East during the civil war with Caesar, and his military service earned praise from Pompey (II.45). He and his father returned to Italy and were pardoned by Caesar in 47. The next year he held office in the family's home town of Arpinum. He wanted to join Caesar in Spain but, in the spring of 45, C. sent him to Greece to study instead, providing him with an allowance, from his mother Terentia's dotal property, sufficient for him to keep up with his aristocratic contemporaries. By then his parents were divorced and his sister Tullia was dead. Even before Caesar was murdered in March of 44, C. contemplated visiting his son in Athens and on 17 July he actually set sail but then returned immediately because of an apparent change in the political situation. Marcus served under Brutus in the civil war against Antony and Octavian and was thus out of Rome when his father was proscribed and killed on 7 December 43. After the defeat of Brutus at Philippi in 42, Marcus joined Pompey's younger son in Sicily. In 39 he was pardoned by Octavian and returned to Rome. After Octavian had defeated Antony at the Battle of Actium, he took Marcus as colleague in the consulship of 30, the year in which statues and monuments of Antony were destroyed. (Antony had been chiefly responsible for his father's death, though Octavian had consented.) He then served as governor of the province of Asia. The evidence suggests that he was an obedient boy and a good soldier but that he lacked his father's intellectual gifts. Later tradition held that he was a hard drinker. (See also Introduction, pp. xvi–xviii.)

ULYSSES, the Roman name for the Greek hero Odysseus, who in Homer's *Iliad* is associated with the stratagem of the Trojan horse. In the *Odyssey* he has many adventures during his ten year journey home after the Trojan War; on his return to Ithaca disguised as a beggar, he is treated as such by his household and the suitors of his wife Penelope, until he slays the suitors and reveals his identity. Other stories of his cunning were told in the later poems of the Homeric cycle and in Greek tragedy. When Paris abducted Helen and all her suitors were obliged (by an oath invented by Odysseus himself) to fight the Trojan War on behalf of Menelaus, he feigned madness to avoid going but was unmasked (see under Palamedes).

VARRO: see TERENTIUS VARRO

VETURIUS CALVINUS, TITUS. As consul for the second time in 321 BC, he and his army were trapped by the Samnites in the Caudine Forks. For the terms of the *sponsio* made to the Samnites, see under Postumius Albinus.

VIRIATHUS, Portuguese national hero who led his people, the Lusitanians, in maintaining their independence against the Romans by guerrilla warfare in the second half of the second century BC. He defeated Roman commanders in 147–145 BC. After C. Laelius, there were further Roman defeats, including that of Q. Pompeius in 143, until a treaty with Viriathus was made in 140, recognizing him as a friend of the Roman people. But the Senate refused to abide by the treaty, and in 139 Q. Servilius Caepio arranged for his assassination.

XANTHIPPUS, a mercenary soldier from Sparta who helped Carthage against Atilius Regulus, reorganizing their army and using elephants and cavalry to defeat the Romans in 255 BC. After this victory he left Carthage.

XENOPHON. Born at Athens, he left in 401 BC and was exiled in 399. He went to Sparta as a friend of King Agesilaus of Sparta and later to Corinth, before returning to Athens. His works include a history, didactic works, memoirs, including one of Socrates, and a historical novel, the *Education of Cyrus* (see under Cyrus).

XERXES, son of Darius, king of Persia (486–465 BC), who invaded Greece and was defeated at Salamis in 480 BC.

ZENO (*c.*335–263 BC) of Citium in Cyprus was the founder of the Stoic School, named after the Stoa Poikile, a decorated colonnade in which he taught in Athens. Only fragments of his works survive, but all the basic doctrines of Stoicism were credited to him, though they were known for the, most part through the voluminous writings of Chrysippus two generations later.

Index of Persons and Places

(For persons, see also the Biographical Notes which are not covered by this Index.
Individual entries there are indicated here by an *.)

*Diogenes of Babylon 119, 120, 121n.,
  124n., 135
*Dion 60
*Dionysius I 71
*Dionysius II 116
Dolabella: *see* Cornelius Dolabella
Drusus: *see* Livius Drusus

*Ennius 11, 17, 22, 33, 71, 87, 123, 140
*Epaminondas 33, 60, 72n.
*Epicurus xxxvi, 105n., 114n., 145, 146
Epirus 17n.
Erillus: *see* Herillus
Eteocles 131n.
*Euripides 131n., 138n., 142

*Fabius Labeo, Quintus 14
*Fabius Maximus Verrucosus, Quintus
  33, 42
*Fabricius Luscinus, Gaius 18, 106,
  132, 133
*Flavius Fimbria, Gaius 129
*Fufius, Lucius 81
*Furius Philus, Lucius 142

Gaul 98n.
Gracchus/i: *see* Sempronius Gracchus
Greece x, xviii, 96, 97n., 127, 138
Greeks 5, 25n., 42, 55, 59, 69, 117
*Gyges 113, 114, 129
Gytheum 118

Hamilcar 138n.
*Hamilcar (Barcas), father of
  Hannibal 138
*Hannibal 17, 18, 42, 144, 145
*Hecaton xix, 123, 124, 134
*Hercules 46, 109
*Herillus of Carthage (a more accurate
  transliteration of the Greek name
  than C.'s Erillus) xxxv, 4
Hernici 15
*Herodotus 78
*Hesiod 20
Hieronymus of Rhodes 105n.
*Hippolytus 13, 137
*Homer 137, 138n.
*Horatius Cocles 25
*Hortensius Hortalus, Quintus 85, 127
*Hostilius Mancinus, Gaius 142, 143

*Iphigenia 137

*Isocrates 2
Italian War 15n., 94
Italy/Italian xi, xxiv, 92n., 93n., 94
Ithaca 138

Janus 99
*Jason of Pherae 42
*Jove (Jupiter) 139, 140
*Jugurtha 129n., 130
*Julius Caesar, Gaius (the Dictator) ix,
  xi, xii, xiii, xiv, xvii, xxviii, xlvii, 11,
  15n., 19, 25n., 26n., 34n., 44, 63n.,
  64n., 69n., 70n., 71n., 73n., 80n.,
  84n., 94n., 95n., 97nn., 98n., 101n.,
  107n., 131n., 132n.; his assassination
  xii, xxvi, 11, 71n., (72)
*Julius Caesar Strabo Vopiscus, Gaius
  42, 52, 81
*Junius Brutus, Lucius 115
*Junius Brutus, Marcus 82
Junius Brutus, Marcus (the
  tyrannicide) xiii, xiv, 72n., 100n.,
  102n.
*Junius Pennus, Marcus 117
*Junius Silanus, Decimus 85
Jupiter 46 and *see* Jove

*Laelius, Gaius 35n., 36, 42, 78, 106
Latins 17, 144
Lentulus: *see* Cornelius Lentulus
  Spinther
Leuctra 25, 72
*Licinius Crassus, Lucius 42, 52, 80,
  81, 85, 88, 117, 125
*Licinius Crassus, Marcus x, xi, xxviii,
  11, 43, 127, 128
*Licinius Crassus, Publius 85
*Licinius Lucullus, Lucius 54, 81, 85
*Licinius Lucullus, Marcus 81, 85
*Livius Drusus, Marcus 42, 94n.
Lucretius, Roman Epicurean poet 61n.,
  67n.
Lucullus/i: *see* Licinius Lucullus
*Lutatius Catulus, Quintus (1) 43, 51,
  52
*Lutatius Catulus, Quintus (2) 30, 43,
  51, 52
*Lutatius Pinthia, Marcus 129
*Lycurgus 30, 31n.
Lydia 114
*Lysander (1) 30, 31n., 43
*Lysander (2) 96

*Terence (P. Terentius Afer), Roman
playwright 12, 58
*Terentius Varro, Gaius 117n., 145
Terentius Varro, Marcus, Roman
scholar 10n., 16n., 63n.
Thales 106n.
Thapsus 69n.
*Thebe 71
Thebes/Thebans 25n., 45n., 60, 72n.
*Themistocles 30, 31n., 42, 68, 91, 118
*Theophrastus 2, 84, 88, 89
*Theopompus 78
Thermopylae 25
*Theseus 13, 136, 137
Thyestes 140n.
*Timotheus 45
Tiro (Marcus Tullius Tiro), C.'s ex-
slave and secretary 103n., 147n.
Transpadani 134
Troezen 117, 118n.
Tubero: *see* Aelius Tubero
Tullia, C.'s daughter xi
*Tullius Cicero, Marcus, C.'s son xvi,
xvii, xviii, 1, 2, 31, 63, 79, 99n., 101,
102, 103n., 112, 147

Tullius Cicero, Quintus (1), C.'s
brother x, xvii
Tullius Cicero, Quintus (2), son of the
above xvi, xvii
Tusculum/Tusculani 9, 15

*Ulysses 44, 138
Utica 44n.

Varro: *see* Terentius Varro
Verres, Gaius (Governor of Sicily,
73–71 BC) x
Veseris River 144
*Veturius Calvinus, Titus 142
*Viriathus 78
Volsci 15

*Xanthippus 138
Xenocrates 43n.
*Xenophon 41n., 46, 79n., 99
*Xerxes 118

*Zeno 28n., 49n., 113

Index of Subjects

Moderation: *see* restraint; *see also* limit, intermediate
Modesty 80–1; *see also* Cynics, restraint
Money: *see* wealth
Moral choice: *see* 'rule', duties: sources of, duties: priority, duties: in particular circumstances
Mos maiorum: *see* ancestors

Nature 6–7, 40–3, 49–50, 51, 57, 105, 112–13, 117; social human xxv, xxviii, 6–8, 9–10, 19, 38–9, 61; individual 20, 29, 42–7; law of 40, 108–11, 119, 127
Neighbours xxiii, 24
Novus homo ix, 54

Oaths: *see fides*
Officium: *see* Notes on Translation, duties
Old Age xvii, xxi, xxiv, 47–8, 57; *see also* Cicero's works: *Cato Maior*
Optimates 34, 81n, 96
Oratory xii–xiv, 1–3, 24, 25, 47, 50–2, 61, 64, 80–2, 89–90; and education x, xvi, 1–2
Order 7–8, 39, 49
Orderliness 55–6
Ordinary language xx, xxii, 76, 105–6
Ordinary opinion 105–6, 132

Parents, duties to xxiii, 10, 23–4, 60, 62, 80, 110
Passions: *see* agitation of spirit
Patriotism: *see res publica*: one's country
Patronage xiv, xxiii–xxiv, 15, 24n, 90–1
Peripatetics 2, 4, 71n, 84n; Marcus and xvi–xvii, 65–6, 68; *see also* Stoics, goal of life, intermediate, Aristotle, Cratippus, Theophrastus
Philosophers 3, 29, 64–6, 87, 125, 129; and public life 12, 28, 60; *see also* Academics, Epicureans, Peripatetics, Stoics
Philosophy 45, 51, 63–6, 75, 82, 102–3; Cicero and x, xi–xii, xxviii, 1–3, 63–6, 101–3; and education x, xvi, xvii–xviii, 64; and public life x, xvii–xviii, xxviii, 36, 59–61, 63–4; *see also* goal of life, sceptical method, law
Pirates: *see* brigands

Plaetorian Law 123
Pleasure 3, 11, 27–8, 41, 46, 58, 63, 76, 99–100, 109, 116; *see also* Epicureans
Poets: *see* theatre
Poor, the xxiv, 21, 34n, 87–8, 90–2
Populares xi, xxviii, 34, 70, 92, 95
Power 5, 28–9, 43, 66, 70–1, 88, 114, 131; *see also* ambition
Praetor's edict xxvi, 14
Praise: *see* reputation
Prepon 37
Private citizens 48
Probabile: *see* sceptical method
Procreation 6, 23
Professions xv, xvii, xxiv, 18n, 45–7, 57–9
Promises: *see fides*
Property xxviii, 9–10, 19n, 22, 34n, 92–3, 95–7
Proscriptions 19n, 73–4
Prudentia: *see* good sense
Psychology: *see* spirit
Public affairs: *see res publica*
Public office: *see res publica*, magistrates
Public service: *see res publica*, money
Punishment 14, 18, 35, 69
Pyrrhonians 4, 65

Reason 6–8, 21, 31–2, 36, 37n, 39–40, 41, 51, 53, 54–5, 69, 80, 109, 125
Reciprocity xxiv, 10, 20–1, 23–4, 68, 90–1; *cf.* gratitude
Recklessness 32, 40, 90
Regula: *see* 'rule'
Religion 15, 23; *see also* gods
Reproof 24, 53, 57
Reputation xx, 39, 43, 49, 55, 57, 58, 70, 72, 74, 76–7
Res publica: *see* Notes on Translation; Roman republic ix, xiii–xv, xxvii, 15, 31, 63–4, 74, 97–8, 101–2, 131–2, 145; one's country 23–4, 108–11, 116, 117–18, 124, 134–7, 143; public service xiii, xxiv, 1, 12, 28–9, 57, 80, 81–2, 97–8, 101–2; public office xvii, xx, xxiv–xxv, 29–32, 34–6, 63–4, 71, 86–7, 92–9; public affairs 26, 48, 51; foreign affairs: *see* war, allies, empire; *see also* duties, leisure, philosophy, society, magistrates, consulship, body: as political analogy

Cambridge Texts in the History of Political Thought

Titles published in the series thus far

Aristotle *The Politics and The Constitution of Athens* (edited by Stephen Everson)
  0 521 48400 6 paperback
Arnold *Culture and Anarchy and other writings* (edited by Stefan Collini)
  0 521 37796 x paperback
Astell *Political Writings* (edited by Patricia Springborg)
  0 521 42845 9 paperback
Augustine *The City of God against the Pagans* (edited by R.W. Dyson)
  0 521 46843 4 paperback
Austin *The Province of Jurisprudence Determined* (edited by Wilfrid E. Rumble)
  0 521 44756 9 paperback
Bacon *The History of the Reign of King Henry VII* (edited by Brian Vickers)
  0 521 58663 1 paperback
Bakunin *Statism and Anarchy* (edited by Marshall Shatz)
  0 521 36973 8 paperback
Baxter *Holy Commonwealth* (edited by William Lamont)
  0 521 40580 7 paperback
Bayle *Political Writings* (edited by Sally L. Jenkinson)
  0 521 47677 1 paperback
Beccaria *On Crimes and Punishments and other writings* (edited by Richard Bellamy)
  0 521 47982 7 paperback
Bentham *Fragment on Government* (introduction by Ross Harrison)
  0 521 35929 5 paperback
Bernstein *The Preconditions of Socialism* (edited by Henry Tudor)
  0 521 39808 8 paperback
Bodin *On Sovereignty* (edited by Julian H. Franklin)
  0 521 34992 3 paperback
Bolingbroke *Political Writings* (edited by David Armitage)
  0 521 58697 6 paperback
Bossuet *Politics Drawn from the Very Words of Holy Scripture*
(edited by Patrick Riley)
  0 521 36807 3 paperback
The British Idealists (edited by David Boucher)
  0 521 45951 6 paperback
Burke *Pre-Revolutionary Writings* (edited by Ian Harris)
  0 521 36800 6 paperback
Christine De Pizan *The Book of the Body Politic* (edited by Kate Langdon Forhan)
  0 521 42259 0 paperback
Cicero *On Duties* (edited by M. T. Griffin and E. M. Atkins)
  0 521 34835 8 paperback
Cicero *On the Commonwealth and On the Laws* (edited by James E. G. Zetzel)
  0 521 45959 1 paperback
Comte *Early Political Writings* (edited by H. S. Jones)
  0 521 46923 6 paperback
Conciliarism and Papalism (edited by J. H. Burns and Thomas M. Izbicki)
  0 521 47674 7 paperback
Constant *Political Writings* (edited by Biancamaria Fontana)
  0 521 31632 4 paperback

Dante *Monarchy* (edited by Prue Shaw)
  0 521 56781 5 paperback
Diderot *Political Writings* (edited by John Hope Mason and Robert Wokler)
  0 521 36911 8 paperback
The Dutch Revolt (edited by Martin van Gelderen)
  0 521 39809 6 paperback
Early Greek Political Thought from Homer to the Sophists
(edited by Michael Gagarin and Paul Woodruff)
  0 521 43768 7 paperback
The Early Political Writings of the German Romantics
(edited by Frederick C. Beiser)
  0 521 44951 0 paperback
The English Levellers (edited by Andrew Sharp)
  0 521 62511 4 paperback
Erasmus *The Education of a Christian Prince* (edited by Lisa Jardine)
  0 521 58811 1 paperback
Fenelon *Telemachus* (edited by Patrick Riley)
  0 521 45662 2 paperback
Ferguson *An Essay on the History of Civil Society* (edited by Fania Oz-Salzberger)
  0 521 44736 4 paperback
Filmer *Patriarcha and Other Writings* (edited by Johann P. Sommerville)
  0 521 39903 3 paperback
Fletcher *Political Works* (edited by John Robertson)
  0 521 43994 9 paperback
Sir John Fortescue *On the Laws and Governance of England*
(edited by Shelley Lockwood)
  0 521 58996 7 paperback
Fourier *The Theory of the Four Movements* (edited by Gareth Stedman Jones and
Ian Patterson)
  0 521 35693 8 paperback
Gramsci *Pre-Prison Writings* (edited by Richard Bellamy)
  0 521 42307 4 paperback
Guicciardini *Dialogue on the Government of Florence* (edited by Alison Brown)
  0 521 45623 1 paperback
Harrington *The Commonwealth of Oceana* and *A System of Politics*
(edited by J. G. A. Pocock)
  0 521 42329 5 paperback
Hegel *Elements of the Philosophy of Right* (edited by Allen W. Wood and
H. B. Nisbet)
  0 521 34888 9 paperback
Hegel *Political Writings* (edited by Laurence Dickey and H. B. Nisbet)
  0 521 45979 3 paperback
Hobbes *On the Citizen* (edited by Michael Silverthorne and Richard Tuck)
  0 521 43780 6 paperback
Hobbes *Leviathan* (edited by Richard Tuck)
  0 521 56797 1 paperback
Hobhouse *Liberalism and Other Writings* (edited by James Meadowcroft)
  0 521 43726 1 paperback
Hooker *Of the Laws of Ecclesiastical Polity* (edited by A. S. McGrade)
  0 521 37908 3 paperback
Hume *Political Essays* (edited by Knud Haakonssen)
  0 521 46639 3 paperback

King James VI and I *Political Writings* (edited by Johann P. Sommerville)
0 521 44729 1 paperback
Jefferson *Political Writings* (edited by Joyce Appleby and Terence Ball)
0 521 64841 6 paperback
John of Salisbury *Policraticus* (edited by Cary Nederman)
0 521 36701 8 paperback
Kant *Political Writings* (edited by H. S. Reiss and H. B. Nisbet)
0 521 39837 1 paperback
Knox *On Rebellion* (edited by Roger A. Mason)
0 521 39988 2 paperback
Kropotkin *The Conquest of Bread and other writings* (edited by Marshall Shatz)
0 521 45990 7 paperback
Lawson *Politica sacra et civilis* (edited by Conal Condren)
0 521 39248 9 paperback
Leibniz *Political Writings* (edited by Patrick Riley)
0 521 35899 x paperback
The Levellers (edited by Andrew Sharp)
0 521 62511 4 paperback
Locke *Political Essays* (edited by Mark Goldie)
0 521 47861 8 paperback
Locke *Two Treatises of Government* (edited by Peter Laslett)
0 521 35730 6 paperback
Loyseau *A Treatise of Orders and Plain Dignities* (edited by Howell A. Lloyd)
0 521 45624 x paperback
Luther and Calvin on Secular Authority (edited by Harro Höpfl)
0 521 34986 9 paperback
Machiavelli *The Prince* (edited by Quentin Skinner and Russell Price)
0 521 34993 1 paperback
de Maistre *Considerations on France* (edited by Isaiah Berlin and Richard Lebrun)
0 521 46628 8 paperback
Malthus *An Essay on the Principle of Population* (edited by Donald Winch)
0 521 42972 2 paperback
Marsiglio of Padua *Defensor minor* and *De translatione Imperii*
(edited by Cary Nederman)
0 521 40846 6 paperback
Marx *Early Political Writings* (edited by Joseph O'Malley)
0 521 34994 x paperback
Marx *Later Political Writings* (edited by Terrell Carver)
0 521 36739 5 paperback
James Mill *Political Writings* (edited by Terence Ball)
0 521 38748 5 paperback
J. S. Mill *On Liberty,* with *The Subjection of Women* and *Chapters on Socialism*
(edited by Stefan Collini)
0 521 37917 2 paperback
Milton *Political Writings* (edited by Martin Dzelzainis)
0 521 34866 8 paperback
Montesquieu *The Spirit of the Laws* (edited by Anne M. Cohler,
Basia Carolyn Miller and Harold Samuel Stone)
0 521 36974 6 paperback
More *Utopia* (edited by George M. Logan and Robert M. Adams)
0 521 40318 9 paperback

Morris *News from Nowhere* (edited by Krishan Kumar)
   0 521 42233 7 paperback
Nicholas of Cusa *The Catholic Concordance* (edited by Paul E. Sigmund)
   0 521 56773 4 paperback
Nietzsche *On the Genealogy of Morality* (edited by Keith Ansell-Pearson)
   0 521 40610 2 paperback
Paine *Political Writings* (edited by Bruce Kuklick)
   0 521 66799 2 paperback
Plato *The Republic* (edited by G. R. F. Ferrari and Tom Griffith)
   0 521 48443 X paperback
Plato *Statesman* (edited by Julia Annas and Robin Waterfield)
   0 521 44778 X paperback
Price *Political Writings* (edited by D. O. Thomas)
   0 521 40969 1 paperback
Priestley *Political Writings* (edited by Peter Miller)
   0 521 42561 1 paperback
Proudhon *What is Property?* (edited by Donald R. Kelley and
Bonnie G. Smith)
   0 521 40556 4 paperback
Pufendorf *On the Duty of Man and Citizen according to Natural Law*
(edited by James Tully)
   0 521 35980 5 paperback
The Radical Reformation (edited by Michael G. Baylor)
   0 521 37948 2 paperback
Rousseau *The Discourses and other early political writings*
(edited by Victor Gourevitch)
   0 521 42445 3 paperback
Rousseau *The Social Contract and other later political writings*
(edited by Victor Gourevitch)
   0 521 42446 1 paperback
Seneca *Moral and Political Essays* (edited by John Cooper and John Procope)
   0 521 34818 8 paperback
Sidney *Court Maxims* (edited by Hans W. Blom, Eco Haitsma Mulier and
Ronald Janse)
   0 521 46736 5 paperback
Sorel *Reflections on Violence* (edited by Jeremy Jennings)
   0 521 55910 3 paperback
Spencer *The Man versus the State* and *The Proper Sphere of Government*
(edited by John Offer)
   0 521 43740 7 paperback
Stirner *The Ego and Its Own* (edited by David Leopold)
   0 521 45647 9 paperback
Thoreau *Political Writings* (edited by Nancy Rosenblum)
   0 521 47675 5 paperback
Utopias of the British Enlightenment (edited by Gregory Claeys)
   0 521 45590 1 paperback
Vitoria *Political Writings* (edited by Anthony Pagden and Jeremy Lawrance)
   0 521 36714 X paperback
Voltaire *Political Writings* (edited by David Williams)
   0 521 43727 X paperback

Weber *Political Writings* (edited by Peter Lassman and Ronald Speirs)
  0 521 39719 7 paperback
William of Ockham *A Short Discourse on Tyrannical Government*
(edited by A. S. McGrade and John Kilcullen)
  0 521 35803 5 paperback
William of Ockham *A Letter to the Friars Minor and other writings*
(edited by A. S. McGrade and John Kilcullen)
  0 521 35804 3 paperback
Wollstonecraft *A Vindication of the Rights of Men* and *A Vindication of the Rights of Woman* (edited by Sylvana Tomaselli)
  0 521 43633 8 paperback